P9-CAM-284

4 Loaches, flying foxes, and elephant-trunk fishes, pages 90–93

5 Livebearers, pages 94–99

13 Catfishes, pages 135–143

15 Oddities, pages 146–151

How this guide works:

On this flap one representative of each of the 15 fish groups is shown. Every group has a number, which you will also find in the appropriate section of the descriptions of species. The page numbers will help you find quickly the fish group that interests you.

14 Gobies, pages 144–145

One of the many *Geophagus* species from South America shown engaging in brood care. Apparently there was some danger and the parent fish took the young in its mouth to protect them. Now they are being released.

Special advisors:

Helmuth Pinter: Characins, barbs, danios

Harro Hieronimus: Loaches, rainbow fishes, catfishes

Jürgen Schmidt: Labyrinth fishes

Steffen Hellner: Killifishes

Hans Horsthemke: Gobies

Peter Scheinert: Fish diseases

Consulting Editor: Matthew M. Vriends, Ph.D.

Ulrich Schliewen

AQUARIUM FISH

300 fresh-water fishes and plants in community, species, and biotope aquariums. Expert advice on setting up and planting a tank and on caring for and breeding fish.

With color photos by eminent aquarium photographers

Drawings: Heiner O. Neuendorf

Contents

Preface 8

The Vital Element of Fish 10
Water in Nature and in the Aquarium 10
Water Hardness 10
Levels of Water Hardness 10
The Correct Water Hardness 11
Measuring Water Hardness 11
Changing Water Hardness 11
Electrical Conductivity 12
The Acidity of Water (pH) 12
The pH of Water 12
Oxygen—The Element Crucial for Life 13

Photo on page 2/3: A community aquarium for South American fishes that is set up and planted in an exemplary manner. The fish in it are a shoal of bleeding heart tetras (*Hyphessobrycon erythrostigma*), a group of angelfish, and—as surface fishes—x-ray fish (*Pristella riddlei*) and common hatchetfish (*Gasteropelecus sternicla*).

The Plant Nutrient Carbon Dioxide (CO_2) 13
How to Determine the CO_2 Content in the Tank 13
Determining the CO_2 Content in Your Tank 14
Toxins in the Aquarium 14
Ammonia (NH_3) 14
Nitrate (NO_3) 15
HOW TO: Water Chemistry 16

Setting Up, Planting, and Maintaining an Aquarium 18
The Right Tank 18
Safety Around the Aquarium 18
The Right Light for the Aquarium 20
Heaters 20
The Right Filter 21
Filter Types 21
Filter Materials 21
Accessories for Maintaining an Aquarium 22
Setting Up and Decorating the Tank 22
Bottom Material 22
Rocks 22
Roots 22
Setting Up the Tank 22

Buying and Introducing the Fish 23
Basic Rules for Combining Different Species 24
Schedule of Chores 24
HOW TO: Plants 26

Setting Up Biotope Aquariums 32
Suggestions for Biotope Aquariums 32
Sand and Open-water Biotopes of the Great African Lakes 32
Tank for Rock Cichlids from Lake Malawi (Mbunas) 33
Rocky Tanganyika Tank with Sandy Area 34
Tank for Fish from Rocky Rapids 35
South American Root Biotope 36
Tank Type: Southeast Asian Still Water with Dense Vegetation 36
Black-Water Tank for Southeast Asian Fishes 37
Tank Type: Rainforest Stream 37

A Healthy Diet 38
Dry Food 38
Live Food 38
Frozen Food 38

A Dutch plant aquarium, where plants predominate.

Live Food Animals 38
Vegetable Food 40
Vitamin Supplements 40
Feeding Rules 40

Preventing and Treating Fish Diseases 42
Recognizing and Treating
   Diseases 42
Poisoning 42
Carbon Dioxide Poisoning 42
Ammonia Poisoning 43
Nitrite/Nitrate Poisoning 44
Poisoning through Medication 44
Poisoning through Tap Water 44
Checklist for Spotting Mistakes in
   Care 45
HOW TO: Diseases 46

Breeding Aquarium Fishes 50
Selecting the Parent Fish 50
What Encourages Fish to
   Spawn 50
Advice for Breeding 52
Transfer into a Breeding Tank 52
Transferring Eggs, Larvae, or
   Fry 52
Feeding the Brood 53
Ongoing Breeding 53
HOW TO: Breeding Fish 54

How Fish Ensure the Survival of Their Species 56
How Fish Reproduce 56
Egg-laying Species 56
Livebearers 56
How Different Fishes Raise Their
   Brood 56
Egg-layers without Brood
   Care 57
Egg-layers with Brood Care 58
Family Forms in Fish 59
HOW TO: Body Shapes 60

An Aquarist's Glossary 62

Popular Aquarium Fishes 72
Notes on the Instructions for
   Care 72
Group 1: Characins 74
Group 2: Barbs and Danios 81
Group 3: Rainbow Fishes,
   Silversides, Rice Fishes 86
Group 4: Loaches, Flying Foxes,
   and Elephant-trunk Fishes 90
Group 5: Livebearers 94
Group 6: Killifishes 100
Group 7: Labyrinth Fishes 105

Cichlid Family 110
Group 8: Tanganyika
   Cichlids 112
Group 9: Malawi Cichlids 116
Group 10: Other African
   Cichlids 120
Group 11: Central American
   Cichlids 125
Group 12: South American
   Cichlids 129
Group 13: Catfishes 135
Group 14: Gobies 144
Group 15: Oddities 146

Species and Subject Index 152

Literature and Addresses 158

How to Turn Your Hobby into an Experience of Nature

Preface

There is one thing all aquarium hobbyists have in common, whether they are young or old, beginners or seasoned aquarists: They are continually tempted by new fish. This is not surprising. With their iridescent colors and intriguing behavior, tropical freshwater fish turn a tank of water into a lively scene that supplies fascinating experiences of nature and suspenseful entertainment every day, right in your own home. That should not lead anyone to put too many fish into a tank, however, let alone to combine in the same tank species that have differing requirements. If you want to experience the watery world of your aquarium in its full beauty and variety without having to worry about unforeseen disasters, you have to know what conditions different fishes and plants need to thrive. You also need to know the technical aspects of aquarium maintenance.

Keeping fish properly: What this entails is explained here by Ulrich Schliewen, an expert aquarist. He supplies practical advice and precise instructions—easy to follow even for neophytes—on setting up, planting, and maintaining different types of aquariums: tanks for a single species of fish, tanks for fish communities, and biotope aquariums. Information on the important chemical processes that go on in water, accompanied by many practical suggestions on preparing the correct aquarium water and, just as important, on maintaining water quality, is presented in concise form on blue HOW TO pages. Other HOW TO pages with vivid illustrations and easy-to-follow instructions present the know-how needed for the proper care of plants, for treating common fish diseases, and for breeding aquarium fishes. In addition there is a glossary where specialized terms having to do with aquarium keeping are explained.

The special topic of this volume is how to set up and arrange biotope aquariums. The key to keeping fish properly is knowing the kind of conditions in which the fishes in your tank live in their native habitat. Consequently the author not only has devoted a special chapter to setting up tanks offering conditions similar to those of nature but also, in the section on the different fish species, has supplied detailed information on the original biotope of each species.

The photos in this book: Brilliant color shots, taken by the best European photographers specializing in aquarium photography, depict healthy fish in their natural colors—the way they look in a tank when properly cared for.

Descriptions of species: This large section of the book with a horizontal blue arrow at the top of each page covers 15 large fish groups. Here the hobbyist finds individual instructions for the care of more than 250 popular aquarium fishes, including some species that are not commonly kept. Precise information is given on water properties, special requirements, and proper feeding, and there are valuable tips on combining different kinds of fishes. What makes this section special: The instructions for the care of fish groups with which the author himself has little practical experience have been checked and, where indicated, supplemented by recognized specialists. Thus the knowledge and extensive practical experience of many experts are incorporated in this book—for the benefit of all aquarists who want to pursue their hobby further.

The author and the editors wish you much enjoyment with your aquarium and many hours of exciting fish watching.

The author and the publisher wish to thank all those who have contributed to the success of this book. We would like to express special thanks here to the artist, Heiner O. Neuendorf, for his clear illustrations, to the photographers for their outstanding pictures, as well as to Walter Foersch, Maurice Kottelat, Rainer Stawikowski, and Arthur Werner for their expert advice.

A red cichlid from West Africa protecting its brood. ▷

The Vital Element of Fish

Fish are in much closer contact with water than land-dwelling creatures are with air. Their gills not only serve as breathing organs but also absorb substances dissolved in the water, substances every fish needs to live. It is because fish depend so greatly on the element that surrounds them that correct aquarium water plays such a crucial role in keeping fish.

Water in Nature and in the Aquarium

If the aquarist fails to take appropriate measures, the aquarium will not be a healthy environment for the fish. There are good reasons for this:

In nature the factors determining water quality are in balance as long as we are dealing with a smoothly functioning ecosystem, such as a healthy lake. Animals, plants, and bacteria cooperate in sustaining a biological cycle that prevents a dangerous build-up of toxic metabolic products. Consequently the water is alive.

In an aquarium the situation is quite different. The water that comes out of the tap is biologically almost dead. It has to be revived before fish can live in it (see Setting Up a Tank, page 22). After that, the aquarium has to be constantly monitored and kept up to par, because in a water world of such limited dimensions, the conditions necessary for biological equilibrium can be imitated and maintained only with the help of filtering and water-conditioning technology. Incorporating beneficial plants and bacteria can enhance this process.

Water quality in the aquarium: It doesn't take a degree in chemistry to provide the proper water quality for your fish, but you do need some awareness of the "invisible" processes going on below the water's surface. For this you need a basic understanding of the factors that account for good water quality: water hardness, acidity or alkalinity (pH), nitrite/nitrate content, and the gases of oxygen and carbon dioxide that are dissolved in the water.

Water Hardness

The hardness of water depends on the amount of mineral salts present in the water in dissolved form. Important among these are carbonates and hydrogen carbonates. If only these are taken into account, we use the term "carbonate hardness."

Carbonate hardness (°dCH): Carbonate hardness has to be watched closely because it affects the pH of the water (see page 12) and the amount of carbon dioxide (see page 14). Just how these values, on which the well-being of fish and plants depends, interact is shown in the drawing on page 17. The level of carbonate hardness is always indicated in German degrees (°dCH).

Noncarbonate hardness (°dNCH): In addition to carbonates there are other salts, such as sulfates, that contribute to water hardness. They account for what is called noncarbonate hardness. Compared to carbonate hardness, it plays a relatively minor role in the aquarium.

General (or Total) hardness: Ordinarily, carbonate and noncarbonate hardness are added together to give us general or, as it is sometimes called, total hardness. Total hardness is expressed in this book in °dH. Each degree corresponds to 30 mg of calcium or magnesium carbonate per liter of water.

Levels of (Total) Water Hardness

The following terms are generally used to describe the various degrees of hardness:

very soft water	= 0° to 4° dH
soft water	= 5° to 8° dH
medium hard water	= 9° to 12° dH
hard water	= 13° to 19° dH
very hard water	= 20° dH and up

Neolamprologus marunguensis, a cichlid species from Lake Tanganyika that was first discovered in 1988.

The Correct Water Hardness

For fish: The great majority of aquarium fishes can be kept in medium hard to hard water. Precise requirements of individual species are given in the descriptions of species, pages 74–151.

For plants: If you want to have thriving plants in your tank, the carbonate hardness should be between 4° and 8°dCH.

Important: Carbonate hardness should not drop below 3° dCH; otherwise, there is a danger that the pH will sink too low. If that happens, we speak of water with a poor pH "buffer" because carbonate hardness helps cushion fluctuations in acidity, which are more likely to occur if carbonate hardness is low.

Measuring Water Hardness

Aquarium dealers sell liquid reagents that can be used to measure both total and carbonate hardness. Subtract carbonate hardness from total hardness to get noncarbonate hardness.

Note: When you measure, the figure for carbonate hardness may turn out to be higher than the one for total hardness. This anomaly is caused by special salts in the water that behave differently from those the measuring kit is designed to test for. For practical purposes you may in such a case simply regard the high carbonate hardness as the total hardness.

Changing Water Hardness

If your tap water is not of the hardness you need for your fish and plants, you can adjust it by lowering or raising the carbonate or the total hardness.

Lowering carbonate hardness: This is often necessary if you want to breed soft-water fishes. Ways of lowering carbonate hardness are:

• Peat filtering (see Glossary, page 67). The organic acids in the peat slightly acidify the water.

• Using a cation exchanger (available at aquarium stores).

• Adding completely desalted water to the water you start with until the desired carbonate hardness is reached (see page 17). Desalted water can be obtained from a reverse osmosis apparatus or from an ion exchanger that removes salts completely. With this method, noncarbonate hardness drops by the same percentage as carbonate hardness. The resulting water is too low in salts and has to be

Dwarf gourami male building a bubble nest.

When the female is ready, she comes to the nest.

slightly hardened again until the desired concentration is reached.

Lowering total hardness: If excessive hardness is due primarily to noncarbonate hardness, it may, depending on the requirements of the fish, make sense to lower the total hardness. This can be accomplished with a reverse osmosis apparatus or an ion exchanger that removes salts completely.

Raising carbonate hardness: Water too low in carbonates often has an unstable pH; that is, it is more likely to undergo fluctuations in pH that are harmful to fish. For this reason, carbonate hardness should be raised: Filter the water through crushed coral for as many days as it takes to reach the desired carbonate hardness; measure the hardness daily.

Electrical Conductivity

Water hardness also influences electrical conductivity. Conductivity indicates how many electrically charged particles (ions) are present in the water. The greater the hardness, the higher the conductivity, because the hardeners generally account for the largest portion of ions formed.

Conductivity can be measured with an electrical conductivity meter, but the value obtained does not indicate anything about the origin of the ions (carbonate or noncarbonate hardness). Therefore measuring conductivity is, in my opinion, of little use to an aquarist.

The Acidity of Water (pH)

Acidity—expressed in units of pH—indicates the amount of acids and bases present in the water. Acidity depends primarily on carbon dioxide—which is present in the water in part as carbonic acid—and on carbonate hardness. The proportions in which these are present make up the pH. There are also some other substances, such as humic acids, that affect acidity.

For most aquarium fishes, water that is just slightly acidic (pH 6 to 6.9) is optimal.

The pH of Water

The pH range of interest to aquarists lies between 4.5 and 9, and the following terms are generally used to indicate different levels within this range:

very acidic	= below pH 6
slightly acidic	= pH 6 to 6.9
neutral	= pH 7
slightly alkaline (or basic)	= pH 7.1 to 8
very alkaline (or basic)	= pH 8.1 to 9

Measuring the pH: Aquarium stores sell various reagents and kits for measuring the pH of water, such as test strips and liquids that turn different colors to indicate different pH ranges. There are also permanent indicators that are placed in the tank next to the thermometer.

Embraced by the male, she deposits the eggs.

The aquarist has to be aware of and pay attention to two properties of oxygen in water:
• The higher the temperature, the less oxygen is dissolved in the water.
• Water can absorb a maximum amount of oxygen from the air only if there is aeration. One alternative to aeration is the use of an oxygen-generating device, a so-called oxidator (see Glossary, page 67), which gives off pure oxygen into the water (be sure to follow the instructions for use!).
Plants produce more oxygen than they need for breathing when daylight permits photosynthesis, but at night they change from oxygen producers into oxygen consumers.
Fish use oxygen. In addition, they produce organic waste that has to be broken down by bacteria. This process, too, consumes oxygen. Consequently the presence of too many fish in a tank or overfeeding further worsens oxygen conditions.

The Plant Nutrient Carbon Dioxide (CO_2)

Carbon dioxide is the second gas—after oxygen—that has to be present in the water in sufficient quantity for plants to grow well. Dissolved in water, some of the carbon dioxide turns into carbonic acid. Carbon dioxide is an essential nutrient for aquarium plants, without which they cannot exist in the long run.
CO_2 deficiency can arise because of the substances that form carbonate hardness. These substances trigger a chemical reaction that removes CO_2 that would otherwise be available to the plants. This means that the higher the carbonate hardness, the less CO_2 is available in the water and—unfortunately—the higher the pH tends to rise (see page 17).
Calcium rims on the leaves of plants are a clear warning sign that there is not enough carbonic acid.
Remedy this by fertilizing with CO_2 or by reducing carbonate hardness. If you want to check whether there is adequate CO_2 for your plants, you can figure out the CO_2 content with the help of the pH value and the carbonate hardness and by referring to the table "Determining the CO_2 Content in Your Tank," page 14.

• Measure the pH daily after setting up a tank. As a rule, the pH stabilizes after a few days or weeks. From then on, measuring is required only every one or two weeks, assuming, of course, that you are not making major changes in the tank.
• Check the pH immediately if you notice changes in the fish or the plants.
My tip: Always measure at the same time of day. Only in this way are comparisons to earlier measurements meaningful, for the pH in a functioning tank fluctuates with the time of day.
Lowering the pH: For practical purposes it is important to know that the lower the carbonate hardness of the water, the easier it is to lower the pH. Lowering carbonate hardness—often combined with peat filtering (see Glossary, page 67), which acidifies the water with humic acids and reduces carbonates—is therefore the most common method of lowering the pH.
Fertilizing with carbon dioxide (CO_2) also lowers the pH, but this method presupposes an intimate knowledge of the way fertilizing devices work and of the interrelationship between pH, CO_2, and °dCH (see HOW TO page 17 on "Water Chemistry").

Oxygen (O_2)—The Element Crucial for Life

Oxygen is present not only in air but also in water. Fish and underwater plants depend on it for breathing just as much as "land dwellers" do.

How to Determine the CO_2 Content in the Tank

Plants need an adequate supply of CO_2. By using the table below you can find out whether there is enough CO_2 in your aquarium water.

(The table is not applicable if peat filtering has been used.)
This is what you do: Measure pH and °dCH; locate the values you have obtained in the table. Where the two lines intersect you will find the CO_2 amount present in the aquarium, given in milligrams per liter (mg/L).
If the CO_2 content is below the minimum requirement for your plants (see HOW TO pages 26–29 on "Plants"), you have to supply them with additional CO_2 or lower the carbonate hardness. Alternatively, you can replace your plants with species that are less demanding. If there is too much CO_2, remove some if the fish are visibly uncomfortable. Too much CO_2 does not harm plants, except for a few *Cryptocoryne* species.

Toxins in the Aquarium

Even in a tank that is optimally set up, water quality deteriorates with time. This happens because of the excreta of the fish and substances produced during the intermediary stages of bacterial breakdown. At higher concentrations these substances become toxic and have to be further broken down and removed by bacteria.
In nature this job is done by bacteria and plants that use these substances as nutrients and are able to transform them into nontoxic substances. These natural processes can also be put to use in an aquarium:
Plentiful planting with fast-growing plants (be sure

to supply adequate light and trace elements) will have the effect of turning organic waste products into plant substance.
Bacteria, fungi, and other microorganisms introduced into a bottom material that is not too fine-grained and therefore is well "aerated" and oxygen-rich also help break down waste products.
Important: HOW TO pages 16 and 17 will tell you how to deal properly with waste substances in your aquarium.

Ammonia (NH₃)
Ammonia is one of the toxic substances produced by organic waste and decaying animal and plant matter. Ammonia is closely related to and can change into its much less toxic "brother" ammonium (NH_4^+)—and vice versa. Depending on the pH of the water, dangerous ammonia changes into the less dangerous ammonium. If, for instance, the pH is below neutral (that is, below 7), almost all the ammonia is present in the form of less harmful ammonium. Remember, therefore:
• If the pH is below 7, this waste product has a less toxic effect.
• When you change the tank water, the pH may suddenly rise well above the neutral point—if, for instance, the tap water has a higher pH. If the tank water previously had a fairly high level of waste products (because of overpopulation or because the water had not been changed for a long time), the relatively harmless ammonium may suddenly change into toxic ammonia, and you will observe

Determining the CO_2 Content in Your Tank

°dCH \ pH	6.0	6.4	6.8	7.2	7.6	8.0
1	30	11	4.5	2.0	1.0	0.5
2	59	24	9.5	3.5	1.5	0.5
3	87	35	14.0	5.5	2.0	1.0
4	118	47	18.5	7.5	3.0	1.0
5	147	59	23.0	9.5	3.5	1.5
6	177	71	28.0	11.0	4.5	2.0
8	240	94	37.0	15.0	6.0	2.5
10	300	118	47.0	18.5	7.5	3.0
15	440	176	70.0	28.0	11.0	4.5
20	590	240	94.0	37.0	14.5	6.0

• This table is not applicable if peat filtering has been used.
• The darker shaded area indicates CO_2 values that are too high for fish.
CO_2 values = mg/L

How to use the table: Measure pH and °dCH and locate the values you have obtained in the table. Where the two lines intersect, you will find the CO_2 content of your aquarium water. If the pH and °dCH do not match the numbers in the table, use the numbers closest to your measuring results.

alvin's cichlid ("*Cichlasoma*" *salvini*)—this pair is having a harmless "marital" squabble.

gns of poisoning: The fish pant heavily and often
re directly below the water surface. This condition
an be mistaken for oxygen deficiency.
emedy the situation either by carefully changing
0 percent of the water (to dilute the poison) or by
autiously lowering the pH below 7.

itrate (NO₃)

litrates are salts normally produced in an aquarium
uring the breakdown of organic wastes. Unfortu-
ately the tap water in many rural areas is often
ontaminated with nitrate, so that relatively high
itrate levels may occur even in tanks that are opti-
ally set up and maintained.
hecking nitrate: Aquarium dealers sell simple test
ticks with which you can measure how much
itrate is in your tap water and your aquarium. If
he test of the aquarium water reads over 25 ppm
= .0025 percent), a partial water change is recom-
ended. Although most fishes can survive in water
rith up to 80 ppm nitrate, no fish thrive under such
onditions in the long run (risk of increased suscep-
bility to disease).

My tip: You can also find out from your water company what the nitrate level of your tap water is. If it is
too high, you have to "dilute" the tap water with fully
desalted water to reduce the nitrate concentration.
Preventing high nitrate levels: Preventive measures
an aquarium hobbyist should be familiar with are:
• In a tank with vigorous plant growth and a low fish
population density there is no chance for nitrate to
build up.
• Frequent partial water changes remove dissolved
waste products. Rule of thumb: Change ¼ to ⅓ of
the water every week or two.
• Siphoning debris off the bottom with a hose
(when cleaning the filter and changing the water)
removes waste products that are not (yet) dissolved
in the water.
• Regular cleaning of filter.
Note: Tap water may also contain herbicides—such
as atrazine—that are harmful to fish in the long run.
If you live in an area where herbicides are found in
the water, you should filter with activated carbon,
which effectively removes many poisonous substances.

HOW TO
Water Chemistry

Aquarists who are familiar with the processes that go on in the tank water are less likely to make mistakes in maintenance procedures such as water changes, filtering, and fertilizing. It is useful to have a working knowledge of a few symbols of chemistry:

O_2 = oxygen
CO_2 = carbon dioxide (in gaseous form)
"CO_2" = carbon dioxide (dissolved in water)
NH_4^+ = ammonium
NO_2^- = nitrite
NO_3^- = nitrate
NH_3 = ammonia

Organic Waste Products in Aquarium Water
Drawing 1
Exchange of gases at the water surface: Water can to some extent absorb gases (O_2, CO_2) from the air. This absorption is greatest if the surface water is in motion. Motion (aeration) is created primarily by the outflowing water of the filter. Aeration increases the O_2 content of water but also gets rid of the important plant nutrient CO_2.
• **Tip:** Make sure there is adequate aeration. Use diffusers or air stones in a tank that is planted only if absolutely necessary, so that not too much CO_2 is removed.
The metabolism of fish affects the water quality as follows:
1. Through breathing, fish use up oxygen and release carbon dioxide, thus lowering oxygen and increasing carbon dioxide levels.
2. The excreta of fish (organic waste products) pollute the water. The ammonium (NH_4^+) that is excreted plays an important role here.
• **Tip:** A well balanced fish population helps prevent a build-up of metabolic products.
Conversion of ammonium (NH_4^+): NH_4^+, which is relatively harmless, is converted into the toxic intermediary product nitrite (NO_2^-) by bacteria present in the bottom material, in the filter, and in the water. In a well-kept tank other bacteria immediately transform nitrite into harmless nitrate (NO_3^-), which, however, also becomes poisonous at high concentrations. If the bacterial balance is upset, as through medications or if the bottom material gets mucky because of poor aeration, too much nitrite may build up, which can lead to symptoms of poisoning in the fish.
Note: Ammonium and other organic waste products also result from leftover food that is rotting and from decaying parts of organisms (plants, fish, snails, and so on). If there is an excess of waste products, bacteria can no longer keep up the conversion process.
• **Tip:** A good climate in the bottom material helps the process of breaking down toxic metabolic products.
The role of plants: Plants have two important functions in an aquarium:
1. They absorb ammonium as a nutrient, bind it, and thus contribute to the reduction of metabolic products.
2. Plants need both CO_2 and O_2 to live. During daylight hours they contribute toward an increase of oxygen in the water by absorbing

1 The most important chemical processes taking place in the aquarium water are the exchange of gases, the influence and effect of organic waste products, and the effects of plants and filter.

O₂, some of which they convert
to O₂ and give off in that form. In
this process, called photosynthesis,
plants produce more O_2 than they
consume in breathing.

Important: At night photosynthesis
stops. Consequently no CO_2 is used
up, but plants keep breathing oxygen (as they do during the day).
That is why the oxygen content of
the water decreases at night.

Tip: If plants do not get adequate
light and sufficient CO_2 as well as
other nutrients, they cannot fulfill
their functions in the aquarium.

H level and ammonia (NH₃):
Excessive levels of ammonium or
ammonia occur only in poorly maintained tanks:
If the pH remains below 6.8, only
ammonium, which is relatively
harmless, will be present.
If the pH is above 6.8, ammonium
turns into toxic ammonia. The
higher the pH, the more ammonia
will be in the water.

Tip: Watch out if there are major
jumps in the pH (as after a water
change). The result may be a sudden excess of NH_3. To prevent this
from occurring, never neglect the
maintainance of the water.

Role of the filter: The first job of the
filter is to collect undissolved muck
(mechanical filtering effect). Second, bacteria in the filter further
break down dissolved products of
metabolism (biological filtering
effect). A combination of different
filtering materials helps optimize
both filtering processes (see pages
21 and 22).

Tip: Regular cleaning of the filter
removes undissolved muck but is
no substitute for water changes.

Water changes: Water changes
remove organic, dissolved waste
products (such as nitrate).

Tip: Regular water changes are
the most effective way to keep the
water clean!

Adequate lighting: This is necessary
for good plant growth.

**Carbon Dioxide, Carbonate
Hardness, and pH**

It is necessary to understand the
interconnection between these
three factors to be able to manipu-
late them as needed, as when

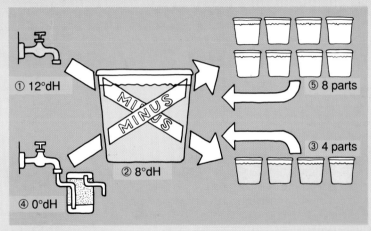

**2 Mixing two kinds of water to obtain a specific degree of hardness in the
aquarium water. Required calculations are described in the text. 1) Tap
water (12°dH). 2) Desired aquarium water (8°dH). 3) Parts of tap water
required. 4) Mixing water, usually fully desalted (0°dH). 5) Parts of mixing
water required.**

plants do poorly because of a lack
of CO_2. Before adding CO_2, however, one should check the carbonate hardness (°dCH) because:
• If the °dCH is high, little CO_2 is
freely available in the water. The pH
will have a tendency to rise because
the acidifying effect of CO_2 is dimin-
ished. If you want to feed the plants
directly with CO_2 in water with a
°dCH of 10 or more, first lower the
carbonate hardness to at most
4°dCH and only then introduce CO_2.
• If you want to make use of the
acidifying effect of "CO_2" to lower
the pH slightly (about one step),
again lower the carbonate hardness
first to 4°dCH at most.
Note: To stabilize a high pH (this is
sometimes necessary for cichlids
from Lake Malawi) when the °dCH
is very low (less than 3°dCH), raise
the °dCH by filtering over crushed
coral.

Mixing Water
Drawing 2
If your tap water is not the right
hardness for your fish, you can mix
in water of a different hardness to
achieve the desired level. Calculate
the proportions as follows: Use as
your numbers the degrees of total
hardness (dH) or of carbonate hardness (°dCH). The drawing above
depicts an example using dH values.

• Two steps are necessary:
1. Determine how many parts of
your basic water supply (usually tap
water) you will use by subtracting
the dH value of the desired tank
water (in our example, 8°dH) from
the dH value of the tap water (here,
12°dH). The result, 4, indicates that
you will want to use 4 parts tap
water.
2. Do the same thing to determine
the required parts of mixing water
(as a rule, completely desalted
water); that is, subtract the dH value
of the mixing water (here, 0°dH)
from the dH value of the desired
tank water (here, 8°dH). The result,
8, indicates that you will want to use
8 parts mixing water.
• If the numbers of parts of each
kind of water you have thus calcu-
lated are combined, you will have
tank water of the desired hardness.

Setting Up, Planting, and Maintaining an Aquarium

By choosing the right kind of tank, equipment, and plants you lay the basis for healthy conditions in your aquarium. It is up to you to set up the "water world of your aquarium" in such a way that it will be an environment in which your fish can thrive.

The Right Tank

Aquarium dealers sell many different kinds of tanks. The most solid ones are all-glass tanks whose joints are caulked with silicon rubber. They also come with decorative frames made of anodized aluminum.

Tank size: The basic rule is: the bigger, the better. Larger tanks are easier to take care of. The toxic substances released in the breakdown of metabolic products are more dispersed in a larger amount of water, which allows water quality to remain stable longer. Aquarium hobbyists with little experience therefore do better with a fairly large tank. For beginners I recommend a tank measuring 40 x 16 x 16 inches (40 gallons) (100 x 40 x 40 cm [160 L]). A tank of this size is easy to take care of, yet does not take up too much room.

Keep in mind in any case that the equation "small fish = small tank" hardly ever works out. There are many kinds of fish that stay small but nevertheless need a lot of room because, for instance, they may be active swimmers.

Note: Minimum sizes for tanks are given in the descriptions of species on pages 74 to 151.

The cover: No aquarium should lack a cover. A cover reduces evaporation and prevents fish that jump from leaping out of the water. Aquarium stores sell plastic covers with lighting fixtures installed in them. Another good solution is to have a glazier cut a tightly fitting cover into several panels (jumping fish!), so that it is never necessary to remove the entire cover when cleaning the tank or feeding the fish.

Safety Around the Aquarium

Water damage and insurance: The nightmare of many an aquarist—that the tank will burst—hardly ever becomes reality, but you should be prepared for such an eventuality. Water damage—which, by the way, can also result from overflowing or a leak in the tank—generally costs a lot to repair. It is therefore a good idea to include your aquarium in your property insurance policy. Ask your insurance agent which costs the insurance will cover in case of a mishap.

Important: Use only tanks with a symbol indicating that they have been tested for safety and whose caulking is guaranteed to last several years.

Even a solid tank may crack easily if unevenness of the surface it rests on causes tension in the glass. For this reason, place the tank on a styrofoam pad about ¼ to ½ inches (½–1 cm) thick that evens out any irregularities and keeps tension from developing.

When you choose the tank size, be sure to keep in mind how much weight the tank stand can support. A tank 40 inches (100 cm) long, with everything inside it, will weigh about 500 pounds (250 kg). This is an enormous weight to be supported by a relatively small area. You should therefore find out whether the floor will be able to withstand this pressure (ask a structural engineer) and whether the tank stand or cabinet is solid enough. Furniture especially designed to support aquariums is sold by aquarium dealers.

Precautions against accidents caused by electricity: Various electrical devices, such as filters, heaters, and lights, are necessary to create the proper conditions for fish and plants in an aquarium.

A pair of veil-finned Siamese fighting fish shortly after depositing eggs below a bubble nest. The white eggs are immediately picked up and spat into the bubble nest. ▷

Red fresh-water crab

Malayan snail

In the photos: Not only fish but also some other lovely and often useful creatures can be kept in an aquarium. The requirements of the creatures depicted in these photos are given on page 73.

Brine shrimp

Ramshorn snail

Striped dwarf shrimp

Everybody knows that the combination of electricity and water spells danger. That is why you should be sure to observe the following safety rules:

• Make sure any electrical appliance you buy is Underwriter's Laboratory (UL) approved.

• Appliances to be operated in the tank must carry a notation that they are suitable for such use.

• Buy a circuit breaker (available from electricians or at pet shops) and install it between the outlet and the appliances. If there is a defect in the wiring or in an appliance, the current is immediately interrupted.

• Unplug all wires before you do anything inside the tank or remove any electrical device from it.

• If anything needs repairing, always have the work done by a licensed electrician.

The Right Light for the Aquarium

Plants need light to grow. Aquarium dealers sell special lighting fixtures for tanks. The choice is between fluorescent tubes and mercury vapor lights.

Fluorescent tubes work very well for tanks up to 20 inches (50 cm) tall. The tubes should be about as long as the tank. Whether one or more tubes are needed depends above all on the light requirements of your plants (see HOW TO pages 26–29 on "Plants").

Replace fluorescent tubes once a year because their light output decreases significantly over time. The best fluorescent lights are the "daylight" ones. They cast a natural light. "Warm-tone" lights and plant lights, which contain a high proportion of red, cast an artificial-looking light and should be used only in combination with "daylight" tubes.

Mercury vapor lights are practical for tanks that are taller than 20 inches (50 cm) because their strong beam delivers enough light even to the lower water strata. Their one drawback is that they use a lot of electricity. It takes a few minutes after they are first turned on before the light reaches its full intensity.

Important: The lights should be on 12 to 14 hours a day. The easiest way to regulate them is to use a timer switch that will turn them on and off reliably every day—even when you are away. Purchase only UL approved equipment, which must carry the statement that it is safe for use under water.

Heaters

If you keep tropical fresh-water fishes, an aquarium heater is necessary even in a heated room. Automatic heaters with built-in thermostats that turn the eat on and off in response to changes in the water temperature are best. There are three types:

rod-type heaters that are attached vertically to the back wall of the tank with suction cups;

bottom heaters, whose heating cables are installed on the floor of the tank before everything else is placed in it (ask your dealer for advice). The less powerful bottom heaters serve primarily to circulate the water through the bottom material and thus create good growing conditions for the plants. Hobbyists who care about healthy plants often use them in addition to rod-type heaters.

Thermofilters are a combination of heater and filter. As the water flows through them, it is cleaned and slightly reheated.

Heater capacity: One half watt per quart of water is sufficient at normal room temperature (66–72°F or 19–22°C). For cooler rooms the heating capacity should be about 1 watt per quart.

Important: If you are going to be away for some time during the winter, keep the room warm enough for the room temperature together with the capacity of the aquarium heater to maintain the proper temperature in the tank.

Thermometer: You need a thermometer to check whether the aquarium heater is functioning properly. The most practical ones are those that are glued to the outside of the glass wall; they are easy to read and do not get covered with algae.

The Right Filter

Filters contribute to the necessary cleaning of the water in two ways:

Mechanical filtering action collects dirt particles. The water is conducted through a filtering material with minuscule pores in which the tiny dirt particles get caught. The dirt is easily washed off the material.

Biological filtering action breaks down waste substances. The large surface area of a second, coarser, filtering material gets covered with huge colonies of microorganisms (bacteria and fungi that occur naturally in the water). These organisms convert dissolved as well as undissolved waste products into other dissolved substances that then have to be removed by means of periodic water changes.

Important: Clean the mechanical part of the filter every week or two when you change the water (see Schedule of Chores, page 24). Clean the biological part only every tenth time you change part of the water, rinsing it with cold water so that the microorganisms are not killed.

Filter Types

Most filter types work essentially by the mechanical principle, with biological filtering being not much more than a side effect. Purely biological filters, which are available from dealers, always have to be used in combination with mechanical filters. There are so many different kinds of filters on the market that it is best to ask the dealer or salesperson for advice on which to choose. We therefore survey the field only briefly here.

Motorized filters (inside or outside filters) are driven by a water pump that creates circulation and agitates the surface water. In this process, oxygen is introduced into the water. This effect can be increased if a spray pipe or a diffuser is attached to the outflow opening. Diffusers and spray pipes are not recommended for fish species that dislike moving water or if plants are being fertilized with CO_2 (the CO_2 is flushed out of the water again). If you have a tank with fishes that like calm water, turn the motorized filter to a low setting.

Important: Be sure to observe the instructions for use!

Air-driven inside filters are good only for small tanks with fish species that dislike moving water, such as many labyrinth fishes. An air pump is used to operate this type of filter.

Filter Materials

You can use combinations of filter materials in almost all types of filters. The finer materials, such as fine foam and filter wadding, function as mechanical filters; coarser materials that last for a long time, such as coarse foam and tiny clay tubes, are used for biological filtering.

Foam that is sold in aquarium stores is long-lasting, so that beneficial microorganisms (fungi and bacteria) that break down organic metabolic products can get permanently established on them. Combine fine and coarse foam, using ¼ fine foam where the water enters the filter and ¾ coarse foam in the next layer. Clean the fine part at the weekly water change and the coarse part about every three or four weeks. Rinse the foam under running, *cool* water, squeezing it vigorously, until the water you squeeze out is clear.

Filter wadding can be used in place of the fine foam. Clean it by rinsing it under a strong jet of water, and replace it when it no longer gets clean.

Coarse nylon fibers or clay tubes can be used instead of the coarse foam and are combined with filter wadding or fine foam. The fibers or tubes last a long time. For cleaning, wash or rinse them under a strong jet of water.

Special filter materials: These are not designed for permanent use but are resorted to only for specific purposes.

• Activated carbon is used when medications have to be removed from the water after fish have been treated for an illness. Since activated carbon varies a great deal in quality, look for reputable brands.

• Peat is sometimes used to lower pH and carbonate hardness (see Peat filtering, page 67).

Accessories for Maintaining an Aquarium

Regular cleaning is an important part of maintaining a tank. Cleaning involves a partial water change, cleaning of the bottom, and cleaning of the glass. For this chore you need the following:

• A hose with a debris siphon: For a partial water change, use the hose to siphon off the water (outside diameter of hose: ½–⅝ inches or 12–16 mm). To clean the bottom, attach the debris siphon to the hose; it will suck up debris and water but not gravel. Never press down too hard on the gravel, or you will destroy the fine structure of the plants' root network.

• Buckets (10–15 quarts) to be used only in connection with the aquarium.

• A window squeegee for getting dirt and algae off the tank walls.

• Fish nets (one large and one small): Use only fine-mesh nets designed for aquarium use (available from aquarium dealers).

• A CO_2-fertilizer diffuser: If the water properties are such that there is not enough CO_2 present for the more demanding plants, CO_2 fertilizing is recommended (see pages 26–29 for requirements of plants). Please be sure to follow very closely the instructions for use of the device you have.

Setting Up and Decorating the Tank

All kinds of materials can be arranged to give shape to the interior of an aquarium: gravel, sand, stones, roots, caves, and plants. Arranging a tank is not just a matter of aesthetics; all the various materials have certain functions.

Bottom Material

Quartz gravel and river sand that contain no calcium are suitable bottom materials (both available at aquarium stores). If the fish have no special requirements, gravel of an average grade (1–3 mm) is adequate for any aquarium. For bottom-dwelling fish that like to burrow in sand, a separate sandy area should be planned, preferably in the unplanted foreground of the tank. Wash at least the top layer of the gravel.

My tip: Most fish act shy in a light-colored tank. A thin layer of lava gravel (added after the plants are put in place) has the effect of darkening a tank considerably. But watch out: Lava gravel has sharp edges! Don't use it with fish that burrow into the bottom!

Rocks

You can build caves and entire rock structures out of rocks. Rocks provide fish with shelters, places to hide, and brooding cavities. They also demarcate separate territories, which are essential to many kinds of fish. Calcium-free rocks like sandstone, granite, slate, and lava are good for this purpose. Build any rock structure directly on the bottom glass before you add the bottom material. This way the fish cannot dig underneath the structure and cause it to collapse.

My tip: Place a thin layer of styrofoam underneath large rocks or rock structures to prevent pressure points that might cause the bottom glass to crack.

Roots

Roots make good hiding places for the fish; they also provide sites for epiphytic plants and are a source of roughage for various corydoras catfishes and many other armored catfishes that gnaw on roots. However, don't use roots if you have fish—many livebearing ones—that need alkaline water. Roots acidify the water. Use only roots from bogs that have lain in airtight acid soil for long periods of time. Roots from the woods cannot be used because they rot in the water.

Note: Not only rocks and roots but also clay pipes and cavities of fired clay, pieces of bamboo cane, and even plastic pipes can provide hiding places for fish. All these items can be bought at aquarium stores.

Setting Up the Tank

1. Place rock structures in the tank. If large rocks or structures are used, place them on a thin layer of styrofoam.

2. Add the bottom material. For a tank with different kinds of fish, use quartz gravel of medium grade (1–3 mm).

First put down a layer about ¾ inch (2 cm) deep, ith soil fertilizer for the plants.

Top with 1½ to 2½ inches (4–6 cm) of gravel. Rinse the gravel for the top layer in a bucket until e water runs clear, or use prewashed gravel.

3. Install the filter: Locate the water intake and e outflow as far from each other as possible to ovide maximum water circulation throughout the nk. Important: Fill the outside filter with water. ollow the manufacturer's instructions.

4. Install the heater, but don't plug it in yet.

5. Install all other technical equipment.

6. Place roots and other decorative materials in uch a way that they hide the technical devices.

7. Add plants that will thrive in the kind of water e functioning tank will have. For the beginning, st-growing plants are a good choice.

8. Pour the water into the tank through a hose in uch a way that the bottom material is not stirred o. Possible methods: Pour the water onto rocks or unto a plate you have placed in the tank for this purpose.

9. Install the lighting.

10. Turn on all the technical equipment.

11. Run the aquarium for two weeks without fish. In the course of this time, establish the water properties the fish and the plants will need (see descriptions of species, pages 74–151).

12. Add the fish.

Buying and Introducing the Fish

• Before you buy, find out what the requirements of the fish are (water properties, kind of food, possible combination with other species).

• Before you buy, create the conditions in the tank that the fish require.

• The fish in the dealer's display tank should look well fed: Their bellies should not be concave but should have rounded contours (use the illustrations

he neon tetra (*Paracheirodon innesi*) is less demanding than the cardinal tetra (*P. axelrodi*).

as a guide). However, the fish don't necessarily have to display their full coloration in the dealer's tank. Full color often doesn't develop until the fish reach maturity and unless they live under optimal conditions, conditions a dealer cannot offer.

• The fish have to be healthy: no clamping of the fins, no rubbing, no panting. They should be as active as is typical of their temperament.

• Don't buy any fish that have been kept in the same tank with sick fish (they might be infected).

• Depending on the length of your trip home and the time of year, have the fish packed with sufficient insulation (it might be a good idea to take a cooler along as insulation against low temperatures).

Introducing the fish into the tank: Let the plastic bag with the fish float on top of the water for 20 minutes, then open the bag and let some tank water flow in (about half again as much as was in the bag originally). Leave the fish in the bag another 10 mintues and then release them carefully into the tank.

Basic Rules for Combining Different Species

• Combine only species that require the same water properties.

• Combine only species that tolerate each other's food.

• Species with different temperature requirements can be combined only if they inhabit different areas of the tank.

• Have only one fish species in each tank area—in a tank over 40 inches (1 m) long, at most two species. In addition you may introduce an *Ancistrus* catfish species. Exceptions may be made only for extremely large tanks.

• Fishes that have territorial needs should be combined with other species only if unclaimed space remains in the tank after the territorial needs (especially those of species that engage in brood care) have been met.

Basic rule: The more sparsely a tank is populated, the better it functions and the easier it is to take care of.

Schedule of Chores

Daily
• Observe the fish: Are there any signs of illness? Are some fish being bullied by others?

• Feeding: Are all the fish eating? Institute one day of fasting per week (except for juveniles).

• Check the technical equipment: Does the heater maintain the correct temperature? Is the filter flow good?

• Remove dead fish if there should be any.

Once or twice a week
• Partial water change: Replace ¼ to ⅓ of the tank water with fresh water of the same properties; siphon off debris; add fertilizer if necessary.

• Clean front glass and cover.

• Wash or replace top layer of filter substrate.

• Check food supplies and replenish if necessary.

At irregular intervals
• Thin and cut back water plants.

• Clean water pump as called for by manufacturer instructions.

Vacations
• Before you leave, change water, clean filter, and remove debris.

• Don't install any new appliances before going away. Don't introduce new fish.

• If you will be gone only one to two weeks, no feeding is necessary (except for juvenile fish). Fish undergo periods of fasting in nature, too.

• For longer absences, set up an automatic feeder and/or find and train someone to look after your fish. You may want to prepare food portions ahead. Leave your vet's or aquarium dealer's phone number in case of emergency.

New Set-up
This will become necessary after two or three years, when the bottom material has deteriorated and plants stagnate or decline in spite of good care.

Nymphoides aquatica, sometimes ▷ called "banana plant" because of the shape of its root, needs a great deal of light and is therefore suitable only for brightly lit, shallow tanks. Bury only the bottom fourth of the root and weigh it down somewhat until the plant has taken hold.

HOW TO
Plants

Plants, like fish, have different requirements according to their species. The water properties in particular have to be just right for both the fish and the plants.

Aids for Planning
Drawing 1
The number of plants and their density depend on the kind of fish to be kept.
Also pay attention to the proper placing of the different types of plants:
1. Background: Tall, slender stem plants or *Vallisneria*.
2. Sides and middle: Plants of medium height. For small tanks, solitary plants.
3. Foreground: No plants.
4. Solitary plants for the middle and back areas.
5. Epiphytes.
6. Floating plants.
Note: Popular aquarium plants for the different tank areas are listed on pages 27–29. Also given there are the plants' requirements.

Planting
Drawings 2 and 3
Calcium-free gravel (grade ¹⁄₂₄ to ³⁄₈ inches or 1–10 mm) is suitable for

2 For rosette plants, make a hole with your finger.

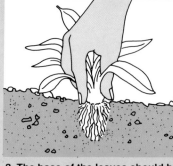

3 The base of the leaves should be just above the surface of the grave

plants. Sand is not desirable. Mix a fertilizer into the bottom layer of gravel.
• Stem plants are planted in clusters, the stems stuck into the ground close together.
• For rosette plants, make a hole big enough to accommodate the roots (if there is a dense root mass, first trim it to 2 inches or 5 cm in length). Place the plant so that the leaf base is just above the gravel.
• Epiphytic plants are tied gently to roots or rocks with nylon or rubber thread. After a while, when the plants have taken hold, the thread can be removed.

Tips for Feeding and Care
Feed with liquid fertilizer. Fertilize a little as possible to prevent algae growth.
There are two types of fertilizer:
1. General fertilizer for aquatic plants. In a new tank, this is applied after one to two weeks. Later add more after every water change or after every second change.
2. Iron fertilizer: Iron, an important trace element that is often lacking, should be replenished when part of the water is changed.
Important: Never use fertilizers designed for house plants!
Nutrient deficiencies: The most obvious sign is leaves turning yellow and glassy (especially new leaves). In such a case, carefully add some fertilizer (half the normal

1 Locations for various plants in the aquarium: ① background, ② sides and middle, ③ foreground, ④ solitary plants, ⑤ epiphytic plants.

mount) and make sure poor plant growth is not due to some other cause. Check light, bottom material, CO_2 concentration, and water properties.

CO_2 *fertilizing*: Plants need to be supplied with CO_2. To make sure they have adequate CO_2, you first have to know their requirements; second, check whether the tank water contains adequate CO_2. The minimum CO_2 requirement of popular aquarium plants is given in the plant descriptions that follow. With the aid of the table on page 14 you can figure out how much CO_2 (mg/L) is in the water. If there is less than the minimum required by the plants in the tank, add CO_2 fertilizer or lower the carbonate hardness—or substitute less demanding plants.

Tips for plant care:

Basic rule: Transplant as little as possible.

Stem plants have to be cut back more or less frequently depending on rate of growth.

If rosette plants develop too many runners, thin them so that they don't deprive each other of light and bottom space. Carefully cut off old, decaying, or algae-covered outer leaves just above the leaf root.

• Loosen the bottom material now and then with a stick, without disturbing the plant roots.

Note: If the bottom climate is not healthy (as with poor aeration), roots will grow upward out of the ground. In this case the bottom has to be carefully loosened. If this doesn't help, the tank has to be newly set up with fresh, washed gravel.

Popular Aquarium Plants

Plants will be healthy if the indicated requirements are met. The numbers for °dCH and pH given in brackets indicate optimum conditions. The CO_2 values represent the minimum required for optimal growth.

Lighting: The light intensity indicated is for a tank 16 to 20 inches (40–50 cm) tall (water depth 12–16 inches or 30–40 cm):

• dim = 1 tube
• medium = 2 tubes
• bright = 3 tubes
• very bright = 4–5 tubes

Plants for the Background

Suitable for this area are tall, slender stem plants or *Vallisneria*.

Example: *Myriophyllum*, a stem plant with feathery leaves.

Copperleaf
Alternanthera reineckii
20 inches (50 cm); CO_2: 20 mg/L; 2–12 [12]°dCH; pH: 6–7.5 [7.4]; 72–82°F (22–28°C); light: medium. Red color shows up only in bright light and with iron fertilizing.

Mud Plantain
Heteranthea zosterifolia
20 inches (50 cm); CO_2: 30 mg/L; 2–15 [3]°dCH; pH: 6–7.5 [6.6]; 72–82°F (22–28°C); light: bright.

Water Hyssop
Bacopa caroliniana
16 inches (40 cm); CO_2: 20 mg/L; 5–12 [10]°dCH; pH: 6–7.5 [7.3]; 72–82°F (22–28°C); light: medium. Similar species: coast bacopa (*Bacopa monnieri*).

Fanwort
Cabomba caroliniana
20 inches (50 cm); CO_2: 30 mg/L; 2–12 [3]°dCH; pH: 6.5–7.2 [6.6]; 72–82°F (22–28°C); light: very bright. Not suitable for most fish tanks. Similar species: *C. piauhyensis* (photo on page 31).

Water Wisteria
Hygrophila difformis
20 inches (50 cm); CO_2: 5 mg/L; 2–15 [6]°dCH; pH: 6.5–8 [7.6]; 73–82°F (23–28°C); light: medium. Hardy.

Hygrophila polysperma
24 inches (60 cm); CO_2: 5 mg/L; 2–15 [6]°dCH; pH: 6.5–8 [7.5]; 68–84°F (20–29°C); light: medium.

Ambulia
Limnophila sessiliflora
20 inches (50 cm); CO_2: 30 mg/L; 3–15 [3]°dCH; pH: 6–7.5 [6.6]; 72–82°F (22–28°C); light: very bright. Very demanding.

Cardinal Flower
Lobelia cardinalis
20 inches (50 cm); CO_2: 10 mg/L; 5–12 [8]°dCH; pH: 6.5–7.5 [7.4]; 68–79°F (20–26°C); light: medium. Hardy.

Marsh-purslane, False Loosestrife
Ludwigia repens
20 inches (50 cm); CO_2: 10 mg/L; 2–15 [10]°dCH; pH: 5.5–8 [7.6]; 68–84°F (20–29°C); light: bright. Hardy.

Parrotfeather
Myriophyllum brasiliense
20 inches (50 cm); CO_2: 40 mg/L; 2–15 [3]°dCH; pH: 5–7.5 [6.5]; 64–82°F (18–28°C); light: very bright. Only marginally suitable for fish tanks.

Broad-leaved Rotala, Loosestrife
Rotala macrandra
20 inches (50 cm); CO_2: 30 mg/L; 2–15 [15]°dCH; pH: 5.5–7.2 [7.2]; 77–86°F (25–30°C); light: medium. Similar species: Round-leaved rotala (*R. rotundifolia*) needs cooler water.

HOW TO
Plants

Arrowhead, Needle Sagittaria
Sagittaria subulata
24 inches (60 cm): CO_2: 20 mg/L;
2–15 [5]°dCH; pH: 6–7.8 [6.9];
68–82°F (20–28°C); light: medium.
Similar species: *S. pusilla*, 4 inches
(10 cm).

Shinnersia rivularis
40 inches (100 cm); CO_2: 5 mg/L;
2–15 [3]°dCH; pH: 5.5–7.5 [7.4];
68–82°F (20–28°C); light: medium.
Fast-growing plant for large tanks.

Vallisneria tortifolia
20 inches (50 cm); CO_2: 2 mg/L;
5–12 [6]°dCH; pH: 6.5–8 [8];
59–86°F (15–30°C); light: dim. Very
undemanding and hardy.

Vallisneria gigantea
40–80 inches (100–200 cm); CO_2:
2 mg/L; 5–15°dCH; pH: 6–8 [8];
64–82°F (18–28°C); light: dim.
Don't plant too densely.

Ammania gracilis
20 inches (50 cm); CO_2: 20 mg/L;
2–12 [10]°dCH; pH: 6–7.5 [7.3];
70–82°F (21–28°C); light: medium.
Plant each stem separately.

Plants for the Sides and Middle
Suitable for this area are plants of
medium height that can also be
used as solitary plants in small
tanks.

Example:
**Cryptocoryne
wendtii, a
species that
requires little
care.**

Cryptocoryne wendtii
4–16 inches (10–40 cm); CO_2:
15 mg/L; 2–15 [9]°dCH; pH: 6.5–7.5
[7.4]; 75–82°F (24–28°C); light: dim
to medium. Similar species: *C.
affinis*.

Water Pennywort
Hydrocotyle leucocephala
20 inches (50 cm); CO_2: 10 mg/L;
2–15 [8]°dCH; pH: 6–7.5 [7.4];
68–82°F (20–28°C); light: bright.
With its small floating leaves, this
plant offers good protection to surface fish.

Water Purslane
Didiplis diandra
6 inches (15 cm); CO_2: 20 mg/L;
5–15 [3]°dCH; pH: 7.4; 72–82°F
(22–28°C); light: medium.

Black Amazon
Echinodorus parviflorus
12 inches (30 cm); CO_2: 20 mg/L;
2–15 [6]°dCH; pH: 6–7.8 [7];
72–82°F (22–28°C); light: medium.
Good solitary plant for small tanks.

Plants for the Foreground
For this area, small plants that form
dense clusters are best.

Cryptocoryne x willisii
5 inches (15 cm): CO_2: 15 mg/L;
2–15 [9]°dCH; pH: 6.5–7.5 [7.4];
72–82°F (22–28°C); light: medium.
Good plant for the foreground,
where it can form dense clusters.

Little Amazon
*Echinodorus quadricostatus x
xinguensis*
2–6 inches (5–15 cm); CO_2:
20 mg/L; 2–12 [6]°dCH; pH: 6.5–7.5
[7]; 72–82°F (22–28°C): light:
medium to bright. Suitable for the
foreground only in large tanks.

Microsagittaria, Pygmy Chain
Echinodorus tenellus
4 inches (10 cm); CO_2: 20 mg/L;
2–12 [6]°dCH; pH: 6.5–7.2 [7];
72–84°F (22–29°C); light: bright.
Forms mats; thin frequently.

Solitary Plants
The middle and back areas of the
tank offer a good place for solitary
plants. Those plants are best that
have a decorative shape and thus
need not be clustered together with
others but stand out attractively by
themselves.

Example:
**Echinodorus
bleheri.**

Aponogeton crispus
20 inches (50 cm); CO_2: 30 mg/L;
2–12 [3]°dCH; pH: 6–7.5 [6.6];
72–82°F (22–28°C); light: medium.
Dormant phase during which leaves
curl up and fall off, but the tuber
survives. Other *Aponogeton* species
are not suited to long-term cultiva-
tion in tanks.

Cryptocoryne balansae
20 inches (50 cm); CO_2: 15 mg/L;
2–15 [9]°dCH; pH: 6.5–7.5 [7.4];
75–82°F (25–28°C); light: dim to
medium. Excellent for very tall and
long tanks where the leaves lie in
the current.

Water Sprite, Water Fern
Ceratopteris thalictroides
20 inches (50 cm); CO_2: 5 mg/L;
5–15 [9]°dCH; pH: 6.5–8 [7.8];
64–82°F (18–28°C); light: medium.
One of the hardiest aquarium
plants, which, because of its fast
growth, quickly absorbs toxic
substances.

Slender-leaved Amazon
Echinodorus amazonicus
20 inches (50 cm); CO_2: 20 mg/L;
2–12 [6]°dCH; pH: 6.5–7.2 [7];
72–82°F (22–28°C); light: medium.

Echinodorus bleheri
Over 20 inches (50 cm); CO_2: 20 mg/L; 2–12 [6]°dCH; pH: 6.5–7.2 [7]; 72–82°F (22–28°C); light: medium. More robust than *E. amazonicus*.

Echinodorus osiris
Over 20 inches (50 cm); CO_2: 20 mg/L; 5–18 [6]°dCH; pH: 6.5–7.5 [7]; 75–84°F (24–29°C); light: dim to medium. Only the young leaves are red. Similar species: *E. horemanni*.

Swordplant, Elephant Ear
Echinodorus cordifolius
Over 20 inches (50 cm); CO_2: 20 mg/L; 5–15 [6]°dCH; pH: 6.5–7.5 [7]; 72–82°F (22–28°C); light: medium. Solitary plant, only for very tall tanks (over 20 inches or 50 cm).

Hygrophila corymbosa
24 inches (60 cm); CO_2: 5 mg/L; 2–15 [6]°dCH; pH: 6.5–7.8 [7.6]; 72–82°F (22–28°C); light: medium. The red-leafed variety needs stronger light.

Nymphaea zenkeri
10–20 inches (25–50 cm); CO_2: 30 mg/L; 2–12 [3]°dCH; pH: 5.5–7.5 [6.6]; 72–82°F (22–28°C); light: bright. Cut off floating leaves; they create too much shade.

Barclaya longifolia
10–20 inches (25–50 cm); CO_2: 30 mg/L; 2–12 [3]°dCH; pH: 6–7 [6.6]; 72–82°F (22–28°C); light: bright.

Epiphytic Plants
These plants are not set in the ground but carefully tied to roots or stones with nylon or rubber thread.

Example: Java fern or swordfern (*Microsorium pteropus*) is a popular plant.

Anubias barteri var. nana
4 inches (10 cm): CO_2: 35 mg/L; 2–15 [13]°dCH; pH: 6–7.5 [7.2]; 72–82°F (22–28°C); light: medium. Plant a lot of them; they grow slowly.

Bolbitis heudelotii
8–20 inches (20–50 cm); CO_2: 30 mg/L; 2–12 [3]°dCH: pH: 6–7 [6.6]; 72–79°F (22–26°C); light: medium.

Java Fern, Swordfern
Microsorium pteropus
8 inches (20 cm); CO_2 20 mg/L; 2–12 [3]°dCH; pH: 5.5–7.5 [6.8]; 70–82°F (21–28°C); light: dim. Gets covered with algae quickly because of its slow growth.

Java Moss
Vesicularia dubyana
CO_2: 5 mg/L; 2–15 [3]°dCH; pH: 5.8–7.5 [7.4]; 68–86°F (20–30°C); light: medium. Good spawning plants for characins, barbs, and rainbow fishes.

Floating Plants
These plants, which are simply placed on the surface of the water, shade the water, help in nest building, and serve as hiding places for fry or as a spawning substrate.

Example: Crystalwort (*Riccia fluitans*).

Hornwort, Coontail
Ceratophyllum demersum
20 inches (50 cm); CO_2: 5 mg/L; 5–15 °dCH; pH: 6–8; 64–86°F (18–28°C); light: medium. Can also be cultivated in the ground.

Water Lettuce
Pistia stratiotes
4–6 inches (10–15 cm) in diameter; CO_2: 10 mg/L; 5–15 [8]°dCH; pH: 6.5–7.5; 72–79°F (22–26°C); light: very bright. Does not tolerate peat water!

Crystalwort
Riccia fluitans
CO_2: 10 mg/L; 2–15 [15]°dCH; pH: 6–8 [7.4]; 59–86°F (15–30°C); light: medium. Ideal nest building plant for labyrinth fishes.

Najas guadelupensis
CO_2: 10 mg/L; 2–12 [8]°dCH; pH: 6–7.5 [7]; 72–82°F (22–28°C); light: dim to medium. Forms loose, voluminous cushions at the water's surface.

Floating Fern
Salvinia auriculata
8–12°dCH; pH: 6–7; 68–81°F (20–27°C); light: bright. Strong light and dissolved nutrients in the water are important. The CO_2 content plays a secondary role.

Ceratopteris pteridoides
CO_2: 5 mg/L; 5–15 [9]°dCH; pH: 6.5–8 [7.8]; 68–86°F (18–28°C); light: medium.

1 *Echinodorus osiris.*

The plants in the photos:

1 *Echinodorus osiris* is an attractive solitary plant. Only the young leaves are reddish.

2 *Ceratopteris pteridoides* is easy to propagate.

3 Crystalwort (*Riccia fluitans*) is a floating plant, but it will also grow on a substrate. This plant is useful for providing shade, as a spawning substrate, and as protection for the fry.

4 *Cryptocoryne x willisii* is planted in clusters in the foreground of the tank.

2 *Ceratopteris pteridoides.*

3 Crystalwort (*Riccia fluitans*).

4 *Cryptocoryne x willisii.*

Nymphaea zenkeri.

6 Echinodorus horemanni.

Anubias barteri blossom.

8 Barclaya longifolia.

Cabomba piauhyensis.

10 Fanwort blossom (Cabomba caroliniana).

5 *Nymphaea zenkeri* is a good solitary plant for large aquariums.
6 *Echinodorus horemanni*, a solitary plant, should be fertilized regularly (with iron).
7 *Anubias barteri* will flower only if it rises above the water surface and receives daylight as well as some sun.
8 *Barclaya longifolia*, a solitary plant, requires strong light.
9 *Cabomba piauhyensis* can be planted anywhere in the aquarium.
10 Fanwort *(Cabomba caroliniana)* rarely flowers and needs a great deal of light.

Setting Up Biotope Aquariums

There are many good reasons for setting up a tank that tries to recreate a natural "biotope" for your fish. For one thing, we know more today about the ecology of individual fish species than ever before. For another, habitat destruction is becoming a greater and greater threat to the survival of many animal and plant species. All the various attempts to halt this trend—as through habitat preservation and through protection of endangered species— have made one fact clear to nature lovers: One can protect only what one knows. Is this not a convincing motivative factor for aquarists to set up a biotope aquarium? With such an aquarium the hobbyist begins to look beyond his or her living-room fish tank. Of course, we cannot be too strict in our standards for setting up a biotope aquarium. Trying to recreate the natural environment of a fish species in an aquarium down to the most minute detail would be a hopeless undertaking. We would, for instance, often have to use materials, like mud, that would be detrimental in the limited confines of an aquarium. Therefore we follow the motto: Attempt only what is feasible.

Suggestions for Biotope Aquariums

The natural habitats of aquarium fishes are extremely varied, so that there are many possibilities for setting up a biotope aquarium. The following examples are meant, on the one hand, as a survey of possibilities and, on the other, as inspiration for aquarists to create biotopes that suit their own fish. The necessary information for turning your own ideas for an aquarium into reality is given in the instructions for the care of individual fish species (pages 74–151) under the heading "Biotope." Always remember: Use only those natural materials that are suitable for an aquarium! Ask your aquarium dealer for advice.
Note: Turn to HOW TO pages 26–29 on "Plants" for help in choosing the right kinds of plants.
My tip: In a normal community tank you can give individual areas a natural look by using some natural materials as structural elements. With *Apistogramma* species, for instance, you can have a layer of fall leaves. There are other suggestions of this kind in the descriptions of species on pages 74 to 151.

Sand and Open-water Biotopes of the Great African Lakes

A tank with very few structures separating largish sandy areas for fishes that like the open water.
Population: Several pairs or a breeding group (One male, two or three females). Sand cichlids of the genera *Ophthalmochromis, Cyathopharynx*, or *Xenotilapia*. For the open water area, add a shoal of carp-like cichlids of the genera *Cyprichromis* or *Paracyprichromis*.
Tank size: 60 x 20 x 20 inches (150 x 50 x 50 cm)– a large tank.
Set-up: A 2½-inch (6 cm) layer of sand, some rocks that subdivide the sandy area into territories. Another way to organize the space is to set some largish plants into pots with gravel (pure sand is not a suitable plant soil).
Special technical requirements: None.
Water: pH: 7.5–9; medium hard to hard; 77–81°F (25–27°C).

The sand cichlid *Xenotilapia ochrogenys*.

rocky aquarium for *aufwuchs*-eating cichlids from Lake Malawi in East Africa (Mbunas).

anks for Rock Cichlids from Lake Malawi
Abunas)

or mouthbrooders from Lake Malawi that feed on
icroorganic growth (see *aufwuchs* in Glossary,
age 62). (Mbuna tank).

opulation: Two to three Mbuna species (two males,
to 6 females), one each of the higher-backed and
e slimmer types from the genera *Pseudotropheus*,
Melanochromis, and *Labeotropheus*. Others that
ay be added: Mochocidae catfishes from Lake
lalawi, *Synodontis nyassae* or *S. petricola* from
ake Tanganyika, and Loricariidae catfishes of the
enus *Ancistrus* to clean up algae.

ank size: 60 x 20 x 20 inches (150 x 50 x 50 cm).

et-up: Medium-grade gravel for the bottom. Along
e sides and in the back, rock structures made of
at rocks, sandstone, or granite slabs piled in such
way that there are many caves and cave-like
Innels. Build the structure right up to the water
Irface! If you want plants, try epiphytic species
Jch as Java fern (*Microsorium pteropus*).

pecial technical requirements: None.

Vater: pH: 7.5–8.5; medium hard to hard;
7–81°F (25–27°C).

In the photo: In this tank *Melanochromis johannii*, *Pseudotropheus*
species, and *Labeotropheus*
species live together. Because
the tank is so large, it can also
accommodate sand cichlids (*Cyrtocara moorii*). In imitation of the
rocky zones of Lake Malawi, flat
rocks have been incorporated into
the tank in such a way as to create
many caves. The fish occupy these
caves as territories. In the natural
habitat there are no higher plants,
such as the *Anubias* and Java fern
seen here, but these plants can be
kept in a biotope aquarium.

Chalinochromis brichardi

Neolamprologus calliurus

In the photos: Both pictures were taken in Lake Tanganyika. They show fishes in their typical biotopes: *Chalinochromis brichardi* **inhabits a rocky biotope; the snail cichlid** *Neolamprologus calliurus* **shown here is living near an accumulation of snail shells where sandy bottom and rock meet.**

Rocky Tanganyika Tank with Sandy Area

For fish that breed in rock caves and for snail cichlids from Lake Tanganyika.

Population: One pair of small cavity-brooding cichlids (up to 2¾ inches [7 cm] long) belonging to the genera *Julidochromis* or *Neolamprologus* (for example, *J. transcriptus* or *N. buescheri*) and one pair of *Lamprologus ocellatus* or another snail cichlid species from Lake Tanganyika. In a very large tank (over 60 inches or 150 cm long and 20 inches or 50 cm tall), you can introduce a shoal of carp-like cichlids into the open-water area and also keep somewhat larger cavity brooders (for example, *Neolamprologus longior*).

Tank size: 40 x 16 x 16 inches (100 x 40 x 40 cm).

Set-up: Build stone structures in the back and along one side, reaching almost or all the way up to the water surface. Build them in such a way that many small and medium-size caves are formed. In the front part of the tank, spread a layer of sand (about 1–1½ inches or 3–4 cm deep) and distribute many empty snail shells over it.

Special technical requirements: None.

Water: pH: 7.5–9; medium hard to hard; 77–81°F (25–27°C).

Rapids in the Río Amapá in northeastern Brazil.

Tank for Fish from Rocky Rapids

For small, mostly bottom-dwelling fish from very fast-moving waters.

Population: One pair or harem (one male, two or three females) of cichlids from fast-moving water from the genera *Steatocranus*, *Teleogramma*, or *Lamprologus*; depending on their size, two to five Loricariidae catfish from the genus *Ancistrus*; also a group of slender characins that like moving water.

Tank size: 40 x 16 x 16 inches (100 x 40 x 40 cm).

Set-up: Sand or gravel bottom (medium grade), flat rocks placed horizontally; long, flat roots that stick up against the back wall.

Special technical requirements: A water pump that creates strong water circulation.

Water: pH about 7; soft to medium hard; 79°F (26°C).

Steatocranus spec. aff. ubanguiensis

In the photos: Fishes that live in the rapids of streams and rivers have largely lost the ability to swim in open water. They have become bottom dwellers that often move in a hopping or creeping manner or that have suction devices that allow them to hang on to rocks.

In the photos: The angelfish shown in the photo also occur in black water. They can therefore be kept a root biotope aquarium because peat filtering imitates black water conditions. To be sure, the extrem water properties of natural black water should be established only for the breeding of some species (a few characins).

A group of angelfish (*Pterophyllum altum*).

Black-water biotope.

South American Root Biotope

A tank for largish, calm South American fishes, often from black-water rivers.

Population: One shoal of surface-dwelling characins (for example, 12 hatchetfish); four to six angelfish, discus fish, or *Uaru amphiacanthoides*; either two to four *Ancistrus* or two to three *Sturisoma* catfish (the two kinds do not tolerate each other); armored catfishes.

Tank size: 48 x 20 x 20 (or 24) inches (120 x 50 x 50 [or 60] cm)—a tall tank.

Set-up: Spread a thin layer (¾–1⅛ inches or 2–3 cm) of sand or gravel to provide a fine-grade bottom material; organize the space exclusively with roots, some of them lying flat on the bottom, but leave enough open sand; arrange other large and multi-branched roots upright so that many spacious shelters are created. No plants.

Special technical requirements: Create only slight circulation by turning on a motorized filter at a low setting. Use only one fluorescent tube for light

(these fishes like it dark!).

Water: Peat-filtered water; pH about 6; carbonate hardness about 4°dCH; total hardness not over 8°dH; 82°F (28°C).

Tank Type: Southeast Asian Still Water with Dense Vegetation

This is a tank for slow-moving labyrinth fishes that build bubble nests, for small barbs or danios, and for catfishes.

Population: Smallish, Southeast Asian catfishes, a group of coolie loaches, a shoal of danios, two or three pairs of honey gourami or dwarf gourami.

Tank size: 40 x 16 x 16 inches (100 x 40 x 40 cm).

Set-up: For the bottom use dark gravel that doesr have sharp edges (these fish burrow). Supply hidir places in the form of coconut shell halves with entr holes. Add roots that stick up in the back of the tan and plant all areas densely, some of them with lea plants; also add Java moss cushions and enough floating plants to cover ½ to ⅔ of the water surface

special technical requirements: Set the filter at a low setting; never let it create strong circulation.
Water: pH about 6.5; soft to medium hard; 82°F (28°C).

Black-Water Tank for Southeast Asian Fishes
This tank is for demanding fishes from Southeast Asia.
Population: A large shoal of danios consisting of 30 Rasbora hengeli or R. heteromorpha; 15 to 20 R. alochroma or R. pauciperforata, two pairs of pearl gouramis, and five to eight clown loaches.
Tank size: 60 x 20 x 20 inches (150 x 50 x 50 cm).
Set-up: The bottom material should be fine-textured and dark. Supply pipe-shaped hiding places for the clown loaches, preferably pieces of bamboo cane about 2¼–3 inches (6–8 cm) thick. Place roots in the back and on the sides, with some of them reaching to the water surface. There should be a partial cover of floating plants that don't require much light.
Special technical requirements: Only slight water circulation; use only one fluorescent tube for light.
Water: pH 5.5–6.5; hardness: up to 8 dH° (4°dCH); 79–82°F (26–28°C).

Tank Type: Rainforest Stream
This is a tank for smaller fishes from small, shaded, clear rainforest streams.

Population: One pair of dwarf cichlids of the genus *Pelvicachromis* or a harem (one male, two or three females) of an *Apistogramma* species; two Loricariidae catfish (*Ancistrus*), and a shoal of characins, danios, or lamp-eyes.
Tank size: 40 x 16 x 16 inches (100 x 40 x 40 cm).
Set-up: Dark bottom material of any grade. Add some round pebbles or some brown beech leaves (dried previously) in the foreground. Place roots in the back, making them stick up to the water surface in one corner, and add some medium to tall plants. Two small caves.
Special technical requirements: None.
Water: pH about 6.5; soft to medium hard; 75°F (24°C).

In the photo: In the natural biotope of discus fishes there are no plants, only roots. Nevertheless discus fishes can be kept unproblematically in a planted aquarium. If you want to keep these fishes in an environment resembling their natural habitat, set up a root biotope tank as described on page 36.

shoal of blue discus fish.

A Healthy Diet

Deficiency symptoms that can turn into diseases, problems of digestion, and obesity are conditions that affect not only humans but fish as well—if they are not fed properly. Providing a healthy diet means giving the fish varied foods containing plenty of roughage. In addition you should check to see whether the food you offer your fish is the kind your particular species thrive on (see descriptions of species, pages 74–151). Food for aquarium fish includes dry food, live food (including frozen live food), and vegetable food.

Dry Food

You can buy dry fish food made up of animal and/or plant matter at aquarium stores, and it is a good basic staple, except for fish that will eat only live food (see descriptions of species, starting on page 74). Always store dry fish food in a dry place, and never use food from cans that have been open for more than two or three months (loss of vitamins and nutrients). Dry fish food comes in the form of flakes, granules, tablets, and pellets.
Flakes and granules are light and float on top of the water. They sink to the bottom only slowly. This kind of food is good primarily for fish that feed at the surface or in the open water. Flakes come in various sizes (big flakes for big fish; small flakes for small fish).
Important: Use as your basic staple those kinds that contain a lot of roughage (check list of ingredients).
Tablets sink to the bottom quickly and are therefore good for bottom-dwelling fish.
Pellets: This is dry food compressed into stick-like shapes. Pellets are an excellent extra ration for big fish with a big appetite.
Important: Supplement pellets with food that is high in vitamins and roughage (for example, vegetable food and small crustaceans).

Live Food

The term "live food" is used for both live and frozen food animals. There is no difference in nutritional value between them, but some fish species will not eat food animals unless they still wriggle (see descriptions of species, starting on page 74).

Frozen Food

Aquarium stores sell frozen fish food in bars similar to chocolate bars. The bars are then stored in your freezer. Before feeding time, break off a piece and either thaw it in a small dish of water or move it back and forth in the surface water of the tank until it is completely thawed.

Live Food Animals

The most common food animals are mosquito larvae, small crustaceans, *Tubifex* worms, and flies. Not all of these are available live at aquarium stores. Some can be obtained only from mail-order dealers (addresses in aquarists' magazines), and some you have to raise yourself.
Mosquito larvae: Red mosquito larvae, black mosquito larvae (biting mosquito), and white mosquito larvae ("phantom midge") can be used as live food animals. They are suitable for all fishes that like live food except very tiny ones, for whom the larvae are too large.
• Live white mosquito larvae are available at aquarium stores, but only during the cold season. Store them in buckets of clear water in the cellar or outdoors.
• Aquarium stores sell live red mosquito larvae year round. Keep the larvae wrapped in damp newspapers or cloth.
• Black mosquito larvae are sold only frozen.
Important: Don't feed your fish too many red mosquito larvae, because they come from polluted waters and may contain harmful substances. Those imported from Southeast Asia are the safest. When you buy these larvae, ask at the store where exactly they are from.

seudotropheus "bright blue" feeding in Lake Malawi.

mall crustaceans: The most common crustaceans
d to fish are *Daphnia*, *Cyclops*, Bosmidae, *Artemia*
rine shrimp), and opossum shrimp (*Mysis*). They
re a good supplemental food because, with their
digestible shells, they are a good source of rough-
ge. All these crustaceans are available in frozen
rm, *Daphnia* sometimes live as well.

Smaller fish species accept *Daphnia*, *Cyclops*,
osmidae, and *Artemia* nauplii.

Larger species can also be given opossum
hrimp and fully grown brine shrimp.

ote: Small crustaceans contain carotenoids, which
ring out the natural red coloration in fish. Caroten-
ids are also found in paprika (sprinkle over food).

ubifex worms should be used only in small
mounts to supply additional fats and proteins.
hey are often polluted. To get rid of some of the
ollutants, keep the worms in pails of water for two
 three days, changing the water daily. Aquarium
tores sell *Tubifex* only live.

In the photo: Fishes that feed on
***aufwuchs* have teeth and mouth**
shapes that are especially adapted
for scraping off *aufwuchs*. Auf-
wuchs is the word used for algae
and the microorganisms living
among the algae growing on a
substrate. Among the *aufwuchs*
feeders there are some that eat
both the algae and the microorgan-
isms, and others that because of
the particular adaptation of their
teeth eat primarily the one or the
other.

Croaking spiny catfish hiding among plants.

pieces of raw potato. Make up a largish batch and freeze in serving portions.

Important: Leftover food has to be removed after one or at most two days because it will decay and pollute the water.

Vitamin Supplements
A lack of vitamins weakens the resistance to disease in fish. To add extra vitamins you can sprinkle a multivitamin powder over the food or coat the food with the powder, but if you feed your fish properly stored dry food or a varied selection of live food, they should not need vitamin supplements.

Feeding Rules
• Feed the fish a varied diet.
• It is best to feed small portions several times a day, but feed at least twice, in the morning and in the evening.
• Feed only as much as is eaten within a few minutes. Vegetables are an exception.
• Impose one fasting day a week—it benefits digestion. This does not apply to juvenile fish that are still growing. They need food every day.
• Give shy, nocturnal fish an extra feeding after the aquarium light is turned off.

My tip: Take advantage of the daily feeding time to watch your fish closely. Physical changes or changes in behavior may be symptoms of disease, results of improper care, or a sign of poisoning. More about this in the next chapter, which deals with fish diseases.

Fruit flies (Drosophila): When these flies are fed to the fish they "swim" on top of the water. They are good for surface and middle-strata fish that like to catch insects. You have to raise fruit flies yourself (instructions on HOW TO pages 54–55, "Breeding Fish").

Important: Many kinds of fish, especially killifishes, have to be fed Drosophila.

Fish and mussels: Fish filets and mussel meat cut in strips can also be used and are easy to store in the freezer. This kind of food can be used as the basic staple for large fishes, but you have to supply extra roughage, as by feeding the fish vegetable food or small crustaceans.

Vegetable Food

Many fishes, especially Loricariidae catfishes and many cichlids, have to get vegetable food. You can buy dry vegetarian fish food at aquarium stores or give your fish fresh vegetables. Suitable vegetables include spinach and lettuce leaves briefly blanched, Brussels sprouts cooked for five minutes, and small

A shoal of diamond tetras ▷
(Moenkhausia pittieri) in a
densely planted community
aquarium.

Preventing and Treating Fish Diseases

If your tank is set up properly and you maintain excellent water quality, feed a diet appropriate for your particular fish, and combine the right species, your fish will rarely get sick. However, mistakes in care weaken fish and will very likely result in disease. It is rare for diseases to be introduced from outside or for strong, healthy fish to be struck by disease.
Important: Don't buy fish that show even the slightest sign of sickness! Take your time when you choose them and, if at all possible, watch to see whether they eat well and are as active as is characteristic of their species.

Recognizing and Treating Diseases

Changes in the body and color as well as in behavior are warning signals! If you know your fish well and observe them closely every day, you are not likely to overlook these signs. Figuring out why a fish is not well, however, is a different matter and a challenge even for experienced aquarists.
Rule 1: If you spot anything suspicious, immediately check the environmental conditions (see Checklist, page 45) and correct them as needed.
Rule 2: Treat only those diseases yourself that you are sure you can diagnose correctly on the basis of unmistakable symptoms (see page 47).
Rule 3: In case of doubt, ask an expert. This might be an experienced pet dealer or a veterinarian who is knowledgeable about fish diseases. Some colleges of veterinary medicine offer information and advice on fish diseases. When you consult an expert, you should be able to describe the changes in the appearance and behavior of your fish as exactly as possible.
An alternative for those who observe their fish conscientiously: Study the literature on fish diseases carefully (see Books, page 158). In order to make a diagnosis you have to be able to use a microscope. Check with your local aquarium club to see whether there is someone who can teach you and give you advice.

Please keep in mind: Only if you watch your fish regularly, preferably every day, will you be able to tell, for instance, whether a fish is somewhat shyer or darker than usual. By the way: A single detail you have observed often fails to give a reliable picture. Study the fish, accumulate observations, and then base your conclusions on the overall picture.
Important: Sudden changes in behavior (such as frequent hiding in the brooding cave or trembling of the body) may be part of the reproductive behavior of the species. Check the courtship behavior of the species in question.

Poisoning

Poisoning occurs if an unusually high level of harmful substances has accumulated in the tank water because of mistakes in care or—more rarely—polluted tap water. Fish react, among other ways, by developing breathing problems, being excessively nervous, darting about in the tank, losing color, or generally failing to thrive.
Important: In a case of poisoning you have to respond quickly by immediately detoxifying the water (see measures suggested under the different kinds of poisoning). Poisoning can sometimes be mistaken for a disease. Moreover, a number of different kinds of poisoning have common symptons and are therefore not easy to tell apart. Observe closely and respond correctly!

Carbon Dioxide Poisoning
Plants need carbon dioxide as a nutrient, but fish can react negatively to concentrations that are too high.
Cause: Too much CO_2 fertilizing.
Symptoms: Panting, restless swimming, staggering apathy.
Measures to take: Strong aeration with the help of the filter; water change; reset the device for CO_2 fertilizing.
My tip: Never fertilize at night! Plants don't need carbon dioxide at night.

Juvenile *Baryancistrus spec.* from Rio Xingú, Brazil.

A *Steatocranus spec. aff. ubanguiensis* peeking out of its brooding retreat.

Ammonia Poisoning

<u>Causes:</u> If too much organic waste material is present and cannot be broken down properly, the ammonia concentration in the tank will rise. If the pH is above 7, there is a danger of ammonia poisoning because harmless ammonium turns into poisonous ammonia (see HOW TO page 16 on "Water Chemistry").

<u>Symptoms:</u> Panting; fish hang sluggishly just below the water surface. Especially characteristic is the

Photo above: Conspicuously colored Loricariidae catfishes are jewels in an aquarium. Although many of them grow very large, they grow very slowly. Thus far little is known about their life history, but we do know that wrong diet quickly leads to intestinal disease in these fish. In most species, tank breeding has not yet been accomplished. It would be a worthy task for hobbyists to try to keep these beauties in accordance with their needs and to get them to reproduce.

Photo below: When setting up a community tank and choosing its inhabitants one has to keep in mind the different species' ways of life. Fishes that need hiding places, for instance, can suffer stress that will make them ill if they have no refuges for retreat.

Hole-in-the-head disease in a discus fish.

In the photo: Pit-like depressions in the head region (with or without a whitish film of fungi) are a typical sign of hole-in-the-head disease. This disease is usually the result of improper care, such as vitamin deficiency resulting from improper diet.

lilac discoloration of the gills (take fish out of the tank and gently lift the gill covers).
Measures to take: Lower the pH to below 7, then remove harmful chemicals by changing the water. Correct the condition that has caused the poisoning.

Nitrite/Nitrate Poisoning
When organic waste materials are broken down, one of the by-products is nitrite, which is ordinarily further broken down into nitrate by microorganisms (see HOW TO page 16 on "Water Chemistry"). Nitrite is more toxic than nitrate.
Causes of nitrite poisoning: The water is heavily polluted with organic waste, and the bacteria are no longer able to transform nitrite into nitrate.

Causes of nitrate poisoning: The nitrate content of the tap water is too high, or the tank water contains too much organic waste material. (Check nitrate content, see page 15.)
Symptoms of nitrite/nitrate poisoning: Panting; fish hang sluggishly just below the water surface. An especially characteristic sign is that the colors of the fish are often strikingly bright.
Measures to take: Carefully change the water until the symptoms disappear, then correct the condition responsible for the poisoning.

Poisoning through Medication
This can occur in fish shortly after medication has been added to the tank water to combat a disease.
Measures to take: Filter through activated carbon (see Special filter materials, page 22); change part of the water.

Poisoning through Tap Water
Several types of poisoning are possible here:
Chlorine poisoning: This can occur (especially during the summer months) if the water has been chlorinated as a precaution against a high bacteria count. You can tell by the chlorine smell.
Correct the situation through vigorous aeration and addition of a water conditioner (available at aquarium stores). Next time you change the water, be sure to aerate the new water (to dissipate the chlorine) or let it stand for a day or two.
Copper poisoning: This can occur if you have copper pipes (often the case with plumbing in old houses). Check the water with a test kit that registers copper (available from laboratory supply dealers). Use a water conditioner; alternatively, if you have a serious problem, it may be worthwhile getting a reverse osmosis device.
Pollutant poisoning: Tap water can also contain various other harmful substances. If you suspect that toxic substances are present, filter through activated carbon—that usually takes care of the problem.

Checklist for Spotting Mistakes in Care

The following questions will help you recognize even those mistakes in care that are not detectable at a glance. If you find a "weak spot," remedy the situation immediately.

Questions	Remedies

Water: Poor water quality means that the fish are living under adverse environmental conditions, which may weaken their resistance to disease.

Questions	Remedies
Has the ammonium level risen above normal?	See page 14.
Is the nitrate/nitrite level too high?	See page 15.
Are there decaying bits of food in the tank?	Remove immediately; observe feeding rules on page 40.
Is there a dead fish in the tank?	Remove immediately; ascertain cause of death (see page 46).
Is the filter dirty?	Clean it (see page 24).
Is the partial water change overdue?	Change water carefully.
Does the water have the correct properties (pH, dH, temperature) for the fishes in your tank?	Check the information on water properties for the fish species you keep (pages 74–151).
Is there enough oxygen in the water?	Aerate (see page 13).
Did you recently add medications or other chemicals to the water?	Partial water change and filtering with activated carbon.

Fish population: Overcrowding and/or wrong combination of species is stressful for the fish and may over time weaken their resistance. Therefore check the following points:

Questions	Remedies
Is the tank overcrowded?	Reduce number of fish.
Are some fish being chased by others?	Remove both the chasers and the chased or create enough hiding places; check combination of species.
Are the more aggressive species keeping the other fish from getting food?	Check combination of species; take more account of the varying behavior of the fish: Feed aggressive eaters first, then the more reserved ones. Feed nocturnal fish after turning off aquarium light.
Have you added new fish and/or species?	Check whether new fish may have introduced disease (see page 47); if fish are incompatible, change the combination.

Diet: A wrong diet can cause deficiency symptoms and digestive problems and can lead to starvation.

Questions	Remedies
Is the food appropriate for the particular combination of fish species in the tank?	Observe the food needs of the fish you keep (see descriptions, pages 74–151). Supply the proper kinds of food; check to see whether fish might be sick.
Are the fish getting enough roughage and vitamins?	Supply substances that may be lacking (see pages 38 and 40).

HOW TO
Diseases

In many cases you will have no choice but to consult a veterinarian or other specialist, either because the treatment calls for prescription drugs or because an aquarist without specialized training simply cannot diagnose the disease reliably.

Aids for Diagnosis and Treatment

In the table on the facing page you will find those diseases which exhibit clear, visible symptoms. The numbers following the name of the disease refer to possible treatments (listed here) based on "home remedies" and on medications available from aquarium or pet dealers.
Important: If you are unable to arrive at a clear diagnosis on the basis of the symptoms mentioned in the table, it is absolutely necessary to consult a specialist.
My tip: Always have the medications mentioned below on hand. With all treatments, be sure that the proper water properties are maintained—except where the recommended therapy involves a change in water quality.

1. Heat Therapy
This treatment is administered in the regular tank.
Helpful for minor cases of infestation with *Ichthyophtirius*, *Oodinium*, and other ectoparasites (*Costia/Trichodina*).
Application: Only in a tank with absolutely clean water and a good supply of oxygen. Raise the temperature by 2°F (1°C) per hour;
• for *Ichthyophtirius*, keep water at 86°F (30°C) for 10 days;
• for *Oodinium*, keep it at 91–93°F (33–34°C) for 24 to 36 hours.
Important: Watch fish closely. If there are any side effects, such as disturbed equilibrium, immediately discontinue treatment.

2. Formalin Bath
This is done in a separate pail. You can buy a 35–40 percent formalin solution at drugstores.
Effective against skin and gill flukes as well as many other ectoparasites.
Application: Add 2–4 ml of formalin solution (35–40 percent) to 10 quarts of water. Place fish in the pail with this water for a maximum of 30 minutes.
Important: If there are signs of disturbed equilibrium, immediately return the fish to the tank.
Caution: Formalin is highly caustic and can cause sickness. Avoid contact with skin, eyes, and mucous membranes. Store where children cannot reach it.

3. Salt Bath
This is done in a separate pail.
Effective against fungus infestation, *Ichthyophtirius*, and minor infestation with skin and gill flukes.
Application: ⅓ to ½ ounce (10–15 g) of table salt per quart of water. Keep fish in the salt solution for 20 minutes, watching them the entire time.
Important: In the case of *Ichthyophtirius*, all the fish in the tank have to be treated and—very important—this initial treatment has to be followed by two more, each after an interval of 48 to 72 hours.

4. Medications Containing Malachite Green Solution
Treatment can be administered in the regular tank. These medications are available from aquarium dealers.
Helpful against infestation with *Ichthyophtirius* and against fungus disease. If any fish are infected with *Ichthyophtirius*, you should always treat all the fish in the tank.
Application: Follow instructions for use.
Important: Aerate tank well. Replenish the medication after water changes.

5. Medications Containing Furazolidon
Treatment can be administered in the regular tank. Various commercial preparations are available, including Furam II and Furazone Light.

Effective against many bacterial infections, such as bacterial fin rot, and sometimes in early stages of ascites.
Application: Follow instructions for use.
Note: Fin rot and ascites are usually caused by poor environmental conditions.

6. Remedies for Hole-in-the-head Disease and Intestinal Flagellate
Can be applied for hole-in-the-head disease with or without intestinal flagellates.
Treatment depends on the stage of the disease:
• If there are only small holes in the head region, adding vitamins to the food (see page 40) may halt the progress of the disease. The disease is often caused by vitamin or mineral deficiency.
• If it seems likely that there are intestinal flagellates (signs: white, stringy excreta), consult a specialist. In all cases, feed a vitamin-rich diet.

Camallanus Infestation
Symptoms: Fish hang motionless in the water with ends of worms protruding from the anus, which is opened wide. If this is the case, consult a specialist.
My tip: Ask whether treatment with Fenbendazol is appropriate.

Taking Fish to the Veterinarian
• It is best if you can take the sick fish to the vet while they are still alive (if possible, two of them).
• Even if one or more fish have died, take (or send) them to the vet or other specialist for diagnosis so that other fish can be treated promptly, if necessary.
• Freeze fish immediately after they have died. Diagnosis is practically impossible for fish that are frozen later than 20 minutes after death.
• Wrap dead fish in wax paper (not plastic) for the transport.
• Send dead fish as frozen merchandise in a styrofoam container with an antifreeze ice pack.
Note: Don't place the fish in formalin or alcohol because this makes diagnosis impossible.
My tip: Ask at your local aquarists' club for names of specialists.

illing a Fish
ometimes it is better to kill fish that ave an incurable disease than to et them go on suffering. In such a ase, sever the spinal cord immedi-tely below the head with a sharp nife or sharp scissors. Large fish hould be stunned first by a blow on e head with a hard, blunt object.

Disinfecting
Before you set up the aquarium again after an episode of sickness (such as neon disease), the tank and all the equipment and accesso-ries used in it (nets, filter, and so on) have to be disinfected. Setting the tank up anew makes sense only if you are going to get all new fish. The old fish that survive are often hidden carriers of the disease and will infect a newly set-up tank.

Disinfectant: Potassium permanga-nate (available at drugstores).
Application: Fill tank or disinfecting container for accessories up to the top with water. Add enough potas-sium permanganate powder to make a dark violet, opaque solution. Place all the equipment in the tank and run the filter without filter material. Let stand three days, then empty. Rinse tank and equipment with water until all trace of violet is gone.

Aids for Diagnosis and Treatment

Symptoms \ Disease and recommended treatment	Ichthyophtirius: treatments 1, 3, 4	Oodinium pillularis: treatment 1	Gill and skin flukes: treatments 2, 3	Ascites: treatment 5	Bacterial fin rot: treatment 5	Hole-in-the-head disease/intestinal flagellates: treatment 6
White dots about 1/16 inch (1.5 mm) in diameter on the body	✦					
Many tiny dots (up to .3 mm) close together, often appearing as a whitish to yellowish film		✦				
Violent and frequent swallowing motions and/or protruding gill covers			✦			
Panting	✦	✦	✦			
Bloated body, often with protuberant scales				✦		
Bulging eyes				✦		
Emaciation						✦
Darkening of the body						✦
Small holes gradually growing larger in the head region; often lined with a white film						✦
White, stringy, slimy excreta						✦
Frayed fins, often shortened, with or without a white rim					✦	
Rubbing against objects in the tank	✦	✦	✦			

What makes the neon tetra glow.

The bright stripe shows up best in a tank arranged in dark colors and with muted lighting. We assume that the neon stripe serves a signal function in keeping the shoal together in dark water. Unlike fireflies, which produce light themselves by means of chemical reactions, neon tetras make use of external light sources. Iridescent particles in the pigment cells of the neon stripe reflect even faint light very effectively. Depending on the light rays' angle of incidence, the stripe lights up in various colors (green to blue). At night, when the fish "turn off" the pigment cells, the stripe is barely visible. Even if there is light now, it strikes the turned-off reflectors at an angle of incidence that barely produces any glow. It takes quite a while until the reflectors are back in working condition again and the stripe glows in full color.

Breeding Aquarium Fishes

Anyone who wants to breed aquarium fishes successfully has to know the requirements of the fish in question and create appropriate environmental conditions, depending on the species, in either the regular maintenance tank or a special breeding tank.

Breeding always implies selection and culling. Sick or malformed juvenile fish should, of course, not be raised, but even among mature fish not all are good bets for breeding.

Selecting the Parent Fish

One prerequisite for successful breeding is the selection of proper breeding stock. Watch for the following:

Traits of the species: The fish should conform in body shape, size, and markings to the characteristic appearance of their species in order to pass these traits on to their offspring. It does not make sense to breed fish with deviant traits.

Health of the parents: Healthy animals are most likely to produce healthy offspring. You will find the signs that distinguish healthy from sick or malformed fish listed on page 23, in the section "Buying and Introducing Fish." The most basic rule is that the fish should appear strong and be as active as is characteristic of their species.

Compatibility of the sexual partners: Sympathy between the partners plays an important role with all fish, regardless of whether they form extended pair bonds or come together only briefly to spawn. That is why you should, if possible, pick partners that get along well in the regular tank or that may already have shown sexual interest in each other. The courtship rituals, in the course of which the fish display special behavior and even colors, will give you the necessary clues.

Crossing different species or different color variants of the same species should be avoided.

What Encourages Fish to Spawn

The right kind of food: Some undemanding fish species will spawn even on a diet of dry food, but many others will spawn only if they are given speci food that closely reflects their special dietary requir ments (see descriptions, pages 74–151). Experi ence has shown, for instance, that characins spaw especially well if they are fed black mosquito larva

The right environment: Many species need hiding places, while others need to live in small shoals to feel at ease. Breeding efforts are successful only the conditions in the maintenance tank or the breeding tank correspond to the requirements of t species in question. Many characins, for instance, need a dark tank. If there is too much light, they hover in a corner, frightened, and refuse to engag in courtship behavior or to deposit their spawn eve though it has formed.

Spawning substrates: Except for species that spawn in open water, all fish need some sort of substrate on which to deposit their eggs.

Spawning rhythm: In nature, most tropical fishes spawn only during the rainy season; in the aquarium, too, signals that the "rainy season" is here are needed by many species to bring about readiness to spawn.

The rainy season affects the water temperature, salt content of the water, water level, and pH. By manipulating these factors, it is possible to simula "rainy season signals" that convince many species Not all species are fooled, however: All attempts t breed the clown loach have failed because no one has yet managed to create the conditions in a tan that will induce these fish to spawn.

Altering the temperature: This is enough to make armored and callichthyd catfishes spawn. Change ¼ of the water daily for several days, until the tank water is about 6–9°F (3–5°C) cooler than when yo started.

Altering salt content, pH, and water level: In many of the more difficult aquarium fish, such as knife

A pair of Tanganiyka clowns (*Eretmodus cyanostictus*) passing eggs from one to the other.

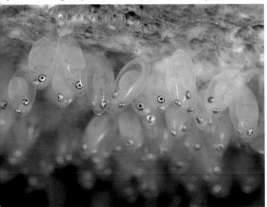

A brood of *Chlamydogobius eremius*.

Photo on left: These larvae of *Chlamydogobius eremius* are just about to emerge from their egg skins. One can clearly distinguish the fully formed eyes and the yolk sac. Because the eggs are transparent, the entire development of the larvae can be observed.

shes, elephant fishes, and probably some other species that have not thus far responded to breeding attempts, the rainy season mood has to be brought about slowly. Try the "Kirschbaum method," which has been successfully used in the case of *Eigenmannia* knife fishes.

The "Kirschbaum method": First reduce the water level to about half, then add daily about 5 percent of the volume of water still in the tank, using fully desalted water, until the tank is full again. Tempera-ture is immaterial in such small quantities of water. Repeat the process for several weeks. If the pH was in the alkaline range initially, it should drop to slightly acid. If the water was slightly acid at the start, the pH will not change. This method is for hard-water fishes only.

My tip: In addition, imitate "rain" by regularly having water splash onto the surface for an hour or so from the spray pipes of a motorized outside filter (use a timer!). When the fish are ready to produce spawn, which you can tell by the swollen bellies of the females, keep the water properties steady where they are.

Important: If all efforts to induce a spawning mood in the fish fail, try again at a different time of year. Fish caught in the wild often have an internal clock that allows them to get ready to spawn only at certain seasons, no matter how favorable conditions are at other times.

Advice for Breeding

What kind of tank to breed your fish in depends on their species. Aquarists divide them into the following groups:

- Species where egg laying, hatching, and growing up of fry all happen in the regular maintenance tank. Many cichlids are in this group.
- Species where the parent fish have to be placed in a separate breeding (spawning) tank because the environmental conditions necessary for breeding (water properties and purity) cannot be met in a normally functioning aquarium. Most characins are in this group.
- Species that spawn in the maintenance tank but whose eggs and/or fry have to be transferred into a rearing tank. Among this group are rainbow fishes (eggs or larvae), armored catfishes (eggs), and Gobiidae (fry).
- Species where one of the parents has to be transferred gently to a rearing tank or where interfering fish have to be removed from the rearing tank. Many mouthbrooders and livebearers belong here.

Transfer into a Breeding Tank
A breeding tank can be:
- a hygienic spawning tank (see HOW TO page 54) from which the parent fish are removed after the eggs have been laid. The brood stays in this tank until it has to be moved into a bigger tank.
- a tank in which the parent fish are kept until the conclusion of brood care.

Important: When the parent fish are transferred into the breeding tank they have to get gradually acclimated to the new water conditions. Place the fish with some water from their regular tank in a bucket. For an hour or two, pour a little water from the breeding tank into the bucket every 10 minutes until the bucket is full. Catch the fish in the bucket with a net and transfer them to the breeding tank. Please keep in mind that the water temperatures in the bucket and the breeding tank have to be the same.

My tip: If you are interested in raising just a few

A pair of kissing gouramis.

young of species that spawn in the maintenance tank, place fry into spawning boxes that are hung into the maintenance tank (see HOW TO page 54)

Transferring Eggs, Larvae, or Fry
Whether or not eggs, larvae, or fry should be moved into a rearing tank depends on their species
Species without brood care: Move eggs or larvae into a tank that holds 10 to 30 quarts. For hygienic reasons it is better not to add any bottom material. The water properties should be the same as in the regular tank. Move the eggs along with the spawning substrate or shake them off the substrate in the rearing tank. The eggs of some species, like those of armored catfishes, stick to their substrate and have to be lifted off with a razor blade. Add to the water an agent that inhibits bacteria and fungi, and be sure to adhere strictly to the instructions for use Larvae that swim at the water's surface can be carefully skimmed off with a ladle. Other larvae are siphoned up with a hose (as when changing the water).

Siphon up excreta and leftover food with a thin hose at least once a day. Replace the water with fresh water of the same temperature and properties. As the fry grow big, move them into as large a rearing tank as possible.

Species with brood care: The larvae and fry of these species are raised in the maintenance tank or in a special breeding tank together with the parent fish for as long as the parents look after them. When this phase comes to an end, the fry are

"Kissing" is part of the courtship.

They embrace during spawning.

placed in as large a rearing tank as possible, where they remain until they are full-grown. The water properties have to be the same in the maintenance and the rearing tank. Change part of the water several times a week, because in most cases the tank will be rather crowded, causing the water to become polluted quickly.

Feeding the Brood

Proper feeding of the brood is essential for the fry to develop into healthy fish. Fish larvae or fry are first fed with special rearing food (such as *Artemia* and paramecia). As they get bigger, they are gradually given somewhat larger food morsels (for kinds of food, see page 55).
• Don't feed larvae while they still have a yolk sac! They would not eat the food, which would pollute the water.
• Start feeding larvae when they have almost emptied their yolk sacs and are swimming around.
• The kind of food has to be appropriate to the size of the brood. Depending on the fry's rate of growth, change to larger kinds of food.
Important: Larvae and fry have to be fed several times a day. They don't have any food reserves yet.
My tip: As soon as the brood swims free, place a few snails in the rearing tank. They serve as "garbage disposal" for leftover food.
To make sure food gets to a shoal of fry in a maintenance tank, a syringe is useful. Attach a piece of thin hose to the syringe (available at drugstores)

and, on the other end, add a rigid plastic tube about 8 to 12 inches (20–30 cm) long (available at aquarium stores).

Ongoing Breeding

If you have fish that do not engage in brood care and if you don't want to move the parent, eggs, or larvae into a separate tank, you can, with many species, still obtain healthy offspring by setting the tank up for ongoing breeding. Proceed as follows:
Population: Keep only a small number of one species in a tank, or add one other very peaceful species, such as a small sucker-mouth catfish.
Set-up: It is important to provide plenty of spawning substrates as well as thickets made up of nonrooting plants, such as Java moss or hornwort, for the fry to hide in during the first few days. Use only a thin layer of sand for the bottom or do without bottom material altogether.
Care: Free-swimming larvae or fry can be given *Artemia* or other food for fry. Under these conditions, some of the young fish always make it to adulthood and are generally especially vigorous specimens.
Important: Don't keep snails that eat spawn in the tank!
My tip: A tank set up for ongoing breeding is especially well suited for fish species that produce tiny larvae. The larvae survive during the first few days on microorganisms that are always present in thick plant growth.

HOW TO
Breeding Fish

Many kinds of fish require special tanks for spawning and rearing. Success in fish breeding is also often dependent on using the right kind of food.

A Spawning Tank
Drawing 1
A hygienic spawning tank for egg-laying fishes that do not engage in brood care.
Tank: 10–30 quarts, cleaned very thoroughly. No bottom material. Instead, place black paper under the bottom pane so that reflections will not irritate the fish. Alternatively, put down a very thin layer of quartz sand.
Protection of spawn: Many egg-layers that don't engage in brood care eat their own eggs. Therefore cover the bottom with glass marbles; the eggs drop between them and are thus out of reach for the adult fish. An alternative for fishes that like acid water: a layer of peat.
Spawning substrates: Different species have different requirements.
• For most characins and barbs: plants with fine, feathery leaves (such

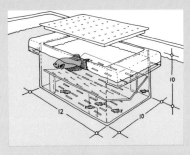

2 Small spawning box that can be hung in the aquarium. Excellent for small livebearers.

as Java moss or *Myriophyllum*).
• For killifishes that attach spawn to substrate: A mop of thick (artificial) fibers that is attached to a cork and floats on the surface has proved reliable.
• Some species prefer broad-leaved plants (many *Rasbora* species) or pieces of pumice stone with grooves filed into them (lamp-eyes).

3 Yolk sac larvae cannot yet swim but hang from a substrate or lie on the bottom. The fat, yellow abdomen is the yolk sac, a food supply to sustain the larvae.

Important: Disinfect all spawning substrates before placing them in the tank. Plants are placed in an alum bath (alum is available from drugstores): 1 heaping teaspoon of alum to 1 quart of water. Immerse plants for five minutes, then rinse well. Other substrates are boiled.
Technical equipment: A carefully cleaned rod-type heater and an air-stone that aerates by gently sending bubbles of air through the water.
How to proceed: Transfer fish that have already demonstrated some reproductive behavior in their regular tank into a spawning tank. Keep this tank dark and disturb it as little as possible (set it up in a quiet corner). If the fish have not spawned after a few days, catch them. It may be a good idea to segregate them by sex. Clean the tank and try again. Once the fish have spawned, wait until the larvae with their yolk sacs hang on the walls of the tank and then begin to swim free. Do not start feeding them until this point.

Spawning Boxes
Drawing 2
Small, rectangular spawning boxes (5 x 4 x 4 inches or 12 x 10 x 10 cm) are useful for small livebearing tooth carps (up to 2 inches or 5 cm). The boxes are hung in the aquarium.
Set-up: Place some crystalwort (*Riccia*) on the water surf ace (gives the fish a sense of safety).
How to proceed: Place gravid female in the spawning box. The newborn fry slip down through the slots in the bottom and are thus out of reach of the cannibalistic mother. After the fry are born, remove the female and the bottom panel of the spawning box.
Boxes for hanging in the tank: Spawning boxes of a larger size (10 x 6 x 6 inches or 25 x 15 x 15 cm) can be used for larger livebearing tooth carps to give birth in as well as for raising smallish numbers of fry of other species. The boxes have stainless steel hooks with which to hang them from the top of the tank wall. For proper aeration a small air-driven foam filter set on low should be hung on the tank wall next to the spawning box, with the filter outflow pipe pointing into the box.

1 A hygienic spawning tank for egg-laying fishes that do not engage in brood care.

Food Animals and Products for Initial and Later Feeding

Artemia nauplii: A nutritious food for initial feeding of brood and later feeding of growing fry. Pour 1 quart of salt water (⅔ ounce or 20 grams of noniodized table salt per quart) into a 2-quart jar and add 2 to 3 level teaspoons of dormant *Artemia* eggs; aerate if needed. Stir to make sure all the eggs are wet. If kept at 75–82°F (24–28°C) (place jars in a water bath with a thermostat heater), the reddish larvae will hatch. Use a food syringe or pipette to suck up larvae but only from near the bottom. Rinse the larvae off (over an *Artemia* sieve) and give immediately to fry. Start a new batch every day so that you will always have enough food. Use of an airstone to aerate the culture is recommended.

Paramecia: First food for tiny fry. Fill jars with water that has been standing a while. Add a few cubes of turnip (only turnip!). Inoculate the water with water from an older culture or start out with oxygen-poor water from a puddle. Paramecia will soon appear in a milky layer just below the water surface. Feed them frequently with drops of evaporated milk. For feeding to fry: Fill a bottle up to the neck with the culture solution, top with a loose wad of cotton wool, and fill the rest of the way with clean water that has been standing. The paramecia will migrate into the upper level of clean water, where they can be sucked up with a food syringe and then given to the fry. Pour the water back in the jar. When the culture stops producing, start new jars.

Whiteworms (*Enchytraeus*): For older fry that feed near the bottom. Soak peat for a few days, then place 2 inches (5 cm) of damp peat in freezer containers (covers with screen section). Add breeding culture and spread a thin layer of feeding mush (in a ratio of 3:3:3—oat meal, whole wheat bread, and powdered milk) over the loosened peat. Moisten slightly with a mist of water, then place in the dark at 68–77°F (20–25°C). Removal: Place a small piece of glass on the peat and press down lightly. The worms will collect beneath the glass, where they can be picked off. Start new cultures every six to eight weeks, if worms start to crawl out of their containers or if the culture is invaded by mites.

Fruit flies (*Drosophila*): Strains that cannot fly are best (available from mail-order firms). Place ¾ to 1¼ inches (2–3 cm) of feeding mush (see below) in several small laboratory jars, sprinkle some dry yeast over it, top with some crumpled paper, add 20 to 30 flies, and close jars with foam rubber stoppers. Give adult flies (after 12–20 days) to fish soon (they don't live long). Removal: Place jars in refrigerator for a short time to immobilize the flies before you feed them to the fish. Start new cultures every few days.

Feeding mush: Puree one can of plums, one packet of oat flakes, one orange with peel, one banana, and 1 cup of vinegar in a blender; add water if needed to obtain a runny, but not watery, consistency.

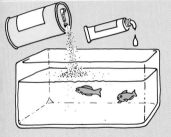

Dry and liquid commercial foods

Other, commercially available and ready-to-feed foods for fry that will eat them: pulverized dry food and infusorians (single-celled microorganisms) in liquid form for very tiny fry (labyrinth fishes). Don't give too much of these foods and make especially sure the tank stays clean. Dry food, in particular, decomposes very quickly. If the fry are swimming free, add two or three snails, which will consume any food remains.

How Fish Ensure the Survival of Their Species

It is hard for us humans to imagine living in water. That is one reason why it is so fascinating for hobbyists to watch how fish manage to exist in this environment, find food and reproduce there.

On HOW TO pages 60 and 61 on the "Body Shapes of Fishes" you can see how different kinds of fish have adapted to be able to inhabit certain environments or to take advantage of particular food sources. In the text that follows you will get a glimpse of the fascinating techniques of reproduction and the development of the young fish. If you plan to breed fish in your aquarium (see Breeding Fish, pages 50–55), you will find here the basic information on the most important forms of fish reproduction, development, and rearing.

How Fish Reproduce

There are fishes that lay eggs and others that give birth to live offspring (livebearers).

Egg-laying Species

The majority of fishes lay eggs that are given off into the open water (open-water spawners), attached to a substrate (substrate spawners), or deposited on the bottom (bottom spawners).

The eggs: The size and number of the eggs can vary greatly depending on the species. Consider two familiar species: Kissing gouramis (*Helostoma temminckii*) lay several thousand eggs, each about 1 mm in diameter. *Tropheus duboisi*, by contrast, usually lay fewer than 10 eggs, but each egg measures almost ⅜ inch (1 cm). Species that lay a small number of large eggs usually look after their brood for some time. Others, like the kissing gouramis, which don't look after the young, produce more, but smaller, eggs to make up for the high mortality rate due to absence of parental care. Big eggs are the size they are because of the yolk, which serves the young organism as a food supply. Large eggs with a lot of yolk take longer (several days) to develop

into larvae. Very tiny eggs hatch into larvae after just one day.

From larva to fry: During the first few days of life almost all larvae carry along a yolk sac to provide them with food. It is not until the larvae swim free that they accept food offered by the aquarist (see HOW TO pages 54 and 55 on "Breeding Fish"). Larvae differ significantly from fry in external appearance. Instead of dorsal, caudal, and anal fins, all they have is one continuous fin fringe. It is from this fringe that fins with rays develop. This is when the larvae turn into fry, or baby fish.

Important: The larvae of a few species, such as rainbow fishes, have almost no yolk sac. They swim free immediately after hatching and have to be fed right away.

Livebearers

Some species, such as guppies, engage in a highly developed form of brood care. They don't lay eggs; instead the egg cells are fertilized and develop into complete baby fish within the mother's body. Once the young are born, they are immediately independent. There are two types of livebearers: In one, eggs form in the female's body and hatch shortly before they are born (ovoviviparous type). In the other (viviparous type), no eggs are formed, and the embryos are fed through a kind of umbilical cord.

How Different Fishes Raise Their Brood

Most species of fish deposit their eggs and then pay no further attention to them. Other egg-laying fishes have developed various special forms of brood care. Giving birth to live offspring (as livebearers do) can be regarded as the most highly developed form of brood care.

Anyone wishing his or her fish to reproduce in an aquarium has to start by creating the kind of conditions that permit the form of egg laying and brood care that the particular species engages in.

One of the few snail cichlids of Lake Malawi.

Egg-layers without Brood Care

Here one distinguishes among three main variations:

Open-water spawners drop their eggs in the open water, often without even leaving the shoal. The eggs either drift to the bottom or remain suspended in the water, or float along on the surface. The larvae hatch after just one day.

Substrate spawners deposit their eggs on some surface (substrate) to which the eggs adhere because they are sticky on the outside. Depending on the species of the fish, the substrate can be a feathery-leaved or broad-leaved plant, wood, or stones, the last often with tiny grooves in them.

Bottom spawners either deposit their eggs in the upper layer of the bottom material, or both partners burrow into the bottom and deposit the eggs there, buried a couple of inches deep. These latter fish, among them many killifishes, are sometimes called "bottom divers." Of course, all bottom spawners need appropriate bottom material (see descriptions of species, pages 74–151).

In the photo: *Pseudotropheus lanisticola*, a snail cichlid from Lake Malawi, is a good example of how animals make use of features in their environment. The sandy bottom characteristic of the environment of snail cichlids offers little in the way of protection. Fish therefore usually have to resort to flight or burrowing into the bottom. This cichlid, however, takes advantage of empty snail shells lying around to hide in. In nature, this cichlid often shares its hiding place with a small catfish species.

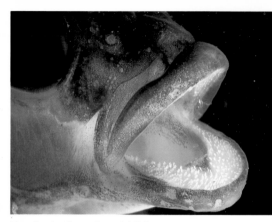

Mouth of a fin-eating cichlid.

Photo above: A number of fish species have turned to highly unusual food sources. Among them are the *Corematodus* species of Lake Malawi that feed on the scales and fins of other fishes.

Underside of a fin-sucker catfish.

Egg-layers with Brood Care

What is meant by brood care is that the parents look after their brood and guard them against predators. Brood care is subdivided according to two aspects: One is how long the care lasts (that is, until what developmental stage the brood is cared for); the other is the brooding manner. Here we find many different kinds of behavior. The three most common ones are care of eggs and larvae with yolk sacs while they adhere to the substrate; care until the brood reaches the fry stage; and mouth-brooding.

Brood care of eggs and yolk sac larvae on the substrate: The eggs and the larvae are fanned (to increase oxygen supply), and the parents keep the brood clean with their mouths. Parental care often ceases when the larvae start to swim free.

The bubble nest builders represent a special and interesting case. These are fishes that make a nest for their brood out of bubbles. They swim to the surface, take an air bubble in the mouth, enclose it in a tough layer of saliva, and spit it out again, usually close to the water surface. They repeat this process until a nest of bubbles is produced, into which the female deposits the eggs. Such a spawning place is especially rich in oxygen because it is close to the surface. Bubble nests are built by fishes that live in oxygen-deficient biotopes and come to the surface to get air. Many labyrinth fishes build bubble nests, as do some callichthyd catfishes.

Brood care of eggs, larvae, and fry: Many brood-caring species, such as cichlids, still look after their young when these swim free as larvae and even longer, after they have turned into fry. The parents attack and drive away predators and in many cases actively feed the brood as well. Discus fish secrete a food substance on the surface of the body, and other species stir up the bottom, thus making food particles available for their young.

Mouthbrooding: This highly specialized form of brood care is found in the most varied fish groups. The eggs that have been spawned are picked up by the parents in the mouth, where they stay until the larvae can swim free (ovophile mouthbrooders). In some species only the larvae are picked up in the mouth, the eggs having been looked after while

In the photo: Some fish species have adapted quite different organs to serve as suction devices. Sometimes—as in the case of the fin-sucker catfish in the photo on page 58, left—it is the pectoral or ventral fins that have been reshaped. Very often it is the mouth, which is changed into a sucker-mouth, as in the *Chaetostoma* genus.

Chaetostoma spec., a sucker-mouth armored catfish.

they remained attached to the substrate (larvophile mouthbrooders). The young swim out of the mouth in search of food but return there if danger threatens and at night.

Family Forms in Fish

As varied as the methods of reproduction are the "family relationships" of fish, ranging from brief sexual contact to longer bonds between sexual partners and, in some cases, extending to offspring. In most fish species no pair bond is established, and contact between the sexual partners is limited to spawning (fertilization and depositing of the eggs). This form of relationship is called agamy. Monogamous relationships also exist among fish, however, and are by no means rare. In addition, one finds polygyny, where one male mates with several females, and polyandry, where one female mates with several males.

When discussing fishes that engage in brood or parental care, we even speak of family forms, which can be divided into three basic groups: the parental family, father or mother families, and extended families.

Parental family: Both sexes perform the same brood care tasks.

Father/mother family: The sexes assume different parental care tasks.

Male-with-harem family: It is the male's job to defend a large territory, within which usually several females gather and tend the brood.

Mother or father family: One parent (in tropical fresh-water fishes, generally the mother) performs the brood care without help from the partner.

Family with brood care helpers: Brood care is performed by the parents together with offspring from earlier spawnings.

What Body Shape Tells Us About Fish

It is well worthwhile for an aquarist to take a closer look at the shapes of his or her fishes, because quite a bit can be learned from this about their diet, environment, and habits. The large drawing on the right shows a fish of average shape that dwells in the middle strata of the water. This type includes, among others, the characins and the barbs. The detail drawings show adaptations in form and function of individual organs.

The gills

Probably the most important adaptation of fish to their environment—water—is the gills. Gills are highly effective breathing organs capable of absorbing oxygen and giving off carbon dioxide. Since water contains only about 5 percent as much oxygen as air does, large amounts of water have to be moved across the surface that absorbs this gas, and this surface itself has to be large. The skin also serves fish as a breathing organ, but the main job has to be done by the gills. That is why
• the surface area of the gills is amazingly large, and
• fish use the mouth and the gill cavity as a very effective pumping system that moves the water through the gills.
Note: Quite a few species have developed additional breathing organs that allow them to breathe air above the water surface. One of these is the labyrinth organ, which labyrinth fishes are named after.

Head region

Several organs in this region tell us something about the way of life of the fish (for instance, the mouth and the eyes).

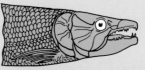

Predatory fish with wide mouths at the tip of the snout (end-positioned) usually hunt for prey in open water.

Fish with a sucker-type mouth feed off substrates and use their mouths to cling to rocks and other objects.

Fish with barbels (tactile and taste organs) can locate food even at night.

Body covering

This consists of skin and scales or bony plates; it serves as protection. The skin is also a breathing organ. The coating of scales gives the body firmness. Many fishes don't have scales or have only tiny ones. Spiny catfishes have bony plates and spines on their skin.

Ventral fin

Serves to provide stability in swimming

The ventral fin is often modified, as in the case of the gouramis, where it has become a thread-like tactile organ.

Bottom-dwelling fishes

The bodies of these fishes are flattened at the bottom or have rounded ventral fins for resting on. In many of them the swim bladder is atrophied, so that they can swim only awkwardly in open water.

Dorsal fin

Lends stability in swimming.

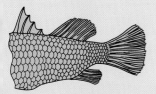

Large dorsal fins are used as "show-off" organs to impress potential sexual partners or intimidate rivals.

n many fishes the dorsal fin is divided n two. The anterior part often has piny rays while the posterior part as soft rays.   The spines serve s defense   against predators.

Caudal fin

In most fishes, the caudal fin, or tail, is the main propelling organ. Fishes that are tireless swimmers have forked tails (see drawing of a fish body on left).

Round caudal fins with a large surface area are effective for quick starts from immobility. They are characteristic of many predators.

Anal fin

Lends stability in swimming.

Lateral line organ

This organ, which is visible as a line of perforated scales, allows fish to register changes in pressure—even from different directions and at great distances. This highly sensitive "teletactile organ" furnishes the fish with additional information about their environment.

Long-drawn-out caudal fins are often "show-off" organs, like the "sword" of the swordtail (*Xiphophorus helleri*).

This fin is often modified into a fin fringe that acts as a propelling force by undulating (in knife fishes, for instance).

Surface-dwelling fishes

Their bodies are flattened at the top, and the mouth is usually undershot. They feed primarily on insects that land on the water and on small surface-dwelling fish. Some even jump out of the water to catch flying insects.

An Aquarist's Glossary

A

Acidic
Water with a pH of less than 7 is acidic.

Acidifiers
These are responsible for a low pH of the water. The most important acidifiers for the aquarist are CARBONIC ACID and HUMIC ACIDS.

Acidity
See pH.

Algae
Primitive type of aquatic plants that live on a substrate or float in the water ("green water"). Overfertilizing and poor WATER PROPERTIES give rise to increased algae growth. This problem can be dealt with by introducing fishes that feed on algae and adding fast-growing, undemanding plants that will compete with the algae for available nutrients. *Important*: Don't resort to chemical algae killers.

Alkaline
Also called "basic." A pH between 7.0 and 14 means that the water is alkaline.

Ammonia (NH$_3$)
A gas that if present in dissolved form in high concentrations is toxic for aquarium fish. Ammonia is present in aquarium water only if the pH is above 6.8. If the pH is below 6.8, ammonia takes on the form of nonpoisonous ammonium (NH$_4^+$). Ammonium and ammonia are produced by the breakdown of ORGANIC WASTE PRODUCTS.

Ammonium (NH$_4^+$)
See AMMONIA.

Andropodium
A mating organ that has evolved from the anal fin in the families Goodeidae and Hemirhamphidae.

Artemia
Also known as brine shrimp. Small crustacean (about ⅜ inch or 1 cm long) belonging to the order Anostraca. Lives in very salty waters. Brine shrimp form resting eggs from which larvae hatch, the so-called *Artemia nauplii*. Aquarium stores sell *Artemia* resting eggs, which will hatch if treated the right way. The nauplii are a universal food for rearing fry. Adult brine shrimp are also sold frozen and are an excellent food for aquarium fish.

Artemia nauplii
See ARTEMIA.

Ascites
Fish disease characterized by an accumulation of fluid in the abdomen. Symptoms: Fish become obese; scales often stick out from body; and eyes bulge. Sometimes there are other manifestations. Ascites is usually caused by bacteria and is often incurable. Easily confused with FISH TUBERCULOSIS.

Aufwuchs
A German word that has gained currency among aquarists to describe microorganisms—such as bacteria, algae, small crustaceans, and single-celled organisms—that colonize substrates, covering them like sheets.

B

Bacteria
Microorganisms, some of which perform useful functions in an aquarium, such as transforming ammonium into NITRITE and NITRATE. Some others act as pathogens, attacking primarily weakened fish and causing diseases such as ASCITES.

Basic
See ALKALINE.

Biotope
The natural environment of an organism.

Biotope aquarium
An aquarium that in its set-up and combination of fishes aims to imitate the natural biotope.

Black water
Water that has a dark, cola-like color caused by HUMIC ACIDS and many other substances. The pH of black water is often below 5, and the water hardness (see GENERAL OR TOTAL HARDNESS) is too low to be measured. The most famous river carrying black water is the Río Negro in Brazil. Trying to recreate these water properties in an aquarium is not recommended, except for breeding a few black-water species (such as *Parosphromenus deissneri*).

Bog roots
Remains of roots after the outer parts have rotted away in a bog. Found, for instance, when peat is dug (available at aquarium stores). The roots have to be soaked in water until they sink to the bottom. necessary, weigh them down with rocks at first. Roots from Scottish moors are an exception: They sink right away.

Bottom spawner
Term describing fish that deposit their eggs in the upper layers of the bottom material. This type of spawning is common among SEASONAL FISHES, whose native waters dry up periodically.

Breeding (spawning) tank
An aquarium set up specifically for breeding fish.

Brood care
Behavior of fish intended to protect and enhance the chances of survival of their offspring.

C

Camallanus
Endoparasitic worms that hang out of the anus of infected fish. Visible only when the fish are not moving. Consult a specialist for treatment.

Carbonate hardness
That part of total hardness that is formed by the ions of carbonates (CO_3^-) and of hydrogen carbonate ions (HCO_3^-). Carbonate hardness is given in °dCH. Because of the inter-relationship between CARBON DIOXIDE and pH, it is important to know the carbonate hardness if one wants to influence the carbon dioxide content and the pH of the tank water. Under normal conditions, 4 to 8°dCH is ideal for most aquarium fishes and plants. Greater hardness is of benefit to "hard-water" fishes.

Carbonates
See CARBONATE HARDNESS.

Carbon dioxide (CO_2)
Important plant nutrient. Even though a small proportion of it changes into carbonic acid, aquarists, for simplicity's sake, speak only of carbon dioxide. The amount of carbon dioxide available to plants is directly related to the carbonate hardness and the pH of the water. That is why it is possible to determine the carbon dioxide content of the tank water by measuring carbonate hardness and pH. The table on page 14 helps find the CO_2 content.
If the carbon dioxide content is too low for the plants in the tank, you can either fertilize with CO_2 (see next entry) or lower CARBONATE HARD-NESS. For most aquarium plants, 4–6°dCH is optimal. If you have fish that prefer alkaline water, choose plants that need only a very low concentration of carbon dioxide.

Carbon dioxide fertilization
A method of making up for carbon dioxide deficiency. In the list of plants (pages 27–29) the amount of CARBON DIOXIDE they need is given. If carbonate hardness is high, more CO_2 fertilization is required than if it is low.
While fertilizing with CO_2, do not use airstones or DIFFUSERS because they would get rid again of the carefully introduced carbon dioxide. Since carbon dioxide fertilization affects the pH, CO_2 fertilization has to be adjusted to the pH requirements of the fish.

Carbonic acid
See CARBON DIOXIDE.

Carbonic acid fertilization
See CARBON DIOXIDE FERTILIZATION.

Cation exchanger
An ion exchanger that exchanges only the cations in the aquarium water, replacing them with acidity-forming hydrogen ions. Suitable for softening water with high CARBONATE HARDNESS and low NONCARBONATE HARDNESS. The water softening process produces a lot of carbonic acid, which is removed from the water through intensive aeration. Water thus treated has a low pH. Before such water is used in an aquarium, it should be hardened with tap water until it is about neutral (a pH of around 7).
Some cation exchangers have an indicator that changes color when they are exhausted.

Clear water
Bodies of waters that are neither muddied by particles suspended in the water nor colored by organic substances. The WATER PROPERTIES can vary widely, but clear water is never as acid as BLACK WATER.

Communities
Different species of fish kept in the same aquarium.

Community tank
An aquarium in which several fish species of different geographical origins are combined.

Complete desalting
Removing all SALTS and thus all hardeners from the water by using ION EXCHANGERS or REVERSE OSMOSIS devices.

Conductivity
See ELECTRICAL CONDUCTIVITY.

Costia
Protozoan ectoparasites that produce cloudy skin in the afflicted fish. Can be treated, like *Ichthyophtirius*, with a bath in salty water.

Courtship display
Special behavior exhibited by animals when courting a mate. In many fish species, this behavior is accompanied by changes in coloration.

Crushed coral
A material that is high in calcium and can because of this quality be used in filters to harden the water in a tank.

Cyclops
Small crustaceans. High-quality food for smaller aquarium fishes. Not suitable for fry because *Cyclops* attack and kill fry. Available frozen at pet stores.

D

Daphnia
Water fleas. A fish food that is high in roughage. Because *Daphnia* are low in nutritive value, a fish diet should not consist exclusively of *Daphnia*. Available at aquarium stores frozen and sometimes live.

Diffuser
An aeration device in an aquarium attached to the outflow opening of a motorized filter. The outflowing water pulls along air from a small air hose and mixes with it.

An Aquarist's Glossary

Drosophila
Genus of fruit fly that can be raised as live food for fish (see page 55). An important food for surface-dwelling aquarium fish.

Dry food
Manufactured fish foods that—if they are of good quality—contain all the important nutrients, vitamins, and trace elements. Dry food comes in the form of tablets, flakes, and PELLETS. Once a package is opened, it should not be used longer than two to three months, and it should be closed carefully after every feeding. Humidity in the air can quickly affect the quality of dry food and cause it to spoil.

Dry season
In the tropics, certain times of year when there is very little precipitation. In some regions several dry and RAINY SEASONS occur within one year. Tropical fish often gear their spawning season to these times.

Dust food
Rearing food of the finest grade for extremely small fish larvae, for which ARTEMIA NAUPLII are too large. The most important components of dust food are PARAMECIA and ROTIFERS.

E

Ectoparasites
Parasites that live on the body surface of host animals; for example, ICHTHYOPHTIRIUS.

Electrical conductivity
Measure of the total concentration of dissolved salts in the water. When salts dissolve in water, they give off electrically charged IONS. These ions conduct electricity. The more ions there are in the water, the greater the electrical conductivity or current (assuming constant voltage). Because there are practically no ions in distilled water, it has almost no conductivity. Hard water, which contains more salts and thus more ions, has a high conductivity. The measured conductivity is expressed in µS/cm (micro-Siemens per cm). Water low in salts has less than 100 µS/cm, medium-salty water has 100-300 µS/cm, and water high in salts has 300 µS/cm and above.
Because measured conductivity does not indicate anything about the kinds of SALTS in the water, it is of little significance for aquarists.

Endoparasites
Parasites that live within the body of host animals, often in specific organs, such as the intestines.

F

Family
A term used in the classification of organisms. A family is made up of related genera (see GENUS).

Filtration
A procedure to maintain good water quality. Minute undissolved particles in the aquarium water are caught in the filter substrate (mechanical filtration), and dissolved substances are converted into different ones by microorganisms present in the filter (biological filtration). Chemical filtration takes place if the water is intentionally changed by being filtered through special substances, as in PEAT FILTERING.

Fin rot
Condition caused by bacteria, usually as a result of inadequate water maintenance. Weakened fish become infected with bacteria that destroy tissue, especially on the fins. Fins become shorter or frayed. Often accompanied by a fungal infection, which can be recognized by the edges of the fins turning white.

Fish tuberculosis
Bacterially caused disease (*Mycobacterium*). The symptoms often resemble those of ASCITES. They are bloated or emaciated body, darkening of color, sometimes deformation of the spine. Cannot be definitely diagnosed except by autopsy. There is a slight possibility that fish tuberculosis may be communicable to humans. Do not, therefore, touch afflicted fish or reach into the tank if you have an open wound on your hand. If the disease becomes epidemic, disinfect the tank and start over.

Frozen food
Frozen live food.

Fry
Baby fish that, unlike LARVAE, are fully formed small fish. All the fins have rays and the YOLK SAC has been used up.

G

Gas exchange
Gas exchange takes place at the surface of the water, where gases dissolved in the water (oxygen, carbon dioxide) dissipate into the air and are absorbed by the water from the air. Gas exchange in an aquarium is increased through aeration.

General or total hardness

This term is used to indicate the salt content of water that is caused by ions of the so-called alkaline-earth compounds. Important for the aquarist are the magnesium and calcium compounds. These are the substances that form

- carbonate hardness if they are magnesium or calcium (hydrogen) carbonates
- noncarbonate hardness if they are primarily magnesium or calcium sulfates.

The sum of carbonate and noncarbonate hardness is the total hardness. Under certain special conditions of water chemistry a situation that appears paradoxical can occur: Measured carbonate hardness may exceed total hardness. In that case, simply use carbonate hardness instead of total hardness. Total hardness is indicated in degrees of dH.

Genus

A term used in the classification of organisms. A genus is made up of similar species. The scientific names of plants and animals are made up of two parts: The first indicates the genus, the second, the species. Example: Various tetras belong to the genus *Hyphesso-rycon*. This genus includes many species, among them *H. pulchripin-nis* (lemon tetra), *H. rubrostigma* (bleeding heart tetra), *H. scholzel* (blade-lined tetra), and *H. callistrus* (jewel tetra), several of which are mentioned in this book.

Gill flukes

Parasites that belong to the egg-laying genus of hookworms *Gyro-dactylus*. They gradually destroy the gill tissues that are crucial for breathing.

Gonopodium

A penis-like mating organ evolved from the anal fin, characteristic of livebearing tooth carps (Poeciliidae). This organ makes possible the fertilization of egg cells inside the body of the female and thus vivipa-rous reproduction.

Group fish

Aquarium fishes generally kept in small groups of five to six.

H

Hole-in-the-head disease

Common fish disease, especially in cichlids. There is still debate about its cause. It is probably brought on by vitamin deficiency (wrong or unbalanced diet). Symptoms: small holes, gradually getting bigger, primarily in the head region. The holes may be filled with white material. Often accompanied by INTESTINAL FLAGELLATES. Treatment: Improve diet and, if indicated, get rid of flagellates.

Humic acids

Organic acids that account for the low pH and cola-like color of BLACK WATER. If needed, they are introduced into the aquarium water by means of PEAT FILTERING.

Hydrogen carbonates

See CARBONATE HARDNESS.

I

Ichthyophtirius multifiliis

Single-celled ectoparasite that causes the common white-dot disease or "ich" in fish. Small white dots about 1/16 inch (1.5 mm) in diameter form on the skin and gills of the fish and feed on the dermal tissue. Each parasite remains on the fish for about four days before leaving and forming several thousand daughter cells that then attack the fish anew. If these cells cannot find a host, they die within a few days. Medications kill the daughter cells only. Repeat treatment several times at intervals of at least three days (see page 46).

Intestinal flagellates

Protozoan ENDOPARASITES that live in the intestines of host animals. Symptoms: white, stringy excreta; often found together with HOLE-IN-THE-HEAD DISEASE.

Ion exchangers

Synthetic resins that because of their special chemical properties are able to change certain ions that are not desirable in a tank into more desirable ones. For instance, cations that cause carbonate hardness can be transformed into hydrogen ions, which reduces CARBONATE HARDNESS (action of a cation exchanger). There are also anion exchangers that, if used together with cation exchangers, desalt the water completely. Ion exchangers are available at aquarium stores. Because REVERSE OSMOSIS apparatuses are being used more and more, the importance of ion exchangers for lowering water hardness is declining.

Ions

Electrically charged particles present in the water after salts have dissolved. All water hardeners are ions, such as carbonate ions and hydrogen carbonate ions, but dissolved ORGANIC WASTE PRODUCTS can also be present as ions: ammonium ions, nitrite ions, and nitrate ions. (The word "ion" is often omitted.)

K

Kirschbaum method

A method, named after Dr. Kirschbaum, of stimulating reproduction in fish by simulating rainy season conditions. The method derives from the realization that many species require exposure to rainy season conditions for several weeks before they get ready to spawn. For instructions, see page 51 in the chapter "Breeding Fish."

L

Larvae

Not yet fully formed fry. One characteristic feature is the "larval fin fringe." Unlike adult fish, they don't yet have distinct unpaired fins with rays that lend them rigidity, but only a fringe without rays. Young larvae that still have a yolk sac are called YOLK SAC LARVAE.

An Aquarist's Glossary

Larvophile mouthbrooders
See MOUTHBROODERS.

Live food
This term is used for small food animals, either live or frozen.

Long-term (ongoing) breeding
Method of breeding aquarium fish. Fish to be bred are kept at low population density in specially set-up tanks (see page 53).

M

Maintenance tank
The aquarium in which the fish are kept. It differs from a BREEDING TANK in the conditions that prevail there, conditions that suit the permanent needs of the fish kept. Many fish species can be bred and reared in a maintenance tank, however.

Mbunas
Common African name for rock cichlids from Lake Malawi that is also used by dealers and hobbyists. Most Mbunas belong to the genera *Pseudotropheus*, *Melanochromis*, and *Labeotropheus*.

Metabolism
Process by which certain substances are transformed by the living body. For instance, proteins are absorbed and transformed until they leave the body in the form of nitrogenous ORGANIC WASTE PRODUCTS, such as urea and AMMONIUM.

Mosquito larvae
Larvae of various kinds of mosquitoes that lay their eggs on the surface of water. The hatched larvae are found in mud (red mosquito larvae), in open, cool water (white mosquito larvae), or hanging down directly from the water surface (black mosquito larvae). Mosquito larvae are a high-quality food for fish and can be bought either live or frozen at aquarium stores.
Caution: Red mosquito larvae are often contaminated, and they don't agree with quite a lot of fish species.

Mouthbrooders
Fishes that care for their offspring in the mouth until they can fend for themselves. Mouthbrooders are divided into ovophile mouthbrooders, such as MBUNA species, which pick up the eggs immediately after spawning, and larvophile mouthbrooders, such as *Bujurquina* species from South America, which spawn against a substrate and wait until the eggs have hatched into larvae before picking them up. Many species continue to look after their brood even after the young swim out of the mouth, picking them up again at night or if there is danger.

N

Neon disease
Incurable disease caused by the bacterium *Pleistophora*. It affects primarily characins. Symptoms: Fading of some color areas; often a deformed spine.

Nitrate (NO$_3^-$)
Mildly poisonous end product of the breakdown of nitrogenous ORGANIC WASTE PRODUCTS in the aquarium. Can be further transformed only by means of certain chemical procedures that reduce it to nitrogen in gas form. (Several appropriate products are available in pet stores.) Normally nitrate is removed from the tank through water changes.

Nitrite (NO$_2^-$)
Toxic intermediary product created in the process of breaking down ORGANIC WASTE PRODUCTS. It occurs between AMMONIUM and NITRATE in the breakdown sequence.

Nitrogen
Element that is an important component of much food, especially PROTEINS; also ORGANIC WASTE PRODUCTS

Noncarbonate hardness
That portion of water hardness that is not caused by carbonates (see CARBONATE HARDNESS) but primarily by SULFATES.

O

Oodinium
Single-celled ectoparasite that causes velvet disease. If heavily infested, the fish look as though they had been dusted with whitish or yellowish powder.

Open-water spawners
Fishes that drop their eggs in the open water. Opposite: SUBSTRATE SPAWNERS.

Order
A term used in the classification of organisms. Related families make up an order. Thus, the families Loricariidae and Mochocidae, together with many other catfish families, form the order of catfishes, Siluriformes. The scientific names of most orders within the animal kingdom have the suffix –*formes*.

Organic waste products
What remains after fungi and bacteria have broken down animal and plant matter. High concentrations of AMMONIUM and NITRATES indicate an excess of organic waste products.

Ovophile mouthbrooders
See MOUTHBROODERS.

Ovoviviparous
Adjective describing a form of livebearing in which the embryos mature in eggs within the female's body (for instance, in Poeciliidae).

xidator

n oxygen-generating device that pplies the tank water with oxygen oduced by a chemical reaction. ne starting substance for the reac-n is hydrogen peroxide, which eaks down into water and oxygen. aution: Hydrogen peroxide is ustic and has to be stored our of ach of children.

xygen (O₂)

as present in the air that is crucial life. Through gas exchange at the ater surface, oxygen becomes ssolved in the water. The warmer e water, the less oxygen dissolves it. Measures to increase the xygen content of water include eration, lowering of the tempera-re, and removal of waste products at use up oxygen. Overcrowding so can lead to oxygen deficiency a tank.

aramecia

lipper animalcules." A protozoan, aramecium caudatum, used as st food for minute fry. See DUST OOD.

eat

lter material that is used because its HUMIC ACID content for softening nd acidifying the tank water. Only nfertilized black peat or peat gran-es (available at aquarium stores) re used. Unfortunately many peat roducts are high in NITRATES, and ne nitrate concentration should be necked if peat is used. Harmless ubstances in the peat lend the ater a brownish color.

Peat filtering

A method of chemical filtering that lowers the CARBONATE HARDNESS and pH of the tank water. The filtering material used is PEAT.
Rule of thumb: It takes about 7 ounces (200 g) of peat to lower the hardness of about 25 gallons (100 L) of water by about 10°dCH. Fill the outside filter or an air-driven inside filter with peat, then monitor the softening and the dropping pH. Replace the peat after about three days. Repeat until the desired water properties are obtained. When changing the water after peat filter-ing, it is best to use peat-filtered water with about the same proper-ties as those of the tank water.

Pellets

Compressed DRY FOOD designed for bigger fish, such as large cichlids. It comes in the shape of short sticks (available at aquarium stores).

pH

Measuring unit indicating the de-gree of acidity of water. The degree of acidity or alkalinity is determined by the relative amounts of acids and bases in the water. If both are present in equal proportions, we speak of neutral water (pH = 7). If there are more acids than bases, the water is acid (pH below 7). If bases predominate, the water is alkaline or basic (pH above 7). Aquarists describe water in the following terms:
very acidic = pH below 6
slightly acidic = pH 6 to 6.9
neutral = pH 7
slightly alkaline/basic = pH 7.1 to 8
very alkaline/basic = pH 8.1 to 9

pH buffering

Water with a certain pH is called well buffered if, when small amounts of acidifying or alkalizing substances are added, the pH does not change or changes only slightly. Water containing carbonates is better buffered than carbonate-deficient water. That is why larger amounts of CARBON DIOXIDE or HUMIC ACID are needed to acidify water high in carbonates than are needed for the same quantity of water low in car-bonates. What is of practical signifi-cance for the aquarist is that a minimum carbonate hardness of 4°dCH should be maintained in order to avoid fluctuations in the pH.

Photosynthesis

A process in which plants use light and CARBON DIOXIDE to produce sugar (glucose) as food for themselves.

Plant spawners

SUBSTRATE SPAWNERS that favor plants as a spawning substrate.

Proteins

The basic building blocks of all living organisms. Proteins contain nitrogen. When they are broken down in the body, nitrogenous ORGANIC WASTE PRODUCTS are created, namely, urea, AMMONIUM, NITRITE, and NITRATE.

R

Rainy season

In the tropics, those times of year during which there is heavy rainfall. See also DRY SEASON.

Rearing tank

A special tank for raising baby fish. Because maintenance chores (such as water changes and siphoning debris off the bottom) have to be performed frequently in these tanks, a rearing tank should be kept simple: only essential objects, no bottom material or only a thin layer.

An Aquarist's Glossary

Reverse osmosis
A modern procedure for removing from the water not only all compounds that form salts (see SALTS), but also other molecules (such as the herbicide atrazine). In contrast to ION EXCHANGERS, reverse osmosis devices require little tending and do not use chemicals. For the amount of desalted water produced there is a lot of leftover water, but this water can be recycled in the household, as for flushing the toilet.

Rotifers
Also called wheel animalcules. A DUST FOOD that is available at aquarium stores in the form of rotifer eggs. A good rearing food that can be used in place of paramecia. Consult the literature listed on page 158.

Roughage
Indigestible parts of food. Many fishes are adapted to eating food with a high proportion of roughage. If these fish get too little roughage, they suffer from digestive problems and become susceptible to diseases of the digestive system.

S

Salts
Chemical compounds made up of negatively and positively charged particles (see IONS). Many salts readily dissolve in water, breaking down into the ions they are made up of. These salts determine the hardness and ELECTRICAL CONDUCTIVITY of the water.

Scientific name
The first word indicates the organism's genus, the second, its species. If another word in quotation marks follows, this is generally the place where the fish was found. This last information is necessary if a species consists of several populations from different geographic sites and often with different coloration. Example: *Biotodoma cupido* "Santarem." Santarém is the city on the Amazon River near which this beautifully colored strain of fish was caught. If the name of the genus is in quotation marks, the species does not properly belong to this genus but its exact scientific classification has not yet been determined.

Seasonal fish
Also called annual fish. Fishes, such as bottom-spawning killifishes, which in nature live in waters that dry up periodically. In the wild they live no more than a few months, but their offspring survive the next dry period as eggs buried in the bottom mud. In an aquarium most seasonal fishes live two to three years.

Shoaling fishes
Fishes that in nature always live together in large numbers. In an aquarium one should always keep at least six individuals of a shoaling species; otherwise, they will fail to thrive.

Skin flukes
These belong to the livebearing hookworm genus *Gyrodactylus*. Ectoparasites that attack the skin of fish and, in severe infestations, also the gills.

Snails
As a rule snails are useful in an aquarium. Malayan snails (*Melanoides tuberculata*) stay hidden in the bottom material during the day and help by using up food remains and aerating the bottom. Other snails (common water snails or *Ampullaria*, ramshorn snails or *Planorbis corneus*, and small muc snails) are useful as disposers of leftover food and can also serve a a "cleaning crew" in a rearing tank In case of mass reproduction, collect the snails from the glass at night, or place food tablets on a saucer overnight. The snails will gather there and can be lifted out the water on the saucer. Mass reproduction may result from inappropriate care (overfeeding, dead fish in the tank).

Spawning rhythm
Many tropical fishes spawn only a certain intervals or under certain conditions (for instance, during rai periods). This rhythm can be alter in the aquarium by creating appropriate conditions. Despite this, wil catches generally adhere to their natural spawning rhythm. Thus many armored catfishes caught in the wild tend to spawn during our winter season.

Spawning substrates
Surfaces on which fish like to deposit their eggs. Harlequin fish (*Rasbora heteromorpha*), for instance, spawn against the underside of big plant leaves, while man other *Rasbora* species prefer feat ery leaves.

Species tank
An aquarium in which only one species of fish is kept.

Substrate-dependent
Fish that always seek closeness t objects are said to be substrate-dependent. Sucker-mouth armore catfishes, for instance, attach ther selves to the glass of the tank.

ubstrate spawners
sh that deposit their sticky eggs
a surface or substrate. They
clude mostly killifishes, characins,
rbs, and rainbow fishes. In the
age of aquarists, this term does
t include substrate spawners that
gage in brood care (such as
bies and cichlids).

ulfates
ulfuric salts present in various
mounts in water. They contribute
NONCARBONATE HARDNESS.

wim bladder
organ in fish that is filled with
ses and allows fish to remain
spended in water without sinking
rising. Many bottom-dwelling
ecies no longer have functional
vim bladders because they have
andoned the open water.

wimming free
sh larvae swim free when they
ave used up the food in their YOLK
cs. Larvae that swim free not only
vim in the open water but also
enetrate close to the bottom.

race elements
ubstances that are present only in
inute amounts in the water and in
od but that have important func-
ns in an aquarium. The trace
ement iron, for instance, has to be
vailable for good plant growth. If it
lacking, plant growth will stag-
ate, and iron fertilizing is needed.

richodina
ngle-celled ectoparasite. Infected
sh can be treated, like fish suffer-
g from *Ichthyophtirius*, with salt
ater baths.

ubifex
hese tube-shaped mud worms are
live fish food high in protein but
ntaining little roughage. Available
aquarium stores. Should be given
ly rarely. *Tubifex* first have to be
aked in water for a few days be-
ause they are often contaminated.
or proper storage of *Tubifex*, see
age 39.

Tufa
Calcareous, porous rock with many
small and largish holes that often
have sharp edges. Not suitable,
because of its calcium content, for
aquariums with soft, acidic water.

U

Utakas
Cichlids from Lake Malawi that
swim in huge shoals and feed on
zooplankton in the water. These
mouthbrooders spawn close to the
bottom. The males become colorful
only during the spawning season
and then form whole colonies
engaging in courtship displays.

V

Vegetable food
Vegetables rich in fiber, such as
blanched spinach, potatoes, and
Brussels sprouts.

Viviparous
Producing live young rather than
eggs. The embryos mature without
a shell in the female's body and
often, as in the case of the
Goodeidae, get their nourishment
through a kind of umbilical cord (see
OVOVIVIPAROUS).

W

Water hardness
See GENERAL OR TOTAL HARDNESS.

Water properties
These determine the quality of the
water. The properties of interest to
aquarists are total hardness, carbonate hardness, noncarbonate
hardness, electrical conductivity,
ammonium or ammonia, nitrate,
nitrite, carbon dioxide, oxygen, pH,
and temperature.

White water
The water of rivers in Amazonia that
is an opaque white color because
of the suspended materials in it
(anorganic sediments). One can
see through only 4 to 20 inches
(10–50 cm) of such water. This
water typically has a pH between
6.2 and 7.2 and is soft (rarely, medium hard). Theoretically the term
can also be applied to waters of
different geographical regions.

Y

Yolk sac
See YOLK SAC LARVA.

Yolk sac larva
See drawing on page 54. Fish larva
that is not yet able to swim and is
equipped with food in the form of
yolk.

Z

Zooplankton
Minute animal life suspended in
water. For example: Daphnia. See
CYCLOPS.

Diversity of species

A spotted-eyed velvet cichlid of the South American cichlid genus *Heros*. Originally it was thought that all South American spotted-eyed velvet cichlids belonged to one species, namely, *Heros severus*. But then it was realized—in part because of information supplied by aquarists with a scientific bent—that spotted-eyed velvet cichlids with different colors and shapes were being imported by dealers of tropical aquarium fishes. Because of this we now assume that there are different kinds of spotted-eyed velvet cichlids in South America. This is not an isolated instance. Quite often what was thought to be one species actually turns out to be several. The newly recognized species are then scientifically described and given their own names. That is one of the reasons why aquarists keep encountering new names. Another reason is the necessary corrections in classification of species that have already been named.

Popular Aquarium Fishes

These days there are innumerable species of fish that can be kept in aquariums. In the following descriptions you will find popular favorites that are kept by many hobbyists, as well as fascinating species that are not yet so familiar. For each species depicted, instructions for care are given, including, among other things, mention of the natural biotope of the species. This information is provided to help hobbyists get to know their fish better so that they can meet their needs more fully and provide conditions closer to the natural habitat. At the same time it is meant to heighten awareness of the importance of nature protection and species protection, which are so crucial in our time. But, many an aquarist may ask, what on earth can I do with an aquarium in my living room to help protect habitats and species? Quite a lot. At least that was the opinion of the famous ethologist Konrad Lorenz when he wrote that keeping animals "provides civilized man, who is getting more and more alienated from nature, with exactly the kind of knowledge whose lack today endangers all mankind." This brings us back to what we said earlier, namely, that we can protect only what we know.

Notes on the Instructions for Care

The following descriptions of species are organized into 15 groups of fish. For ease of reference, each group name is preceded by a number, for instance, 1 Characins, and so on. All the instructions have been checked by experts knowledgeable about the various fish groups.
Name: If there is a popular English name for a species, it is given in addition to the scientific name.
Size: The sizes given are those reached by the fish in nature. Some species grow somewhat larger in an aquarium because they may live longer there than in the wild. A range of size means that there are populations of different sizes or that the exact adult size is not known.
Tank: What is given are the minimum dimensions required for keeping fish properly for their full life span. Juvenile fish can of course be kept in smaller tanks, but when they reach maturity they have to be transferred to a larger tank.
Stratum: This refers to the area in the tank where the fish spend most of their time. Now and then fish will move to other tank areas, as when they are being fed.
bottom = immediately above the bottom or slightly higher
middle = in normal tanks, the largest area
top = near the water surface
substrate-dependent = any area of the tank but always near substrates, such as rocks.

Water: The values given are those that experience has shown to be beneficial to the health of the fish. If no other values are cited under the heading "Breeding," those given at the beginning of the description hold for rearing, too.
Note: The following terms are used to describe water hardness:
very soft = 0° to 4°dH
soft = 5° to 8°dH
medium hard = 9° to 12°dH
hard = 13° to 19°dH
very hard = 20°dH and up
Set-up: Here there are notes on how the tank should be arranged for the species in question; where appropriate, special technical requirements are mentioned.
Tip on communities: Advice on what other fishes the species under discussion can be combined with.
Words indicating size mean:
small = about 3 inches (8 cm)
medium = about 3½ to 5 inches (9–13 cm)
large = over 5 inches (13 cm)
Food: Here suitable foods and foods the fish are especially fond of are indicated, and special behavior associated with eating is mentioned.
Sexual differences: The most important differences in appearance.
Breeding: Information given here includes spawning type (for instance, open-water spawner); for species engaging in parental care, the kind of care provided (for instance, larvophile mouthbrooder) and the type of family (for instance, parental family); also the type of tank in which the fish should be bred and the initial food for the larvae. If special water properties are required, these are given.
Biotope: Whenever known, the preferred biotope of the species in its natural geographical range of distribution is named, so that the hobbyist can picture how and where the fish lives in the wild. This information should be of help in providing conditions that approximate those in nature.
Similar species: Closely related species that require care similar to that of the species depicted. Any differences are noted.

Tips for the Care of Other Tank Inhabitants

Often some other forms of animal life coexist in an aquarium, and these "lower" creatures, which often fulfill useful functions there, have their own requirements that have to be met.

▲ *Channa orientalis* **guiding its young.**

Crustaceans

There are several crustaceans that make good tank dwellers. The trait they all share is that they periodically shed their skins. You may come upon an empty shell and mistake it for a dead animal. In fact, the animal, having just lost its "armor," is hiding until its new, still soft shell hardens.

Striped dwarf shrimp (*Cardina spec.*), 1½ inches (4 cm), photo on page 20: Prettily marked, live-bearing shrimp. Loves thickets of feathery-leaved plants that offer protection. Can be fed dry fish food. Do not combine with large or aggressive fish.

Brine shrimp (*Atyopsis moluccensis*), 4 inches (10 cm), photo on page 20: Unaggressive shrimp. Though large, it eats only food that comes in small morsels (such as disintegrating food tablets and *Artemia* nauplii). If kept in a tank with circulation, it can be seen standing in the current with its fan spread wide to sift small food particles from the water. It also forages for food on the bottom. Do not combine with robust fishes.

Red fresh-water crab from the family of Grapsidae, about 2¾ inches (7 cm), photo on page 20: Needs a dry perch above the water surface. Because these crabs may escape, the cover has to fit on the tank without the slightest crack. Easy to feed with all kinds of food. Likes to have sea salt added to the water.

Snails

These tank inhabitants, which are often inadvertently introduced, turn out in most cases to be useful because they dispose of leftover food and loosen up the bottom material.

Malayan snails (*Melanoides spec.*), photo on page 20: These livebearing snails are the earthworms of the aquarium. They move tirelessly through the bottom material, loosening it up in the process, and consume leftover food.

Ramshorn snails (*Helisoma spec.*), about ¾ inch (2 cm), photo on page 20: Especially good as consumers of leftovers in a rearing tank. Deposit jelly-like egg packets.

Common water snails (*Ampullaria spec.*): These snails get bigger than a pingpong ball. They rise to the surface to breathe, taking up air through a long proboscis. Eggs are deposited out of the water. A closely fitting cover is important to keep the snails from getting out of the tank. Omnivores with a big appetite. If there is not enough food, these snails will also eat plants.

Charancins

Comprising about 1,500 species, characins are found in almost all types of water in South America and Africa. Next to the livebearing tooth carps they are the most popular aquarium fishes suitable for community tanks. Their popularity is due only in part to their lovely, bright colors. Aquarists are also fond of them because, being shoaling fishes, they are kept in groups, and thus there is much to watch. Tanks with characins are always "lively tanks."

What You Should Know about Characins

They belong to the order *Characiformes*.

Characteristic traits: Most characins have an extra fin between the dorsal and the caudal fins, the so-called adipose fin. This fin is not supported by spiny rays. The bodies of characins are covered with scales.

Care: Even though many characins live in the open water, they still need some protected areas in the tank. These may be created through partial dense planting of roots from bogs. The lighting and the bottom material should not be too bright. If necessary, you may have to shade the water partially with floating plants because the lovely colors of these fish don't show well except in dim light.

Water: For most species, slightly acid (pH around 6.5) and soft to medium hard water is ideal. For a few of them, however, and for raising the offspring of many species, very soft and acid water is required.

Communities: Characins can easily be combined with dwarf cichlids, catfishes, and other characin species. Largish fishes that claim territories (many cichlids) should be avoided because they dominate the tank, especially during the brood care period, and bully the characins. Where called for, tips for combining species are given in the descriptions of individual characin species.

Behavior: Most characins are shoaling fishes and do not display their normal behavior unless kept in groups. You should keep a minimum of six individuals of the same species (for exceptions, see individual descriptions). In many species the males at times claim small territories which they defend against other males, but this does not lead to serious fights.

Tips on breeding: Most characins can be bred only if the aquarist is willing to go to considerable trouble. Most species do not engage in brood care but simply deposit their eggs on plants or other substrates. Low water values are often necessary for the eggs to develop, water values that cannot be provided in a community tank. That is why a separate breeding tank for fishes without brood care (see HOW TO page 54 on "Breeding fish") has to be set up, and water has to be prepared to meet the breeding requirements of a particular species. Once the small, delicate larvae swim free, their initial food has to be of the finest grade, such as paramecia. With many species you have to wait several days before feeding them *Artemia* nauplii. Another method of raising characins is long-term breeding in the shoal (see page 53).

Long-finned Characin (*Brycinus longipinnis*)
5 inches (13 cm). *Tank*: 40 inches (100 cm). *Strata*: Middle, top. *Water*: pH 6.5–7.5; soft to hard; 73–79°F (23–26°C). *Set-up*: Large tank arranged in dark colors, no floating plants. Water circulation and effective filtration important. Active swimmers. *Food*: Nutritious live food (mosquito larvae, insects), also food flakes. *Sexual differences*: Males slim, with elongated dorsal fin. *Breeding*: Large breeding tank; water: pH 6–7; very soft (less than 6°dH). Start feeding with *Artemia*. *Biotope*: Transition area between shore vegetation and open water in clear-water rivers of West Africa.

Congo Tetra (*Phenacogrammus interruptus*)
3½ inches (9 cm). *Tank*: 40 inches (100 cm). *Strata*: Middle, top. *Water*: pH 6–7.5; soft to hard; 73–79°F (23–26°C). *Set-up*: Tank arranged in dark colors, preferably with water circulation; plenty of open swimming space; sides and back loosely planted. Shoaling fish. *Food*: Mosquito larvae, small insects; also vegetarian food and dry food. *Sexual differences*: Males bigger, with elongated dorsal and caudal fins. *Breeding*: Large breeding tank; water: pH 6–6.5, very soft. Start feeding with *Artemia*. *Biotope*: The Zaire River watershed.

Arnold's Red-eyed Characin

(*Arnoldichthys spilopterus*)
3 inches (8 cm). *Tank*: 40 inches (100 cm). *Strata*: middle,
top. *Water*: pH 6–7.5; soft to hard; 73–82°F (23–28°C).
Set-up: Requires lots of open swimming space and, if
possible, water circulation; therefore sparse planting.
Lively shoaling fish. *Food*: All food that comes in smallish
morsels, especially mosquito larvae and small insects.
Sexual differences: Males slimmer, with brightly striped
anal fin. *Breeding*: Large breeding tank; water: pH 6–7;
soft; thin layer of peat on the bottom. Start feeding with
paramecia. *Biotope*: Rivers in southern Nigeria.

Neolebias ansorgii

1⅜ inches (3.5 cm). *Tank*: 20 inches (50 cm). *Strata*:
Bottom, middle. *Water*: pH 5–6.5; soft to medium hard;
72–77°F (22–25°C). *Set-up*: Tank arranged in dark colors,
with small hiding places for the males, who defend territories; plant with *Anubias* and floating plants. Keep two males
with several females. Tip on communities: Only small,
delicate fishes. *Food*: Small live food; dry food only now
and then. *Sexual differences*: Females paler, plumper.
Breeding: Breeding tank. Start feeding with paramecia;
young are delicate. *Special remarks*: There are red and
red-and-green strains. *Biotope*: In plant thickets along the
banks of small, clear rivers in Nigeria and Cameroon.

Black Phantom Tetra (*Megalomphodus megalopterus*)

1¾ inches (4.5 cm). *Tank*: 24 inches (60 cm). *Stratum*:
Middle. *Water*: pH 6–7.5; soft to hard; 73–82°F (23–28°C).
Set-up: Tank arranged in dark colors; dense planting
along sides and back, floating plants. Group fish. Tip on
communities: Small fishes. *Food*: All types of fairly fine
grade. *Sexual differences*: Males slimmer, with larger fins.
Breeding: Breeding tank; water: pH 6–7; soft. *Special
remarks*: Males sometimes claim small territories. *Biotope*:
Shaded areas with lots of vegetation in rivers and lakes of
central Brazil. *Similar species*: *M. sweglesi*, more delicate.

Hyphessobrycon bentosi

1¾ inches (4.5 cm). *Tank*: 24 inches (60 cm). *Stratum*:
Middle. *Water*: pH 6–7.5; soft to hard; 73–81°F (23–27°C).
Set-up: Community tank with slight circulation, loosely
planted. Undemanding, lively fish. *Food*: All types of fairly
fine grade. *Sexual differences*: Males with very elongated
dorsal fin. *Breeding*: Breeding tank; water: pH 6–7; soft.
Start feeding with *Artemia*. *Biotope*: Above sandy or pebbly
bottom in clear, sunny, rivers (Guiana, lower Amazon).
Similar species: Bleeding heart tetra (*H. erythrostigma* or
rubrostigma), 2⅜ inches (6 cm), softer water.

Flame Tetra

(*Hyphessobrycon flammeus*)
1½ inches (4 cm). *Tank*: 20 inches
(50 cm). *Stratum*: Middle. *Water*: pH
6–7.5; soft to hard; 72–81°F (22–27°C).
Set-up: Tank arranged in dark colors,
well planted. Undemanding species.
Tip for communities: Small fishes.
Food: All types of fairly fine grade.
Sexual differences: Males slimmer,
colors more brilliant. *Breeding*: Easy.
Breeding tank. Start feeding *Artemia*
or, if necessary, crushed dry food.
Biotope: Vicinity of Rio de Janeiro.
Similar species: *H. bifasciatus*, 2
inches (5 cm).

Callistus Tetra or Jewel Tetra

(*Hyphessobrycon callistus*)
1½ inches (4 cm). *Tank*: 24 inches (60 cm). *Stratum*: Middle.
Water: pH 6–7.5; soft to hard; 75–82°F (24–28°C). *Set-up*: Tank arranged in dark colors, well planted but leaving open space for swimming. Keep in small groups (six to eight fish). *Food*: All types of fairly fine grade. *Sexual differences*: Females plumper. *Breeding*: Breeding tank; water pH 6–7, soft. Start feeding with *Artemia*. *Special remarks*: There are several subspecies, all of which should be tended the same way. *Biotope*: Calm water, often full of vegetation; also in black water in the Amazon Basin.

Darter Characin (*Characidium spec.*)

3 inches (8 cm). *Tank*: 32 inches (80 cm). *Stratum*: Bottom. *Water*: pH 6.5–7.5; soft to hard, clear, oxygen-rich; 73–82°F (23–28°C). *Set-up*: Tank with open sand and gravel areas. Inquisitive fish; they tend to be aggressive if too few are kept. Tip on communities: Small to medium-sized fishes of the middle and upper strata. *Food*: All types of fairly fine grade, especially food tablets. *Sexual differences*: Females plumper. *Breeding*: Breeding tank. Start feeding with *Artemia*. *Special remarks*: There are many hard-to-identify *Characidium* species. *Biotope*: Bottom stratum of many rivers in South America.

Black Tetra (*Gymnocorymbus ternetzi*)

2⅜ inches (6 cm). *Tank*: 24 inches (60 cm). *Stratum*: Middle. *Water*: pH 6.5–7.5; soft to hard; 73–82°F (23–28°C). *Set-up*: Tank that is not too bright, open planting. Undemanding, calm species. Tip for communities: Species up to twice its size. *Food*: All types of fairly fine grade. *Sexual differences*: Males smaller, slimmer. *Breeding*: Breeding tank. Start feeding with *Artemia*. *Special remarks*: The black markings become paler with age. *Biotope*: Shaded, calm zones in rivers of the Río Paraguay watershed in southern Brazil.

Penguin Fish (*Thayeria boehlkei*)

2⅜ inches (6 cm). *Tank*: 24 inches (60 cm). *Strata*: Middle, top. *Water*: pH 6–7.5; soft to hard; 75–82°F (24–28°C). *Set-up*: Loosely planted tank. Calm shoaling fish. *Food*: Dry and live food, especially mosquito larvae and insects, with addition of vegetarian food. *Sexual differences*: Females plumper. *Breeding*: Largish breeding tank; water pH 5.5–6.5; 77–81°F (25–27°C); soft. Start feeding with paramecia. *Biotope*: Among plants in slow portions of the Río Araguaia, Peru. *Similar species*: *T. obliqua*, 3 inches (8 cm).

Moenkhausia sanctaefilomenae

2¾ inches (7 cm). *Tank*: 32 inches (80 cm). *Strata*: Middle, top. *Water*: pH 5.5–8.5; soft to hard; 73–79°F (23–26°C). *Set-up*: Tank with plenty of open space for swimming and preferably with a slight circulation. Undemanding, lively shoaling fish. Tip on communities: Do not combine with calm species of the top stratum; these might feel disturbed. *Food*: All types of finer grade. *Sexual differences*: Females plumper. *Breeding*: Breeding tank; can be bred in medium hard water. Start feeding with *Artemia*. *Biotope*: Central South America: Paraguay, eastern Bolivia, eastern Peru, western Brazil.

Splash Tetra (*Copella arnoldi*)

3 inches (8 cm). *Tank*: 24 inches (60 cm). *Strata*: Middle, top. *Water*: pH 6.5–7.5; soft to medium hard; 75–84°F (24–29°C). *Set-up*: Planted tank, with partial cover of floating plants. Tightly fitting cover because these fish jump. *Food*: Small live food, *Drosophila*, and dry food. *Sexual differences*: Males larger, more colorful, with longer fins. *Breeding*: Spawn outside of the water on plant leaves. Males engage in brood care, splashing the eggs with water. Transfer eggs to rearing tank. Start feeding with paramecia. *Biotope*: Vegetation along banks of clear streams in Guiana, South America.

Glowlight Tetra (*Hemigrammus erythrozonus*)
1½ inches (4 cm). *Tank*: 20 inches (50 cm). *Stratum*:
Middle. *Water*: pH 6–7.5; soft to medium hard; 72–79°F
(22–26°C). *Set-up*: Tank arranged in dark colors, loosely
planted, floating plants. Calm shoaling fish. Tip on communities: Don't combine with lively shoaling fishes. *Food*:
All types of fine-grade foods. *Sexual differences*: Females
plumper. *Breeding*: Breeding tank; water: pH 5.5–7, soft.
Start feeding with paramecia. *Special remarks*: Coloration
is practically identical with that of the glowlight rasbora
from Asia, though the two species are not related.
Biotope: Río Essequibo in Guiana, South America.

Hasemania nana
2 inches (5 cm). *Tank*: 24 inches (60 cm). *Stratum*:
Middle. *Water*: pH 6–7.5; soft to hard; 73–81°F (23–27°C).
Set-up: Tank arranged in dark colors, planted along sides
and back; an open-water swimming area is important.
Lively shoaling fish. *Food*: All types of fine-grade foods.
Sexual differences: Males slimmer. *Breeding*: Breeding
tank; water pH 6–7.5; soft to medium hard. Start feeding
with paramecia. *Special remarks*: One of the few characins without an adipose fin. *Biotope*: Small streams in
southern Brazil, also in black water.

Hemigrammus bleheri
1¾ inches (4.5 cm). *Tank*: 24 inches (60 cm). *Stratum*:
Middle. *Water*: pH 5–6.5; soft to medium hard; 73–82°F
(23–28°C). *Set-up*: Community tank arranged in dark
colors. Undemanding species. *Food*: All types of fairly
fine-grade foods, also vegetarian food. *Sexual differences*: Females plumper. *Breeding*: Difficult. Breeding
tank; water: pH 5.5–6.5; very soft. Start feeding with
paramecia. *Biotope*: Clear, shaded black water, either still
or gently flowing, in the watershed of the Río Negro and
the Uaupe in northern Brazil. *Similar species*: *Petitella
georgiae* and *H. rhodostomus* both differ from the species
described by having red on the mouth, which is reflected
in their English names: false rummy-nose tetra and
rummy-nose tetra. Telling the species apart is difficult.

Cardinal Tetra (*Paracheirodon axelrodi*)
¾–2¾ inches (4.5–6 cm). *Tank*: 24 inches (60 cm). *Strata*:
Bottom, middle. *Water*: pH 4.5–6.5; soft to medium hard;
73–81°F (23–27°C). *Set-up*: Tank arranged in dark colors,
floating plants. Shoaling fish. Tip on communities: Only
small to medium-size species. *Food*: All types of fine-grade
foods. *Sexual differences*: Males more slender. *Special
remarks*: Tank-bred fish are hardier than those caught in
the wild. *Breeding*: Breeding tank; water pH 5–7; 73–79°F
(23–26°C); very soft (up to 10°dH). Start feeding with
paramecia. *Biotope*: Shaded areas, especially clear water
in northwestern Brazil. *Similar species*: Neon tetra
(*P. innesi*), pH 5–7.5, soft to hard, 68–75°F (20–24°C).

Beckford's Pencil Fish (*Nannostomus beckfordi*)
2½ inches (6.5 cm). *Tank*: 24 inches (60 cm). *Strata*:
Middle, top. *Water*: pH 6–7.5; soft to hard; 73–79°F
(23–26°C). *Set-up*: Tank arranged in dark colors, densely
planted. Tip on communities: Very compatible with *Apistogramma* species. *Food*: Varied, including small live and
fine-grade dry food; also *Drosophila*. *Sexual differences*:
Males slimmer, with brighter red. *Breeding*: Breeding tank;
water soft to medium hard. Start feeding with *Artemia*.
Biotope: Thickets of shore vegetation reaching into the water
of rivers and streams in northern South America. *Similar
species*: Three-lined pencil fish (*N. trifasciatus*), 2⅜ inches
(6 cm), softer water.

Inpaichthys kerri
¾ inches (4.5 cm). *Tank*: 20 inches (50 cm). *Stratum*:
Middle. *Water*: pH 6.5–7.5; soft to medium hard, 73–79°F
(23–26°C). *Set-up*: Tank arranged in dark colors, loosely
planted. Tip on communities: Small species. *Food*: All
types of fairly fine-grade foods. *Sexual differences*:
Females smaller, less colorful. *Breeding*: Breeding tank;
water: pH 6–7; 73–77°F (23–25°C); soft. Start feeding
with *Artemia*. *Special remarks*: Males defend small courtship territories. *Biotope*: Río Aripuana, a tributary of Río
Madeira in western Brazil.

Emperor Tetra (*Nematobrycon palmeri*)
2⅜ inches (6 cm). *Tank*: 24 inches (60 cm). *Strata*:
Bottom, middle. *Water*: pH 5–7.5; soft to hard; 73–79°F
(23–26°C). *Set-up*: Tank arranged in dark colors, densely
planted, floating plants. Keep two or three males with
many females. Tip on communities: Other species should
not be too lively. *Food*: All types of fairly fine-grade foods,
including vegetarian. *Sexual differences*: Males have
larger fins; more high-backed with age. *Breeding*: Breeding tank; water pH 5–7; 73–79°F (23–26°C); soft (up to
10°dH). Start feeding with paramecia. *Biotope*: Water-
sheds in western Colombia (Río Atrata, Río San Juan).

Marbled Hatchetfish (*Carnegiella strigata*)
1½ inches (4 cm). *Tank*: 24 inches (60 cm). *Stratum*: Top. *Water*: pH 5–7.5; soft to hard; 79–86°F (26–30°C). *Set-up*: Water partially covered with floating plants. Water surface no higher than 4 inches (10 cm) below tightly fitting cover because these fish jump. *Food*: Black mosquito larvae (also freeze dried), small insects (such as *Drosophila*). *Sexual differences*: When getting ready to spawn (rare), females are plumper. *Breeding*: Breeding has occasionally succeeded in soft water with a pH of 6–7. Start feeding with paramecia. *Biotope*: Shaded still or slightly moving black water in northern South America. *Similar species*: *Gasteropelecus sternicla*.

Striped Headstander (*Anostomus anostomus*)
7 inches (18 cm). *Tank*: 40 inches (100 cm). *Strata*: Bottom, middle. *Water*: pH 6–7.5; soft to medium hard; 73–82°F (23–28°C). *Set-up*: Tank with slight circulation; many hiding places. Keep singly; if you keep several, each must have a separate hiding place. Tip on communities: Small to medium-sized species; can bother slow-moving fish (such as angelfish). *Food*: Small frozen food, vegetarian food; dry food alone is not enough. *Sexual differences*: Mature females larger, plumper. *Breeding*: Natural breeding in a tank is unknown. *Special remarks*: Don't combine with ravenous fishes or this species will starve. *Biotope*: Along the banks of rivers in northern South America.

Boehlkea fredcochui
2 inches (5 cm). *Tank*: 24 inches (60 cm). *Strata*: Middle, top. *Water*: pH 6–7.5; soft to medium hard; 73–79°F (23–26°C). *Set-up*: Tank arranged in dark colors, with circulation; loosely planted, especially with broad-leaved plants. *Food*: All typles of fairly fine-grade foods. *Sexual differences*: Females plumper. *Breeding*: Through a kind of prefertilization the females are almost always fertilized; they deposit their eggs later on the underside of plant leaves. Eggs develop only in soft water. It is best to transfer leaves with eggs on them to a breeding tank. Feed first with paramecia. *Biotope*: Peruvian Amazonia.

Tips on Care of Other Species

Nannostomus eques
2 inches (5 cm). Tank: 20 inches (50 cm). Stratum: Top. Water: pH 5–6.5; soft to medium hard, 79–84°F (26–29°C). Tank arranged in dark colors; small live food, including insects.

Garnet Tetra (*Hemigrammus pulcher*)
2⅜ inches (6 cm). Tank: 24 inches (60 cm). Stratum: Middle. Water: pH 5–6.5; soft to medium hard; 75–82°F (24–28°C). Tank arranged in dark colors or the colors of the fish will not show up.

Head-and-tail-light Tetra (*Hemigrammus ocillifer*)
2 inches (5 cm). Tank: 24 inches (60 cm). Stratum: Middle. Water: pH 6–7.5; soft to hard; 75–82°F (24–28°C). Tank arranged in dark colors.

Black Neon Tetra (*Hyphessobrycon herbertaxelrodi*)
1½ inches (4 cm). Tank: 24 inches (60 cm). *Stratum*: Middle. Water: pH 5–6.5; soft to medium hard; 75–82°F (24–28°C). Tank arranged in dark colors.

Diamond Tetra (*Moenkhausia pittieri*)
2⅜ inches (6 cm). Tank: 24 inches (60 cm). Stratum: Middle. Water: pH 5.5–6.5; soft to medium hard; 75–82°F (24–28°C). Calm species for a tank arranged in dark colors (see photo on page 41).

Barbs and danios are popular shoaling fishes for community tanks. Most of them come from southern and eastern Asia, with a few from Africa. They live in the most varied biotopes.

What You Should Know about Barbs and Danios

They belong to the order of *Cypriniformes*.

Distinguishing traits: Barbs and danios can be recognized by the small barbels at the corners of the mouth, but it takes very close looking. And there are some species without barbels! The body shape is elongated to high-backed (typical fish shape) and slightly compressed laterally.

Barbs and danios are often confused with similar-looking characins, but unlike characins, they never have an adipose fin between the dorsal and caudal fins.

Care: The tank should be set up in dark colors, densely planted but leaving plenty of open water for swimming. The sun-loving *Brachydanio* species have different light requirements; they display their full liveliness only under bright lighting. *Puntius* species like to burrow into the bottom material, some of which at least should therefore be soft.

Water: Neutral to slightly acid water is best for all species—except *Sawbwa resplendens*.

Communities: All species can be combined with other fishes of similar size, as long as their temperaments are compatible. Especially good candidates for a community tank are the Schubert's barb, cherry barb, rosy barb, black ruby barb, and members of the *Brachydanio* species. Some *Puntius* species cannot be combined with calm, long-finned fishes because they like to nibble on the fins of the latter.

Behavior: All the species described in the following pages are shoaling fishes. Therefore at least six of any one species should be kept. All barbs of the genus *Puntius* tend to stay in the vicinity of the bottom and forage for some of their food by burrowing. Danios usually stay in the middle and upper strata and only rarely feed on the bottom.

Hints on breeding: Barbs and danios do not engage in brood care after depositing their eggs. They are therefore raised in a breeding tank for fish without brood care (see HOW TO page 53 on breeding fish). Many species require soft, slightly acid water for breeding. Species whose larvae are too small to eat *Artemia* have to be given paramecia or other dust food at first. Breeding barbs and danios is not easy and requires patience and time.

Hengel's Rasbora (*Rasbora hengeli*)
1⅜ inches (3.5 cm). *Tank*: 20 inches (50 cm). *Strata*: Middle, top. *Water*: pH 5.5–6.5; soft to medium hard; 73–82°F (23–28°C.) *Set-up*: Same as for harlequin fish. The lovely colors show up only under shaded lights and in a tank with dark colors. *Food*: All types of fairly fine-grade foods. *Sexual differences*: Males more brilliantly colored, with larger wedge-shaped mark. *Breeding*: Same as for harlequin fish. *Special remarks*: The correct scientific name may turn out to be *R. espei*. *Biotope*: Judging by the gorgeous, rusty-red color, this must be a black-water fish. Found in central Sumatra and Thailand.

Harlequin Fish (*Rasbora heteromorpha*)
1¾ inches (4.5 cm). *Tank*: 20 inches (50 cm). *Strata*: Middle, top. *Water*: pH 5–7; soft to medium hard; 73–82°F (23–28°C). *Set-up*: Tank arranged in dark colors, with dense planting along sides and back. Lively species. Tip on communities: Small to medium-sized fishes. *Food*: All types of fairly fine-grade foods. *Sexual differences*: Males have a black wedge-shaped mark spanning almost the entire side of the fish. *Breeding*: Breeding tank; water pH 5.5–6.5; soft. Supply small *Cryptocoryne* plants as spawning substrate. Start feeding with *Artemia*. *Biotope*: Still, usually clear water in Southeast Asia.

Ceylonese Fire Barb (*Rasbora vaterifloris*)
1½ inches (4 cm). *Tank*: 24 inches (60 cm). *Stratum*:
Middle. *Water*: pH 5.5–6.5; soft; 73–81°F (23–27°C).
Set-up: Tank arranged in dark colors, with dense bottom
and surface planting. Demanding species. Best not combined with others. *Food*: Small live food, especially black
mosquito larvae and *Daphnia*. *Sexual differences*: Males
slimmer. *Breeding*: If not kept with other species, can be
bred in the maintenance tank. Water pH 5.5–6.5, soft,
73–77°F (23–25°C). Start feeding with paramecia. *Special
remarks*: There are several different color varieties.
Biotope: Shady areas, sometimes quite deep, in clear,
light brownish streams in Sri Lanka.

Dwarf or Spotted Rasbora (*Rasbora maculata*)
1 inch (2.5 cm). *Tank*: 12 inches (30 cm). *Stratum*: Middle.
Water: pH 5–6.5; soft to medium hard; 77–84°F (25–29°C).
Set-up: Tank with dimmed lighting, densely planted. Be
sure to maintain water properties! Tip on communities:
Only "minifishes." *Food*: Tiniest live food and, for a change,
dry food. *Sexual differences*: Females plumper. *Breeding*:
In a maintenance tank with a pH of about 6, very soft
water, and dense bottom and floating plants, some young
survive to maturity. *Biotope*: Near plant-covered banks of
slowly moving and still water (floodplains) in western
Malaysia and western Sumatra. *Similar species*: Ocellated
dwarf rasbora (*R. urophthalma*), up to 79°F (26°C).

Three-lined Rasbora or Scissortail
(*Rasbora trilineata*)
4–6 inches (10–15 cm). *Tank*: 48 inches (120 cm). *Strata*:
Middle, top. *Water*: pH 6–8; soft to medium hard; 73–81°F
(23–27°C). *Set-up*: Long tank, planted densely along sides
and back with plenty of open water. Tip on communities:
Active fishes of the lower and middle strata. *Food*: Small
to medium-sized live and dry food. *Sexual differences*:
Females plumper. *Breeding*: Densely planted breeding
tank (32 inches [80 cm]); water pH 6–7.5; soft. Start feeding with *Artemia*. *Biotope*: Often opaque, still or slightly
moving water (clear water, white water) in Southeast Asia.

Red-line Rasbora (*Rasbora pauciperforata*)
2¾ inches (7 cm). *Tank*: 32 inches (80 cm). *Stratum*: Top.
Water: pH 5–6.5; soft to medium hard; 75–82°F (24–28°C)
Set-up: Tank with peat filtering, floating plants. Active
species. Tip on communities: Species dwelling in the
bottom stratum. *Food*: Small live and dry food; also
Drosophila; will not pick up food from the bottom. *Sexual
differences*: Females plumper. *Breeding*: Breeding tank;
soft water; peat filtering. Start feeding with paramecia.
Biotope: Near the surface where there is vegetation along
the shore of slowly moving black water in Malaysia and
western Indonesia.

Puntius pentazona

inches (5 cm). *Tank*: 24 inches (60 cm). *Strata*: Bottom, middle. *Water*: pH 5–6.5; soft to medium hard; 79–84°F (26–29°C). *Set-up*: Tank arranged in dark colors, peat filtering, dense planting along sides and back to provide refuge for these rather shy fish. Calmer than other barbs. Tip on communities: Don't combine with lively species. *Food*: All types of fairly fine-grade foods. *Sexual differences*: Males slimmer. *Breeding*: Only in soft, peat-filtered water. Start feeding with *Artemia*. *Special remarks*: Lovely orange color shows up only if water quality is good. *Biotope*: Shore areas of slowly moving or still black water in Malaysia. *Similar species*: P. johorensis.

Cherry Barb (*Puntius titteya*)

2 inches (5 cm). *Tank*: 24 inches (60 cm). *Strata*: Bottom, middle. *Water*: pH 6–7.5; soft to hard; 73–81°F (23–27°C). *Set-up*: Tank arranged in dark colors, shaded by plants; bottom material soft in places for burrowing. Calm species. Tip for communities: Calm fishes only. *Food*: All types of fairly fine-grade foods, especially *Daphnia*. *Sexual differences*: Males slimmer, with brighter red coloring. *Breeding*: Breeding tank; water pH 6–6.5; soft, 79–81°F (27–28°C). Start feeding with *Artemia*. *Biotope*: Bottom stratum of dark rainforest streams on Sri Lanka.

Schubert's Barb (*Puntius semifasciolatus* "schuberti")

2¾ inches (7 cm). *Tank*: 32 inches (80 cm). *Strata*: Bottom, middle. *Water*: pH 6–7.5; soft to hard; 68–75°F (20–24°C). *Set-up*: Bright tank, part of it densely planted; with areas of soft bottom material for burrowing. Active, undemanding shoaling fish for community tanks with low temperatures. *Food*: All types of fairly fine-grade foods, including vegetarian. *Sexual differences*: Females plumper. *Breeding*: Relatively easy. Breeding tank. Start feeding with *Artemia*. *Special remarks*: The original form of this species comes from southeastern China. *Biotope*: This is a tank-bred strain that does not occur in nature.

Checkered Barb (*Puntius oligolepis*)

2 inches (5 cm). *Tank*: 24 inches (60 cm). *Strata*: Bottom, middle. *Water*: pH 6–7.5; soft to hard; 73–81°F (23–27°C). *Set-up*: Lighter or darker tanks possible; loosely planted; bottom material soft in places for burrowing. Tip for communities: Compatible with active species. *Food*: All types of fairly fine-grade foods, including vegetarian. *Sexual differences*: Males with dark edges on dorsal and anal fins; females plumper. *Breeding*: Breeding tank, bright, with plants. Start feeding with paramecia. *Biotope*: Still and moving water in hilly country on Sumatra, Indonesia.

Tiger Barb or Sumatra Barb (*Puntius tetrazona*)
2¾ inches (7 cm). *Tank*: 32 inches (80 cm). *Strata*: Bottom, middle. *Water*: pH 6–7.5; soft to hard; 73–82°F (23–28°C). *Set-up*: Loosely planted tank with plenty of open water for swimming; sandy bottom for burrowing. Tip on communities: Only robust, agile fishes (this barb pulls on fins of slow-moving fishes). *Food*: All kinds of fairly fine-grade foods, including vegetarian. Don't overfeed these ravenous eaters. *Sexual differences*: Males slimmer, with brighter colors. *Breeding*: Breeding tank; water pH 5.5–7; soft to medium hard. Start feeding with *Artemia*. *Special remarks*: Cultivated strains exist. *Biotope*: Bottom stratum of slow-moving and still waters on Sumatra.

Angola Barb (*Barbus barilioides*)
2 inches (5 cm). *Tank*: 24 inches (60 cm). *Strata*: Bottom, middle. *Water*: pH 5.5–6.5; soft to medium hard; 72–77°F (22–25°C). *Set-up*: Tank arranged in dark colors, loosely planted, with plenty of open water for swimming. *Food*: All types of fairly fine-grade foods, including vegetarian. *Sexual differences*: Females plumper. *Breeding*: Breeding tank, densely planted; soft water. Start feeding with paramecia. *Biotope*: Probably smallish streams in Angola, northern Rhodesia, southern Zaire. *Similar species*: *B. jae*, 1⅛ inches (3 cm), demanding, for tanks at least 26 inches (40 cm) long.

Zebra Danio or Striped Danio (*Brachydanio rerio*)
2⅜ inches (6 cm). *Tank*: 32 inches (80 cm). *Strata*: Middle, top. *Water*: pH 6–8; soft to hard; 75–81°F (24–27°C). *Set-up*: Tank with good circulation, bright lighting. Lively species. Tip on communities: Smallish to medium-sized fishes that do not require peace and quiet. *Food*: Dry and live food of fairly fine grade. *Sexual differences*: Males smaller, slimmer. *Breeding*: In maintenance tanks with areas of dense planting, some young often survive to maturity, otherwise use a breeding tank. Start feeding with paramecia or dry food crushed fine. *Biotope*: Clear, often fast-flowing streams in India. *Similar species*: Spotted danio (*B. nigrofasciatus*).

Giant Danio (*Danio aequipinnatus*)
4 inches (10 cm). *Tank*: 48 inches (120 cm). *Strata*: Middle, top. *Water*: pH 6.5–8; soft to hard; 73–79°F (23–26°C). *Set-up*: Tank with plenty of open water for swimming. Active species. Tip on communities: Can include largish fishes of the lower strata. *Food*: Live and dry food of medium size, including vegetarian food. *Sexual differences*: Males slimmer. *Breeding*: Large breeding tank. Dry food possible as first food. *Biotope*: Rivers in India and Sri Lanka. *Similar species*: *D. devario*, 3 inches (8 cm), more high-backed; *D. regina*, 5 inches (12.5 cm).

White Cloud minnows are an ideal fish for beginners. They reproduce easily. If one keeps a large shoal in a densely planted, unheated tank, some young always make it to adulthood. The water temperature should be 64 to 72°F (18–22°C). If these fish are kept too warm, their pretty colors fade.

hite Cloud (*Tanichthys albonubes*)
 inches (4 cm). *Tank*: 24 inches (60 cm) *Strata*: Middle,
. *Water*: pH 6–8; soft to hard; 64–72°F (18–22°C).
t-up: Tank with densely planted areas. Undemanding
ecies. Males display their best colors to impress rivals.
od: All types of fairly fine-grade foods. *Sexual differ-
ces*: Males slimmer. *Breeding*: Some young quite often
rvive to maturity in a densely planted maintenance tank.
not, use a breeding tank. Start feeding with paramecia
 fine-grade dry food. This species can also be raised by
e long-term breeding method. *Special remarks*: Don't
ep this species too warm; the lovely colors fade in water
er 77°F (25°C). Juveniles have an especially prominent
minous longitudinal stripe. *Biotope*: Clear mountain
eams in southern China. *Note*: The scientific names
metimes give clues about the geographical origin of a
ecies. Its scientific name
eans: fish from the white cloud mountains. The White
oud Mountains are a mountain range in southern China.
hen this species was introduced in Europe around
40, it was first called "Working-man's Neon" in Ger-
any, a name no longer in use. Unlike neon tetras, which
re very expensive at that time, this species was much
eaper so that people with little money could afford to
y them. White Clouds are comparable in beauty to
on tetras, especially because the juveniles have such
bright neon stripe.

Tips on the Care of Other Species

Bala Shark (*Balantiocheilus melanopterus*)
14 inches (35 cm)! Tank: 8 feet (250 cm). Strata: Bottom, middle. Water: pH 6–7.5; soft to medium hard, 75–82°F (24–28°C). Often available; only for very large tanks; alternatively, keep only as a juvenile.
Sawbwa resplendens
1¾ inches (4.5 cm). Tank: 24 inches (60 cm). Stratum: Middle. Water: pH 7–8.5; medium hard to hard; 70–75°F (21–24°C). Does not display its "glowing" head in soft, acid water.
Purple-headed Barb (*Puntius nigrofasciatus*)
2½ inches (6.5 cm). Tank: 32 inches (80 cm). Strata: Bottom, middle. Water: pH 5.5–6.5; soft to medium hard; 70–75°F (21–24°C).
Rosy Barb (*Puntius conchonius*)
3 inches (8 cm) and supposedly larger. Tank: 32 inches (80 cm). Strata: Bottom, middle. Water: pH 6–8; soft to hard; 64–72°F (18–22°C). Don't keep too warm!
Spotted Danio (*Brachydanio albolineatus*)
2⅜ inches (6 cm). Tank: 32 inches (80 cm). Strata: Middle, top. Water: pH 6.5–7.5; soft to hard; 73–82°F (24–28°C). Lively fish with iridescent colors that show up only if lit from above.

These groups of fishes, though closely related, belong to four different families. Except for their areas of distribution, they have so much in common that all of them can be described together.

What You Should Know about Rainbow Fishes, Silversides, and Rice Fishes

Rainbow fishes belong to the family Melanotaeniidae; the closely related blue-eyed rainbow fishes to the family Pseudomugilidae; the silversides, to the family Atherinidae; and the rice fishes, to the family Oryziatidae. Rainbow fishes are found only in Australia, Papua New Guinea, and Irian Jaya (Indonesia) and blue-eyed rainbow fishes in New Guinea, while silversides exist worldwide in warm water, and rice fishes are found in the Far East.

Distinguishing traits: All the members of these four families have elongated bodies with more or less flattened sides. The often splendid colors generally reach their peak only when the fish reach maturity. Old rainbow fish males often have very high-backed bodies.

Care: All these species are shoaling fishes that do not do well if kept singly. A hobbyist should always keep at least six individuals of a species. The maintenance tank should be planted along the sides and back only, because these lively swimmers need plenty of open water. As protection for the fry, a small part of the water surface should be covered with floating plants. Tufts of Java moss (*Vesicularia dubyana*) serve as spawning substrate. Use roots only sparingly (they acidify the water).

Water: With a few exceptions all these fishes like medium-hard to hard, alkaline water. Water changes are important because the fish lose their color quickly if the water deteriorates.

Communities: All species of these four families can be combined with livebearers, smallish cichlids from Lake Tanganyika, gobies, and catfishes.

Behavior: Most species engage in very interesting behavior that can be observed in an aquarium. Rainbow fishes are an example. They are sometimes called "children of the morning sun" because the males generally perform their courtship display in the morning. Their colors are much more brilliant than in the afternoon.

Hints on breeding: Being long-term spawners, rainbow fishes and silversides, as well as blue-eyed rainbow fishes, deposit a few eggs every day during the reproductive period. Rice fish females carry grape-like clusters of eggs in the anal region and deposit them on plants only after some time. Java moss and a wool mop are good spawning substrates for them. Once the eggs are deposited, pick them off the substrate with your fingers and place them in a rearing tank (same water quality as in the maintenance tank). There the young will hatch after one or two weeks. They swim just below the surface and immediately start taking food. Usually they are first given dust food (or dry food of the finest grade). Only a few species eat *Artemia* from the start. The fry grow very slowly. (Transfer fry that have hatched in a maintenance tank to a rearing tank.)

Only the male salmon-red rainbow fish is red. The female has an olive yellow body with shimmering golden yellow scales.

Salmon-red Rainbow Fish (*Glossolepis incisus*)
6 inches (15 cm). *Tank*: 48 inches (120 cm). *Strata*: Middle, top. *Water*: pH 7–8.5; medium hard to hard; 72–77°F (22–25°C). *Set-up*: Loosely planted tank, cushions of Java moss, lots of open water for swimming. *Food*: Small to medium live and dry food (*Daphnia*, mosquito larvae). *Sexual differences*: Males red and, with age, high-backed. *Breeding*: Transfer eggs to rearing tank. Start feeding with finest-grade dry food, later give *Artemia*. *Biotope*: Near dense vegetation in Lake Sentani in Irian Jaya (Indonesia). *Similar species*: G. wanamensis, 4 inches (10 cm). *Note*: The coloration of the male depends on mood but is also influenced by the rank of the particular individual. Subordinate males do not display bright colors.

Jewel Rainbow Fish

(*Melanotaenia trifasciata* "Goyder River")
4¾ inches (12 cm). *Tank*: 48 inches (120 cm). *Stratum*: Middle. *Water*: pH 7–8; medium hard to hard; 75–82°F (24–28°C). *Set-up*: Tank loosely planted along edges, cushions of Java moss, open water for swimming. *Breeding*: Transfer eggs to rearing tank. Start feeding with finest-grade dry food. *Sexual differences*: Females paler, slimmer. *Special remarks*: Other strains from the Giddy and the Coen Rivers have different colors. The different strains should not be kept together in the same aquarium because hybrid offspring may result. *Biotope*: A number of rivers in northern Australia.

Boeseman's Rainbow Fish

(*Melanotaenia boesemani*)
5½ inches (14 cm). *Tank*: 40 inches (100 cm). *Strata*: Middle, top. *Water*: pH 7–8.5; medium hard to hard; 73–79°F (23–26°C). *Set-up*: Tank loosely planted along edges, cushions of Java moss, lots of open water for swimming. Compatible community fish. *Food*: Live and dry food. *Sexual differences*: Males more brilliantly colored. *Breeding*: Transfer eggs to rearing tank. Start feeding with finest-grade dry food. *Biotope*: Shallow areas with feathery-leaved vegetation in the Ajamaru Lakes, Irian Jaya (Indonesia). *Note*: Since its introduction in 1982, this fish has become one of the most popular aquarium fishes.

Chilaterina bleheri

4 inches (10 cm). *Tank*: 40 inches (100 cm). *Stratum*: Middle. *Water*: pH 7–8.5; medium hard to hard; 73–81°F (23–27°C). *Set-up*: Tank subdivided by a few tall plants; dark bottom material, cushions of Java moss, a few floating plants. Tip on communities: Only fishes that will not be bothered by this active shoaling fish. *Food*: Mosquito larvae, *Daphnia*, dry food. *Sexual differences*: Females less conspicuous. *Breeding*: Transfer eggs to a rearing tank. Start feeding with fine-grade dry food, later with *Artemia*. *Biotope*: Dense shore vegetation and small feeder streams of Lake Holmes (Danau Biru), Irian Jaya, Indonesia.

Celebes Rainbow Fish (*Telmatherina ladigesi*)

2¾ inches (7 cm). *Tank*: 32 inches (80 cm). *Stratum*: middle. *Water*: pH 7–8; medium hard to hard; 77–82°F (25–28°C). *Set-up*: Parts of tank densely planted, open water for swimming, partially covered with floating plants. Clear, clean water and frequent water changes important, otherwise the fish soon ail. *Food*: Small live food as well as dry food. *Sexual differences*: Males have larger, elongated fins. *Breeding*: Carefully transfer eggs to rearing tank. Start feeding with paramecia, fine-grade dry food; later *Artemia*. *Biotope*: Streams with not too much current in hilly country on Celebes, Indonesia.

Iriatherina werneri

2 inches (5 cm). *Tank*: 24 inches (60 cm). *Stratum*: Middle. *Water*: pH 6–7.5; soft to medium hard; 77–81°F (25–27°C). *Set-up*: Dense planting along edges, open water for swimming, partially covered with floating plants. Tip on communities: Only delicate fishes. *Food*: Small live food, especially *Daphnia*, *Cyclops*, and *Artemia*. *Sexual differences*: Males have beautiful, elongated fins. *Breeding*: Like Boeseman's rainbow fish. Start feeding with

finest-grade dry food. *Biotope*: Small, still, or slowly moving bodies of water full of vegetation in northern Australia and southern New Guinea. *Note*: These fish are often kept with poor results because they are combined with the wrong species. They display their full splendor only if kept by themselves or in suitable communities (delicate fishes).

Pseudomugil furcatus
¾ inches (7 cm). *Tank*: 24 inches (60 cm). *Strata*:
Middle, top. *Water*: pH 6–7.5; soft to medium hard;
75–81°F (24–27°C). *Set-up*: Tank with circulation, dense
planting around edges, moss cushions on rocks. Tip on
communities: Peaceful small fishes of the bottom stratum.
Food: Small live and fine-grade dry food. *Sexual differences*: Males more brightly colored. *Breeding*: Pick off
eggs; larvae hatch after two weeks and eat *Artemia* from
the first. *Biotope*: Fast-flowing waters with stony bottom in
northern Papua New Guinea. *Similar species*: P. conniae,
lacks black rims on the caudal fin.

Red-tailed Silverside (*Bedotia geayi*)
6 inches (15 cm). *Tank*: 48 inches (120 cm). *Strata*:
Middle, top. *Water*: pH 7–8; medium hard to hard; 70–75°F
(21–24°C). *Set-up*: Tank with strong circulation, loosely
planted. Bright lighting possible. Peaceful shoaling fish.
Tip on communities: Fishes from moving waters. *Food*:
Vegetable food, live and dry food. *Sexual differences*:
Males slimmer, with brighter colors. *Breeding*: Transfer
spawning substrate or eggs to rearing tank with slight
circulation. Start feeding with *Artemia*. *Biotope*: Clear
mountain streams in Madagascar.

Rice Fish (*Oryzias latipes*)
2¼ inches (5.5 cm). *Tank*: 20 inches (50 cm). *Strata*:
Middle, top. *Water*: pH 7–8.5; medium hard to hard;
64–75°F (18–24°C). *Set-up*: Tank with feathery plants,
plenty of open water for swimming; slight circulation
desirable. Tip on communities: Only small, peaceful fishes
of the lower and middle strata. *Food*: Small live and fine-
grade dry food. *Sexual differences*: Males have larger
fins. *Breeding*: Like all rainbow fishes. *Biotope*: Standing
water. Widespread in the Far East (Japan, China, Korea).
Similar species: Dealers also offer some other *Oryzias*
species from Celebes, Indonesia.

Tips on Care of Other Species

Melanotaenia lacustris
4¾ inches (12 cm). Tank: 48 inches (120 cm).
Strata: Middle, top. Water: pH 7–8.5; medium hard;
72–77°F (22–25°C). Somewhat delicate.

Melanotaenia or Nematurentra splendida
4–6 inches (10–15 cm), depending on subspecies.
Tank: 40–48 inches (100–120 cm). Stratum: Middle.
Water: pH 7–7.5; soft to hard; 73–81°F (23–27°C);
otherwise as for *M. boesemani*. Several subspecies
that should not be mixed together.

Chilatherina fasciata
4 inches (10 cm). Tank: 40 inches (100 cm). Stratum: Middle. Water: pH 7–8; medium hard to hard;
72–79°F (22–26°C). Males have a beautiful, golden
stripe that shows up during courtship.

Pseudomugil gertrudae
1½ inches (4 cm). Tank: 20 inches (50 cm). Strata:
Middle, top. Water: pH 6–6.5; soft to medium hard;
77–82°F (25–28°C). A beauty for a small tank. Small
live and fine-grade dry food; maintenance of water
quality important. Difficult to breed.

Honey Rainbow Fish (*Pseudomugil mellis*)
1½ inches (4 cm). Tank: 20 inches (50 cm). Strata:
Middle, top. Water: pH 6–7.5; soft to medium hard;
75–82°F (24–28°C). Less sensitive than *P. gertrudae*.

A few species from these fish groups are very common in aquariums. Most aquarists keep single specimens as clean-up fish in a community tank. Unfortunately very little is known about the biology of the fishes belonging to these groups, which come from Europe, Africa, and Asia.

What You Should Know about Loaches, Flying Foxes, and Elephant-trunk Fishes

These fishes are part of the order Cypriniformes (carp-like fishes) and belong to various families.

Distinguishing traits: Most species are elongated and round-bodied, with an overshot mouth well adapted for bottom-feeding. Many loaches have erectile spines below the eyes (caution: you can get hurt on these when catching the fish). In order to survive in rapidly moving waters, the sucking loaches and sucker-mouth armored catfish have developed suction organs that allow them to hang on to rocks and plants in spite of strong current.

Care: The most important aspect of the tank is the availability of hiding places. These can be caves or refuges among roots, and, for some species, plant thickets. Many species establish territories around their hiding places; some are nocturnal and use the retreats to rest in during the day. To prevent injuries to the fishes' mouths, do not use bottom material with sharp edges. Sand or fine gravel is best.

Water: Many loaches and elephant-trunk fishes are affected quickly by a build-up of metabolic products. Frequent water changes are therefore crucial. All members of these three groups like slightly acid to slightly alkaline (pH 6.5–7.5) and soft to medium hard water.

Communities: Almost all species can be combined with fishes of the middle and upper water levels. The bottom stratum should not include other fishes, especially in small tanks, because otherwise there will be conflicts over living space. Some species (*Epalzeorhynchus bicolor*) become bullies with age and can terrorize the entire population of a community tank.

Behavior: Some species are very territorial and should be kept singly. Others are sociable and live in small groups. Some species make croaking sounds that are assumed to be associated with aggression or courtship.

Hints on breeding: To date only accidental reproduction—no successful planned breeding—has been reported. Probably seasonal fluctuations in environmental conditions (pH, salt content, temperature?) play a role in inducing readiness to reproduce. Attempts to simulate the rainy season might bring success (see Kirschbaum Method, page 51).

Red-finned Loach (*Botia modesta*)
4¾–8 inches (12–20 cm). *Tank*: 40 inches (100 cm). *Stratum*: Bottom. *Water*: pH 6–7.5; soft to medium hard; 75–82°F (24–28°C). *Set-up*: Loosely planted tank. A refuge for each fish! Keep a small group. Upkeep of water quality important. Tip on communities: No other bottom-dwelling fishes. *Food*: Mosquito larvae, small worms, food tablets. *Sexual differences*: Unknown. *Breeding*: Unknown. *Biotope*: Rivers in Thailand, Malaysia, Vietnam. *Similar species*: B. eos, B. lecontei. All three species are easily mistaken for one another.

Dwarf Loach (*Botia sidthimunki*)
2⅜–3½ inches (6–9 cm). *Tank*: 24 inches (60 cm). *Stratum*: Bottom. *Water*: pH 6–7.5; soft to hard; 79–84°F (26–29°C). *Set-up*: Dense vegetation in part of tank, open water for swimming. Lively shoaling fish that does not do well if kept singly. Tip on communities: Smallish, nonterritorial fishes. *Food*: Small live and fine-grade dry food. *Sexual differences*: Females carrying spawn (rare) noticeably fatter. *Breeding*: Accidental. During courtship the fish change colors and turn paler. *Biotope*: Standing and slow-moving waters in Indochina and northern Thailand.

The popular clown loach can easily be kept in the biotope aquarium described on page 37 as "Blackwater Tank for Southeast Asian Fishes."

Clown Loach (*Botia macracanthus*)
–12 inches (15–30 cm). *Tank*: 48 inches (120 cm). *Strata*: Middle, bottom. *Water*: pH 5–7.5; soft to medium hard; 75–86°F (24–30°C). *Set-up*: Tank with hiding places such as pieces of bamboo cane). Keep groups of at least five fish; if there are fewer there is often fighting among them. Tip on communities: Medium-sized fishes in the middle and upper water levels. *Food*: Mosquito larvae, worms, food tablets, small snails. *Sexual differences*: Older females plumper as viewed from above. *Breeding*: unknown. Probably this species migrates upriver to special spawning grounds. No natural breeding in captivity

thus far reported. *Special remarks*: Do not keep in small tanks! *Biotope*: Rivers and lakes on Sumatra and Borneo, especially in floodplains in the hill country.
Note: Clown loaches are imported in great numbers from Southeast Asia. Many people there make a living catching and selling these fish to middlemen. The method of catching the loaches is simple. Where the fish are found, bamboo canes are placed in certain spots as traps. The loaches swim into them, mistaking them for hiding places. The bamboo canes often yield one or more fish at the daily checks.

Coolie Loach (*Pangio spec.*)
inches (8 cm). *Tank*: 24 inches (60 cm). *Stratum*: Bottom. *Water*: pH 5–7; soft to medium hard; 79–86°F (26–30°C). *Set-up*: Tank with slight circulation, roots, plant thickets for hiding, soft bottom material. Fish stay mostly hidden during the day and come out at feeding time. *Food*: Small live food that drifts to the bottom; also food tablets. *Sexual differences*: Females carrying spawn become obese. *Breeding*: Accidental breeding in tanks with lots of plants reported. *Biotope*: Masses of fish hidden in plant cushions in streams in Southeast Asia. *Similar species*: P. myersi, P. kuhlii, P. semicinctus.

Algae-eater or Sucking Loach
(*Gyrinocheilus aymonieri*)
6–10 inches (15–25 cm). *Tank*: 40 inches (100 cm). *Strata*: All, but not in open water. *Water*: pH 6–8; soft to hard; 75–82°F (24–28°C). *Set-up*: Unproblematic if there is a refuge for each fish. Become aggressive toward each other with age. Tip on communities: No slow-moving fishes with large sides, or they will be "scrubbed" by the algae-eaters. *Food*: Vegetarian, food tablets, small live food. *Sexual differences*: Unknown. *Breeding*: Only accidental. *Biotope*: On the bottom of moving water and rarely of standing water in Indochina and central Thailand.

The genus *Pseudogastromyzon* has developed sucking disks on the fins that allow the fish to hold on to stones or other objects even in strong current. This adaptation allows them to survive in their environment (fast-flowing water). You can see the underside of the suction fin in the photo on page 58.

Pseudogastromyzon cheni

(sucker-mouth armored catfish)
2⅜ inches (6 cm). *Tank*: 48 inches (60 cm). *Stratum*: Substrate-dependent. *Water*: pH 6.5–7.5; soft to medium hard: 72–75°F (22–24°C). *Set-up*: Planted tank with roots and pebbles (direct circulation from filter over them). It is best to keep several specimens. Tip on communities: Do not combine with rivals for food, for this fish does not assert itself and will starve. *Food*: Artemia, small *Daphnia*, mosquito larvae; also dry food. Fish will forage on the pebbles for live food animals that are there or drift by. Not an algae eater; algae are consumed only "on the side." *Sexual differences*: Unclear; red rims on dorsal fin may indicate male. *Breeding*: Unknown. *Special remarks*: Interesting threatening displays. *Biotope*: On algae-covered stones in fast-flowing, clear streams of southern China. Because of this biotope it has often been wrongly assumed that this species is a pure algae eater. In fact, algae do not constitute the main diet for this species in nature or in an aquarium.

Acanthopsis spec.

About 8 inches (20 cm). *Tank*: 40 inches (100 cm). *Stratum*: Bottom. *Water*: pH 6–7.5; soft to hard; 75–82°F (24–28°C). *Set-up*: Sandy bottom material (river sand without sharp edges) in which the fish sometimes bury themselves is important. Tip on communities: Fishes of the middle and upper strata. *Food*: Worms and mosquito larvae. *Sexual differences*: Unknown. *Breeding*: Unknown *Biotope*: Sandy bottom of rivers in Southeast Asia. *Similar species*: Other members of the genus *Acanthopsoides* that remain small; they can be accommodated in fairly small tanks.

Flying Fox (*Epalzeorhynchus kallopterus*)
6 inches (15 cm). *Tank*: 40 inches (100 cm). *Strata*: All, but not in open water. *Water*: pH 6–7.5; soft to medium hard; 77–82°F (25–28°C). *Set-up*: Densely planted tank with circulation. Shoaling fish, should be kept in small groups even when older because if there are too few specimens they are aggressive amongst themselves. Good for cleaning up algae in community tanks, but does not eat every kind of algae. *Food*: Vegetarian dry food, small live food, food tablets. *Sexual differences*: Unknown. *Breeding*: Unknown. *Biotope*: In the current of medium-size to large rivers in hilly country in much of Southeast Asia.

Epalzeorhynchus bicolor
6 inches (15 cm). *Tank*: 40 inches (100 cm). *Stratum*: Bottom. *Water*: pH 6–7.5; soft to hard; 73–82°F (23–28°C). *Set-up*: A refuge for each fish is very important. Territorial species. Keep only one specimen because this fish is aggressive toward others of its own species and other, similar-looking species. Keep several only in a very large tank. Older fish become aggressive toward other kinds of fish as well. Tip on communities: Fishes of the middle and upper strata. *Food*: All types, including vegetarian. *Sexual differences*: Males narrower, with elongated dorsal fin. *Breeding*: Rarely successful. *Biotope*: Clear and muddy rivers with wood and stone in central Thailand.

Epalzeorhynchus frenatus
4¾ inches (12 cm). *Tank*: 40 inches (100 cm). *Stratum*: Bottom. *Water*: pH 6–7.5; soft to medium hard; 75–81°F (24–27°C). *Set-up*: As for *E. bicolor*, but this fish is more tolerant of other members of its species; older specimens are also compatible with other species. *Food*: All types of food, especially fond of vegetable food; also consumes algae. *Sexual differences*: Males slimmer. *Breeding*: Only accidental breeding. *Biotope*: Unknown; found in northern Thailand. Similar species: It may be that fish sold as *E. erythrozonus* are simply large specimens of *E. frenatus*; the classification is uncertain.

Tips on Care of Other Species

Nemacheilus notostigma
3 inches (8 cm). Tank: 32 inches (80 cm). Stratum: Bottom. Water: pH 6.5–7.5; soft to medium hard; 72–75°F (22–24°C). Plants and hiding places. Has been bred in maintenance tanks.

Botia morleti
2¾ inches (7 cm). Tank: 32 inches (80 cm). Stratum: Bottom. Water: pH 6.5–7.5; soft to medium hard; 77–86°F (25-30°C). Keep several specimens. Each fish needs a refuge. Occasionally aggressive.

Pakistani Loach (*Botia lohachata*)
4 inches (10 cm). Tank: 32 inches (80 cm). Stratum: Bottom. Water: pH 6.5–7.5; soft to medium hard; 74–82°F (24–28°C). Refuges. Something of a loner. Needs *Tubifex* worms. Occasionally aggressive.

Zebra Loach (*Botia striata*)
4 inches (10 cm). Tank: 32 inches (80 cm). Stratum: Bottom. Water: pH 6.5–7.5; soft to medium hard; 73–81°F (23–27°C). Soft bottom material. Group fish. Occasionally aggressive.

Pangio anguillaris
2¾ inches (7 cm). Tank: 20 inches (50 cm). Stratum: Bottom. Water: pH 5–6.5; soft to medium hard; 75–81°F (24–27°C). Soft bottom material; densely planted.

Livebearing aquarium fishes belong to several fish families. What they all have in common is that they do not lay eggs like most other fishes but instead give birth to live offspring.

There are some very beautiful wild forms of livebearers, but there are also a great many cultivated varieties that are extremely popular. Through selective breeding their colors and fin shapes have been altered to to create some special effects.

What You Should Know about Livebearers

Among the livebearing fishes generally kept in aquariums are the following:

- livebearing tooth carps (family Poeciliidae) from North, Central, and South America
- the Goodeidae family from Mexico
- the Hemirhamphidae family from Southeast Asia.

Distinguishing traits: Because the egg cells of livebearers are fertilized inside the female's body, the males have a sexual organ in order to accomplish internal fertilization. It consists of a modified anal fin. Because of differences in external appearance, this organ is called the gonopodium in livebearing tooth carps and the andropodium in Goodeidae and Hemirhamphidae. The gonopodium is flipped forward for copulation, whereas the andropodium is folded when inserted into the female's genital opening. The development of the embryos happens in two different ways, depending on genus and family:

- The young develop inside eggs within the mother's body, hatch there, and are then "born"; the guppy (*Poecilia reticulata*) is an example.
- The young develop without an eggshell inside the mother's body, receiving nourishment through an umbilical cord; *Ameca splendens* is an example.

Care: Most livebearers are shoaling fishes, and one should therefore always keep several individuals of a species. It is important that there be more females than males in a shoal because males become too aggressive otherwise and pursue the females too actively.

A tank with dense vegetation along the sides and plenty of open water for swimming is recommended. For most species vegetables are an important part of the diet.

Water: With a few exceptions, livebearing aquarium fishes like medium hard to hard, alkaline (pH 7–7.8) water. Regular water changes are especially important.

Communities: Most livebearers can be combined without problems with other active shoaling fishes, catfishes, and cichlids that are not too large. Again it is important to keep up water quality.

Behavior: Courtship behavior, especially, can be observed well in an aquarium. The males, which engage in courtship displays almost continuously, swim around the female in a hectic manner and often with crescent-shaped movements. If there are several males, a kind of pecking order is soon established. The highest-ranking male drives away the males ranking below him, the second-ranking male drives the third- and fourth-ranking ones away, and so on.

Hints on breeding: Because the young of livebearers start foraging for themselves immediately after birth and are relatively large, some of them always survive to maturity in a sparsely populated and well planted community tank. It is important, however, to supply fine-grade food at the first appearance of the young. If you want to raise a whole batch of young, the gravid female should be placed in a large spawning cage or a separate tank. Either container should include some feathery-leaved plants.

It is sometimes hard to tell when a female is close to giving birth. The best way is to compare the fish before feeding. If the abdomen is very round and the eyes of the young already visible inside the female's body, the birth is imminent.

Because in some species the parents eat their own young, the latter should be transferred to a rearing tank, where they are fed with small crustaceans and crushed dry food.

Swordtail (*Xiphophorus helleri*)
4¾ inches (12 cm). *Tank*: 40 inches (100 cm). *Stratum*: Middle. *Water*: pH 7–8; medium hard to hard; 72–82°F (22–28°C). *Set-up*: Tank with circulation. Males are aggressive amongst themselves and occasionally toward other species. Keep either just one male or enough for the aggression to be spread around. *Food*: Vegetarian food, also nonvegetarian food and food flakes. *Sexual differences*: Males smaller, with a "sword" on the caudal fin; gonopodium. *Breeding*: Isolate highly pregnant females. Feed young with live and dry food. *Biotope*: Rivers in Mexico and Guatemala.

ariegated or Sunset Platy (*Xiphophorus variatus*)
⅜ inches (6 cm). *Tank*: 24 inches (60 cm). *Strata*: Mid-
e, top. *Water*: pH 7–8; medium hard to hard; 70–75°F
21–24°C). *Set-up*: Important to keep up water quality,
herwise this fish soon suffers. Good community fish.
onsumes algae in the tank. *Food*: Vegetarian food, also
mall live food and nonvegetarian dry food. *Sexual differ-
nces*: Males more brilliantly colored; gonopodium. *Breed-
g*: Isolate highly pregnant females. Feed young with dry
od and *Artemia*. *Special remarks*: Many cultivated
arieties, such as the mari-gold platy. *Biotope*: Shallow
reas with little current in rivers in southern Mexico.

Platy (*Xiphophorus maculatus*)
2⅜ inches (6 cm). *Tank*: 24 inches (60 cm). *Stratum*:
Middle. *Water*: pH 7–8; medium hard to hard; 70–77°F
(21–25°C). *Set-up*: Loosely planted tank with a cover of
floating plants where fry can seek shelter. Undemanding
community fish. *Food*: All types of fairly fine-grade foods,
especially vegetarian. *Sexual differences*: Males smaller;
gonopodium. *Breeding*: Isolate highly pregnant females.
Young can be fed dry food. *Special remarks:* Many cultivated varieties, such as the moon platy and the coral
platy. *Biotope*: Lowland rivers on the Atlantic side of
Central America.

**There are many cultivated varieties
of the sunset platy (such as the
yellow sunset platy). The colors
in these strains are often brighter
than those of the original wild
strain. Anyone interested in the
wild variety should turn for information to the American Killifish
Association (see page 158 for
address).**

"Black Molly" and Pointed-mouth Molly
(*Poecilia sphenops*)
3–4⅜ inches (8–12 cm). *Tank*: 32–40 inches (80–100 cm)
Strata: Middle, top. *Water*: pH 7.5–8.5; medium hard
to hard; 68–82°F (20–28°C) (black molly: 79–84°F or
26–29°C). *Set-up*: Robust plants; floating plants to serve
as protection for the young. Frequent water changes.
Original strain undemanding, but cultivated black variety
often susceptible to disease. *Food*: Vegetarian, also dry
and live food. Good algae eater. *Sexual differences*:
Males smaller; gonopodium. *Breeding*: Raise young in
rearing tank on vegetarian dry food and *Artemia*. *Special
remarks*: Both the cultivated and the original forms are
excellent at cleaning up algae. *Biotope*: Wild form in fresh
and brackish water, especially in rivers from Venezuela to
Mexico.
Note: The black variety called "black molly" exists with
differently shaped fins. Although the original strain (see
photo above, right) is hardy and undemanding, the cultivated black form can be susceptible to disease: As in
many other highly bred strains, by changing the shape
and colors of the fish other, invisible, characteristics are
altered as well. Such invisible changes can negatively
affect the hardiness of the animals.

Guppy (*Poecilia reticulata*)
2⅜ inches (6 cm). *Tank*: 24 inches (60 cm). *Strata*: Middle, top. *Water*: pH 7–8.5; medium hard to hard; 68–86°F
(20–30°C). *Set-up*: Densely planted tank with some open
water for swimming. Good community fish. Cultivated
varieties with very large fins are best kept singly. *Food*:
Small live and fine-grade dry food. *Sexual differences*:
Males smaller; gonopodium. *Breeding*: Easy; can be
done in the maintenance tank ("million fish"). Young are
easy to raise on dry food. *Biotope*: Standing and slowly
moving water, originally in northern South America and
the Caribbean.

Sailfin Molly (*Poecilia velifera*)
6 inches (15 cm). *Tank*: 48 inches
(120 cm). *Strata*: Middle, top. *Water*:
pH 7.5–8.5; hard; 77–82°F (25–28°C).
Set-up: Tank with a great deal of open
water for swimming; otherwise, future-
generation males will not develop the
same tall fins. Not suitable for normal
community tanks because this species requires brackish water (add
salt); good candidate for a tank with
brackish water. *Food*: Vegetarian, with
addition of other types of food. *Sexual
differences*: Males have very high
dorsal fin, the so-called sailfin; gonopodium. *Breeding*: About 200 young
are born approximately every four
weeks. Raise them in a rearing tank
on vegetarian dry food and *Artemia*.
Biotope: Coastal areas in Yucatán,
Mexico. *Similar species*: P. latipinna.

Alfaro cultratus
inches (8 cm). *Tank*: 40 inches (100 cm). *Stratum*: Top.
Water: pH 6.5–7.5; soft to medium hard; 75–79°F
(24–26°C). *Set-up*: Tank with circulation. Active species.
Tip on communities: Small and medium-sized Central
American cichlids. *Food*: Mosquito larvae, insects. *Sexual
differences*: Males smaller; gonopodium. *Breeding*:
Females produce up to 80 young about every 30 days.
Isolate female before she gives birth. Raise the fast-
growing brood in a large tank on small crustaceans and
vegetarian dry food. *Biotope*: Near the surface and close
to banks in fast-moving sections of clear-water rivers in
western Central America.

Midget Livebearer or Mosquito fish
(*Heterandria formosa*)
1¾ inches (4.5 cm). *Tank*: 16 inches (40 cm). *Strata*:
Middle, top. *Water*: pH 7–8; medium hard to hard; 64–86°F
(18–30°C). *Set-up*: Tank with dense vegetation, especially
floating plants. Tip on communities: Only small, agile
shoaling fishes. *Food*: Small crustaceans, also *Artemia*
nauplii and food flakes. *Sexual differences*: Males smaller;
gonopodium. *Breeding*: In the maintenance tank. During
the spawning period a few young are born every day.
Biotope: Among plants in the smallest of vegetation-
choked bodies of water in Florida and South Carolina.

Metallic Livebearer (*Girardinus metallicus*, "Blackbelly")
2¾ inches (7 cm). *Tank*: 24 inches (60 cm). *Stratum*:
Middle. *Water*: pH 6.5–8; medium hard to hard; 74–82°F
(25–28°C). *Set-up*: Easy to keep in a tank with some
dense planting and as long as water quality is maintained.
Food: All types of fairly fine-grade foods, including vegetarian. *Sexual differences*: Males are little more than half
the size of females; gonopodium. *Breeding*: Females give
birth about every 28 to 30 days; isolate them beforehand.
Raise fry on crushed vegetarian flakes and *Artemia*.
Biotope: Slow-moving and standing water in Cuba.

Priapella intermedia
2¾ inches (7 cm). *Tank*: 32 inches (80 cm). *Strata*: Middle, top. *Water*: pH 7–8; medium hard to hard; 77–82°F
(25–28°C). *Set-up*: Tank with circulation; loose planting
along sides and back with plants reaching to surface;
plenty of open water for swimming. Tightly fitting cover
because this species jumps. Good water maintenance
important. Peaceful community fish. *Food*: Mosquito larvae
insects (*Drosophila*), also dry food. *Sexual differences*:
Males somewhat smaller; gonopodium. *Breeding*: Female
produce 10–20 young about every four weeks. Isolate
female beforehand. Raise young on *Artemia*. *Biotope*:
Near the surface of fast-flowing, clear rivers in Mexico.

Ameca splendens
4¾ inches (12 cm). *Tank*: 40 inches (100 cm). *Stratum*:
Middle. *Water*: pH 6.5–8; medium hard to hard; 75–82°F
(24–28°C). *Set-up*: Tank with good circulation; plenty
of open swimming area. Peaceful species. Tip on
communities: Other Central American livebearers. *Food*:
Vegetarian food important; also live and dry food. *Sexual
differences*: Males smaller, with yellow rim on caudal fin;
andropodium. *Breeding*: Offspring measuring up to ¾ inch
(2 cm) are born every 40 to 60 days. Raise them on
vegetarian dry food and small crustaceans. *Biotope*: Clear
rivers with rocky sections and plenty of vegetation. Mexico.

Xenotoca eiseni
2¾ inches (7 cm). *Tank*: 32 inches (80 cm). *Stratum*:
Middle. *Water*: pH 6–8; medium hard to hard; 64–79°F
(18–26°C). *Set-up*: Tank with circulation. Undemanding
species. Tip on communities: Do not combine with slow-
moving fishes with long fins. *Food*: All types of fairly fine-
grade foods, especially vegetarian. *Sexual differences*:
Males more colorful; andropodium. *Breeding*: Females
produce up to 50 young every 35 to 70 days. Isolate
female beforehand. Raise young on small crustaceans
and vegetarian dry food. Older females no longer produce
young. *Biotope*: Streams with moderate current in Mexico

Malayan or Wrestling Half-beak
(*Dermogenys pusillus*)
2¾ inches (7 cm). *Tank*: 32 inches (80 cm). *Stratum*: Top.
Water: pH 7–8; medium hard to hard; 75–82°F (24–28°C).
Set-up: Tank with slight circulation; plants that reach up to
the surface, some floating plants. Also brackish-water
tanks with some salt. Good community fish. *Food*: Insects, mosquito larvae; also dry food. Vitamin supplements recommended. *Sexual differences*: Males smaller;
andropodium. *Breeding*: Transfer fry (up to 80) carefully to
a rearing tank. Raise on *Artemia*. *Biotope*: Shallow areas
of rivers in coastal regions of Southeast Asia.

Nomorhamphus liemi
4 inches (10 cm). *Tank*: 40 inches (100 cm). *Stratum*: Top.
Water: pH 6.5–8; soft to medium hard; 68–75°F (20–24°C).
Set-up: Vigorous circulation; floating plants. Frequent
water changes important. Keep one male with several
females because males fight among each other. *Food*:
Nutritious live food, fry, insects, dry food. *Sexual differences*: Males much smaller, more colorful, with a protruding, red lower jaw; andropodium. *Breeding*: Raise fry (¾
inch or 2 cm) in a rearing tank on small live food. *Biotope*:
Fast-moving mountain streams on Celebes (Indonesia) up
to and above 3,000 feet (1,000 m) above sea level.

Tips on Care of Other Species

Characodon lateralis
2½ inches (6.5 cm). Tank: 24 inches (60 cm). Strata:
Bottom, middle. Water: pH 6.5–7.5; medium hard to
hard; 64–75°F (18–24°C). Somewhat sensitive.

Ilyodon furcidens
4¾ inches (12 cm). Tank: 40 inches (100 cm). Strata:
Bottom, middle. Water: pH 6–8; medium hard to hard;
75–81°F (24–27°C). Rocks and circulation; vegetarian food important. Eats young, sometimes bites.

Mosquito Fish (*Gambusia affinis*)
2½ inches (6.5 cm). Tank: 24 inches (60 cm). Strata:
middle, top. Water: pH 6–8.5; soft to hard; 64–86°F
(18–30°C). Undemanding; distributed worldwide.

Phalloceros caudimaculatus
2¾ inches (7 cm). Tank: 24 inches (60 cm). Strata:
middle, top. Water: pH 7–8; medium hard to hard;
64–72°F (18–22°C). Well-planted tank.

Humpbacked Limia (*Limia nigrofasciata*)
2½ inches (7 cm). Tank: 24 inches (60 cm). Stratum:
Middle. Water: pH 7–8.5; medium hard to hard;
77–82°F (25–28°C). Vegetarian food important.

Phallichthys amates
2⅜ inches (6 cm). Tank: 24 inches (60 cm). Stratum:
Middle. Water: pH 6.5–7.5; medium hard to hard;
75–81°F (24–27°C). Densely planted tank. Do not
combine with robust species.

Pike Livebearer or Pike-top Minnow
(*Belonesox belizanus*)
8½ inches (22 cm). Tank: 48 inches (120 cm).
Stratum: Top. Water: pH 6–8; medium hard to hard;
72–79°F (22–26°C). Predatory species! Generally
can be fed only with small to medium-sized fish.

Hemirhamphodon pogonognathus
3½ inches (9 cm). Tank: 40 inches (100 cm). Stratum: Top. Water: pH 6–7.5; soft to medium hard;
75–82°F (24–28°C). Slight circulation. Feed with
Drosophila and other small insects.

Killifishes (Killies) are considered the survival artists among fish because some species manage to live in bodies of water that dry up for considerable periods of the year. These are called seasonal or annual fish. Buried in the mud, only the eggs stay alive through the dry periods, while the parent fish die. When water returns with the rain, the young hatch.

What You Should Know about Killifishes

These fish are part of the order Cyprinodontiformes and, except for Australia and the Arctic, they are found world-wide.

Distinguishing traits: Most killies have more or less elongated bodies that are round in cross-section. Species living close to the surface have a pronouncedly undershot mouth. Species living in the middle and bottom strata are generally more high-backed and have an only slightly undershot mouth.

Care: Coming from areas with shallow standing or slow-moving water, most killies need a densely planted tank without circulation and with a dark bottom and shaded water. The lamp-eyes are an exception; they need slightly circulating water and open water for swimming. A tightly fitting cover is essential because killies are good jumpers.

Water: Most killies prefer soft, slightly acid (pH 6–7) water. The exceptions here are the lamp-eyes from Lake Tanganyika and desert fishes, which need hard, alkaline (pH 7.5–8.5) water.

Communities: Many killies can be combined safely with catfishes, small shoaling fishes, and other nonaggressive, nonterritorial species. Robust species that grow larger or live close to the surface are also compatible with dwarf cichlids. Small, delicate species are better kept in separate, small tanks.

Behavior: Most killies are not lively swimmers. Males are very aggressive among themselves and can fight to the death in tanks that are too confining. In a larger tank one can observe the constant efforts of the males to intimidate each other. Such a tank has to be set up to include hiding places into which individual fish can retreat when needed.

Hints on breeding: There are bottom spawners as well as substrate spawners among the killifishes.

Bottom spawners deposit their eggs in soft bottom material, both parents sometimes diving into it so that the female can deposit or hurl most of her eggs into it. They do not engage in parental care. Anyone wanting to raise bottom spawners should consult specialized literature on the subject (see Books, page 158).

Substrate spawners deposit their sticky eggs on plants or in cracks in wood or rocks; they do not engage in parental care either. Usually aquarists set up a mop or pumice stones with small grooves scratched in them right in the maintenance tank and then remove them to a small rearing tank after a few days. There the hatched fry are usually fed first with *Artemia*. Later they are given *Artemia* and other small live food (*Cyclops*, *Daphnia*). Some substrate spawners are best bred by following the long-term method (see page 53).

Steel-blue Aphyosemion (*Aphyosemion gardneri*)
2⅜–3 inches (6–8 cm). *Tank*: 20 inches (50 cm). *Stratum*: Bottom. *Water*: pH 6–7.5; soft to medium hard; 73–81°F (23–27°C). *Set-up*: Tank arranged in dark colors, densely planted; floating plants; small hiding places. Keep one male with several females. Males are very aggressive toward each other. Tip on communities: No very delicate species. *Food*: Live and dry food. *Sexual differences*: Males more colorful. *Breeding*: Both substrate and bottom spawner. Store eggs in peat, add water after about four weeks. Feed first with *Artemia*. *Special remarks*: Ideal killifish for beginners. *Biotope*: Primarily small bodies of water in the savanna regions of Nigeria.

Aphyosemion striatum
2 inches (5 cm). *Tank*: 12 inches (30 cm). *Strata*: all. *Water*: pH 6–7; soft to medium hard; 70–73°F (21–23°C). *Set-up*: Tank arranged in dark colors, densely planted; floating plants. Tip on communities: In larger tanks (24 inches or 60 cm) this species can be kept with other substrate-spawning *Aphyosemion* species, lamp-eyes, and dwarf barbs. *Food*: Small live food, including *Drosophila*. *Sexual differences*: Males more beautiful. *Breeding*: As for *A. australe*. *Special remarks*: A good species for beginners. *Biotope*: Shallow shore areas of small rivers in northern Gabon.

The male of the golden pheasant gularis is often aggressive toward the female. That is why the tank has to contain plenty of hiding places among plants.

Golden Pheasant Gularis *(Aphyosemion sjoestedti)*
inches (8 cm). *Tank*: 32 inches (80 cm). *Stratum*: Bottom. *Water*: pH 6–7.5; soft to hard; 75–79°F (24–26°C). *Set-up*: Planted tank with hiding places; bottom partially covered with a thin layer of peat. Keep one male with two females. Tip on communities: Can include larger fishes. *Food*: Nutritious live food. No *Tubifex* for adult fish. Feed sparingly. *Sexual differences*: Males larger, with more spectacular colors. *Breeding*: Bottom spawner. Store eggs in peat and add water after one or two months. Start feeding with *Artemia*. *Biotope*: Marshy waters in the coastal rainforest from Nigeria to Cameroon. *Similar species*: A. fallax, 3½ inches (9 cm).

Note: This species, as well as many other bottom spawners, can be bred in a maintenance tank if spawning vessels are supplied, such as freezer containers about 4 inches (10 cm) deep, with covers. Cut a hole below the cover for the fish to enter. Place about ¾ inch (2 cm) of peat in the container and close it. After two weeks, take the container out of the tank, place peat in a net, drain, and squeeze until no more water emerges. Look to see if there are any eggs. If so, let peat dry on three layers of newspaper for about one day, then store in a plastic bag for six to eight weeks, airing it frequently. Then put into a small tank with water and start feeding immediately with *Artemia* nauplii several times a day.

Cape Lopez Lyretail or Lyre-tailed Panchax
(Aphyosemion australe)
2⅜ inches (6 cm). *Tank*: 12 inches (30 cm). *Strata*: All. *Water*: pH 6–7; soft to medium hard; 70–73°F (21–23°C). *Set-up*: Tank arranged in dark colors, with plant thickets. Keep one male and two females in a 12-inch (30 cm) tank. Tip on communities: Dwarf barbs, lamp-eyes, small *Aphyosemion* species. *Food*: Small live food. *Sexual differences*: Males more attractive. *Breeding*: Substrate spawner. Store eggs in a tiny tank or in peat; add water after two or three weeks. Start feeding with *Artemia*. *Biotope*: Shallow, leaf-covered shore areas in Gabon rainforest.

Epiplatys dageti monroviae
2⅜ inches (6 cm). *Tank*: 24 inches (60 cm). *Stratum*: Top. *Water*: pH 6–7; soft to medium hard; 72–79°F (22–26°C). *Set-up*: Tank arranged in dark colors, loosely planted; floating plants; plenty of open water for swimming. Tip on communities: Shoaling fishes of the middle stratum, dwarf cichlids, small catfishes. *Food*: Live food, especially *Drosophila*; also dry food. *Sexual differences*: Males have larger fins. *Breeding*: Substrate spawner. In a maintenance tank with a cover of floating plants, some young survive to adulthood. Start feeding with dry food and paramecia. *Biotope*: Small streams in Liberia.

Yellow Lamp-eye (*Procatopus similis*)
2⅜ inches (6 cm). *Tank*: 24 inches (60 cm). *Strata*: Middle, top. *Water*: pH 6.5–7.5; soft to medium hard; 73–77°F (23–25°C). *Set-up*: Tank arranged in dark colors, loosely planted, with slight circulation. Shoaling fish. *Food*: Small live and fine-grade dry food, *Drosophila*. *Sexual differences*: Males bigger, more colorful. *Breeding*: These fish spawn in cracks. Place pieces of natural cork on the surface, and the fish will deposit eggs in the cracks. Transfer cork into rearing containers. Young hatch after about two weeks. Feed initially with paramecia and crushed dry food and soon after with *Artemia*. *Biotope*: Streams near the coast in western Cameroon.

Red Lamp-eye (*Aplocheilichthys macrophthalmus*)
1⅜ inches (3.5 cm). *Tank*: 12 inches (30 cm). *Strata*: Middle, top. *Water*: pH 6.5–7.5; soft to medium hard; 77–81°F (25–27°C). *Set-up*: Tank arranged in dark colors, densely planted, slight circulation. Good water maintenance important. Keep at least six to eight specimens. Tip on communities: Bottom-dwelling, small rainforest fishes, such as dwarf barbs, small *Aphyosemion* species, and small armored catfishes. *Food*: Small live food, especially *Drosophila*. *Sexual differences*: Males have larger fins. *Breeding*: Substrate spawner; also, like the yellow lamp-eye, spawns in cracks. Start feeding with paramecia. *Biotope*: Small rainforest streams in southern Nigeria.

A pair of Rachow's nothobranch in the process of spawning. The male "embraces" the female with his dorsal fin. Shortly after, the eggs are hurled into the bottom material

Rachow's Nothobranch (*Nothobranchius rachovii*)
2⅜ inches (6 cm). *Tank*: 16 inches (40 cm). *Strata*: Bottom, middle. *Water*: pH 6–7.5; soft to hard; 79°F (26°C). *Set-up*: Tank arranged in dark colors, planted. Keep several pairs. Tip on communities: Small shoaling fishes, catfishes. *Food*: Small live and fine-grade dry food; these fish also like *Tubifex*. *Sexual differences*: Males more colorful. *Breeding*: Bottom spawner. Store eggs in peat. Add water after four to six months. Start feeding with *Artemia* and dry food. *Biotope*: Seasonal fish in waters of the floodplains of the Zambezi and other rivers in Mozambique. *Similar species*: Other *Nothobranchius*

species, such as Guenther's nothobranch (*N. guentheri*), 1¾ inches (4.5 cm).
Note: There can be violent fighting among the spectacularly colored males of the genus *Nothobranchius*. Two males swim toward each other with widely fanned fins and extended gill covers. This intimidation behavior usually suffices to drive the opponent to flight, but in tanks that are too small, the weaker fish may be killed.

Tanganyika Lamp-eye (*Lamprichthys tanganicanus*)
inches (15 cm). *Tank*: 48 inches (120 cm). *Strata*:
Middle, top. *Water*: pH 7.5–8.5; medium hard to hard;
9–81°F (26–27°C). *Set-up*: Loosely planted tank with
open water. Shoaling fish. Tip on communities: Good for a
Tanganyika Lake aquarium; do not combine with *Cyprichromis* species. *Food*: Small crustaceans, mosquito
larvae, insects; several times a day! *Sexual differences*:
Males bigger. *Breeding*: As for yellow lamp-eye. Raise
young on *Artemia* in a large rearing tank. *Special remarks*:
Transport fish singly. Never catch them in a net. Their
dorsal fin can inflict a painful wound. Instead drive them
into a 2-quart jar. *Biotope*: Shore areas of Lake Tanganyika.

Blue Panchax (*Aplocheilus panchax*)
2¾ inches (7 cm). *Tank*: 24 inches (60 cm). *Stratum*: Top.
Water: pH 6–7.5; soft to medium hard; 75–84°F (24–29°C).
Set-up: Densely planted tank with floating plants that
serve as cover for the males, which are somewhat ag-
gressive among themselves. Undemanding species.
Food: Live and dry food; especially fond of insects. *Sexual
differences*: Hard to tell. Females plumper. *Breeding*:
Substrate spawner that deposits eggs on surface plants.
Transfer eggs or fry to rearing tank. Start feeding with
Artemia. *Biotope*: Surface of vegetation-choked marshes
and of rice fields in Southeast Asia.

Rivulus agilae
inches (5 cm). *Tank*: 12 inches (30 cm). *Strata*: All. *Water*:
pH 6–7; soft to medium hard; 72–77°F (22–25°C). *Set-up*:
Tank arranged in dark colors, densely planted, with soft
bottom material in some areas and with slight circulation.
Keep one male with several females. Tip on communities:
Small characins, catfishes. *Food*: Mosquito larvae, *Drosophila, Daphnia, Artemia*. *Sexual differences*: Males more
colorful. *Breeding*: Substrate spawner. Store eggs in
slightly damp peat. Add water after three weeks. Start
feeding with *Artemia*. *Biotope*: Small, shady rivers in the
coastal plain of Guiana; also near the surface of still water.

Rivulus xiphidius
1⅜ inches (3.5 cm). *Tank*: 12 inches (30 cm). *Strata*:
Middle, top. *Water*: pH 6–7; soft; 73–77°F (23–25°C). *Set-
up*: Tank arranged in dark colors with a cover of floating
plants. Sensitive species that is better not combined with
others. *Food*: Live food, specially *Drosophila, Artemia*,
and *Cyclops*. *Sexual differences*: Males more colorful
once they grow beyond 1⅛ inches (3 cm). *Breeding*: As
for *R. agilae*. Substrate spawner. *Biotope*: Small, shady
rivers in the coastal plains of Guiana; also near surface of
still water.

Desert Pupfish
(*Cyprinodon macularius*)
2⅜ inches (6 cm). *Tank*: 20 inches
(50 cm). *Strata*: Bottom, middle.
Water: pH 7.5–8.5; hard; 79–91°F
(26–33°C). *Set-up*: Tank with bright
lighting; with hornwort (*Ceratophyllu*
demersum); addition of sea salt (3
teaspoons per 10 quarts) necessary.
Males establish territories. Keep one
male with several females. *Food*:
Vegetarian as well as live and dry
food; fish have to be fed several time
a day! *Sexual differences*: Females
paler and plumper. *Breeding*: Let fish
spawn on fine nylon fibers and transfer eggs into a tiny tank. Start feeding
with *Artemia*. Biotope: Sandy areas i
water with extreme temperatures an
salt concentrations in the deserts of
North America. Almost extinct in the
wild.

Peruvian Longfin (*Pterolebias peruensis*)
4¾ inches (12 cm). *Tank*: 20 inches (50 cm). *Strata*: Bottom,
middle. *Water*: pH 6–7.5; soft to medium hard; 81–86°F
(27–30°C). *Set-up*: Tank arranged in dark colors, with
dense planting to provide refuges. Keep one male with
several females. Tip on communities: Smaller characins,
catfishes. *Food*: Mosquito larvae, adult *Artemia*, small
amounts of dry food, *Tubifex*. *Sexual differences*: Males
have larger fins. *Breeding*: Bottom spawner. Store eggs in
peat. Add water after five or six months. Start feeding with
Artemia. *Biotope*: Marshy areas that may sometimes dry
up in the floodplain of the Amazon River in Peru.

Tips on Care of Other Species

Aphyosemion bualuanum kekemense
2 inches (5 cm). Tank: 12 inches (30 cm). Strata:
Middle, top. Water: pH 6–6.5; soft; 68–73°F
(20–23°C). Substrate spawner.
Pseudepiplatys annulatus
1½ inches (4 cm). Tank: 12 inches (30 cm). Stratum:
Top. Water: pH 6–6.5; soft; 73–81°F (23–27°C).
Parts of tank densely planted. Substrate spawner.
Can be raised in maintenance tank. Feed with
Artemia, Drosophila.
Playfair's Panchax (*Pachypanchax playfairii*)
3 inches (8 cm). Tank: 32 inches (80 cm). Strata:
Middle, top. Water: pH 6.5–7.5; soft to hard; 72–
79°F (22–26°C). Aggressive toward own and other
species. Combine only with robust species. Substrate spawner.
Black-finned Pearl Fish (*Cynolebias nigripinnis*)
2⅜ inches (6 cm). Tank: 12 inches (30 cm). Strata:
Bottom, middle. Water: pH 6–7; soft to medium
hard; 64–72°F (18–22°C). Bottom spawner. Does
not do well in very high temperatures. Males very
aggressive among each other.

abyrinth fishes are very popular with aquarists because their gorgeous colors and fascinating behavior. With any species, courtship, nest building, and parental care n be observed even in a community aquarium, as long there are not too many fish in it.

hat You Should Know about Labyrinth Fishes

hey belong to the suborder Anabantoidea. Asia is their ain area of distribution, though some species occur in rica. In nature many species live in still or slowly moving ater that is often muddy and low in oxygen.

istinguishing traits: The organ for which this group of hes is named, the labyrinth, is located above the gills d consists of skin folds, or lamelli, filled with blood essels through which oxygen can be absorbed from the r. This anatomical feature enables labyrinth fishes to urvive even in water with extremely low oxygen levels. ne body shape of labyrinth fishes varies from elongated ith only slight lateral compression (*Betta* genus) to leaf-aped (*Belontia* genus).

are: Dark tanks with dense planting, including floating ants, are essential for success with most species. Some enera also like the additional protection of small caves. A w species accept only live food. For species that build ubble nests there should be no circulation.

ater: Almost all species thrive and also reproduce in ghtly acid (pH about 6.5) and soft to medium hard ater. Exceptions are fishes from black water, such as e chocolate gourami and members of the *Parosphro-enus* genus, which require very acid, extremely soft ater for general care and for reproduction. Depending n the species, labyrinth fishes are kept in pairs or small roups.

ommunities: Most labyrinth fishes are calm and should e combined only with bottom-dwelling species or shoal-g fishes of similar temperament. It is better not to com-ne them with cichlids because the latter are territorial, as re labyrinth fishes. Smaller labyrinth fishes quickly suc-umb to larger species in a conflict.

ehavior: Especially during the reproductive period, most ales establish territories, which they defend against thers of their species as well as, usually, against other nds. Brooding behavior varies with the species:

The males of many species build bubble nests within eir territory on the water surface or against the ceiling of aves. The fish then spawn below the nest. Usually the male arries the eggs to the nest in his mouth. The brood care, o, is usually performed by the male.

Many labyrinth fishes, especially those living in moving ater where a bubble nest would not be sturdy enough, enerally protect the young in their mouths. In many of ese mouthbrooding species, the father takes sole re-ponsibility for the eggs and larvae; in others the female oks after the brood by herself.

Some labyrinth fishes are open-water spawners and do t engage in brood care.

Hints on breeding: If labyrinth fishes are provided with appropriate environmental conditions in a thinly populated community tank, the young can be left there until they start swimming free. Then you should proceed as follows:
Bubble nest builders: Transfer larvae to a rearing tank and start feeding them (for first foods, look under individual species). Later, *Artemia* and other fine-grade foods can be given.
Mouthbrooders: Move the mouthbrooding fish very gently to a small tank. After the brood is no longer kept in the mouth, remove the parent fish and raise the young as described under bubble nest builders.
Open-water spawners: Transfer eggs to a rearing tank and feed larvae once they start swimming.
Rearing tank for labyrinth fishes: Water properties the same as in the maintenance tank (where this is not the case it is noted under the individual species). Supply some leafy plants as well as floating plants. It is best to install an interior filter with foam; no bottom material (easier to keep tank clean).

Blue Gourami (*Trichogaster trichopterus*)
4¾ inches (12 cm). *Tank*: 40 inches (100 cm). *Strata*: Middle, top. *Water*: pH 6–7.5; soft to hard; 72–81°F (22–27°C). *Set-up*: Densely planted tank, floating plants. Undemanding species. Males protecting brood can be aggressive in a community tank. Tip on communities: No barbs that pull on fins. *Food*: Dry and live food. *Sexual differences*: Females smaller, with short, rounded dorsal fin. *Breeding*: Same water as in maintenance tank; other-wise as for *T. leeri*. Bubble nest builder. *Special remarks*: Different cultivated varieties exist. *Biotope*: Standing and moving water, even muddy, in Indonesia and Malaysia.

Pearl Gourami (*Trichogaster leeri*) 4¾ inches (12 cm). *Tank*: 40 inches (100 cm). *Strata*: Middle, top. *Water*: pH 5.5–7.5; soft to hard; 73–81°F (23–27°C). *Set-up*: Dark tank, cover of floating plants. Keep in pairs in small tanks. Supply retreats for the female! Tip on communities: Only calm bottom dwellers. *Food*: Live and dry food. *Sexual differences*: Adult males have longer dorsal and anal fin rays and orange to red breast. *Breeding*: Soft to medium hard water. Bubble nest builder. Transfer young to a rearing tank. Start feeding with paramecia. *Biotope*: Shore areas with vegetation or underneath floating plants in standing or slow-moving water in Southeast Asia. Often in shallow areas with leaf-strewn bottom.

Honey Gourami (*Colisa chuna*) 1¾ inches (4.5 cm). *Tank*: 20 inches (50 cm). *Strata*: Middle, top. *Water*: pH 6–7.5; soft to hard; 72–82°F (22–28°C). *Set-up*: Densely planted tank, floating plants. Tip on communities: Only small, delicate fishes of the bottom stratum. *Food*: Fine-grade dry and small live food. *Sexual differences*: Females colorless even when getting ready to spawn. *Breeding*: As for *Trichogaster leeri*. Bubble nest builder. *Biotope*: Close to shore or in slowly moving or standing water in floodplains in northeastern India. *Note*: Usually colorless in dealers' tanks.

Dwarf Gourami (*Colisa lalia*) 2⅜ inches (6 cm). *Tank*: 24 inches (60 cm). *Strata*: Middle, top. *Water*: pH 6–7.5; soft to hard; 75–82°F (24–28°C). *Set-up*: Densely planted tank with cover of floating plants. Keep in pairs or, in tanks larger than 32 inches (80 cm), in small groups. Tip on communities: In small tanks only bottom-dwelling fishes; in larger tanks also peaceful shoaling fishes. *Food*: All types of fine-grade foods. *Sexual differences*: Males are many-colored, females, silvery. *Breeding*: As for *Trichogaster leeri*. Bubble nest builder. *Biotope*: Floodplains of large rivers, canals with dense vegetation, India. *Similar species*: Giant gourami.

etta spec. aff. pugnax

inches (10 cm). *Tank*: 32 inches (80 cm). *Strata*: Bottom, iddle. *Water*: pH 5–6.5; soft to medium hard; 73–81°F 3–27°C). *Set-up*: Tank with circulation, dense planting, ots. Good filtration! Tip on communities: Medium-sized hes of the upper strata; also small catfishes. *Food*: mall, nutritious live food. *Sexual differences*: Males have omewhat more brilliant colors. *Breeding*: Mouthbrooder ale). Transfer male gently into a rearing tank. Start eding young with *Artemia*. *Biotope*: Shore region, with egetation, of clear rivers in Borneo. *Similar species*: outhbrooding fighting fish and Java fighting fish for tanks at least 24 inches (60 cm); 73–77°F (23–25°C).

Siamese Fighting Fish (*Betta splendens*)

2⅜ inches (6 cm); those with veil fins somewhat larger. *Tank*: 20 inches (50 cm). *Strata*: Middle, top. *Water*: pH 6–7.5; soft to hard; 73–81°F (23–27°C). *Set-up*: Densely planted tank, with cover of floating plants. One male can be kept with several females. Never more than one male per tank, otherwise, rivals fight to the death. Good community fish. *Food*: Fine-grade dry and small live food. *Sexual differences*: Females brown, with shorter fins. *Breeding*: Bubble nest builder. Transfer young to a rearing tank; crushed dry food and *Artemia* are possible first foods. *Biotope*: Marshy areas (including rice fields), canals in Thailand.

etta imbellis

inches (5 cm). *Tank*: 16 inches (40 cm). *Strata*: Middle, p. *Water*: pH 6–7; soft to hard; 79–82°F (26–28°C). et-up: Densely planted tank, with cover of floating plants. eep one pair in a 16-inch (40 cm) tank. In a 24-inch 0 cm) tank, two males with several females can be kept. ip on communities: Small fishes of the bottom stratum. ood: Small live and fine-grade dry food. *Sexual differ-* nces: Females inconspicuous. *Breeding*: As for *B.* lendens, but start feeding with paramecia. *Biotope*: arshy areas, canals, floodplains in eastern Thailand nd western Malaysia.

Pygmy Purring Gourami or Green Croaking Gourami (*Trichopsis pumila*)

1½ inches (4 cm). *Tank*: 16 inches (40 cm). *Stratum*: Middle. *Water*: pH 6–7; soft to hard; 73–81°F (23–27°C). *Set-up*: Dense planting. Tip on communities: Catfishes, shoaling fishes of similar size. *Food*: Small live and fine-grade dry food. *Sexual differences*: Males with elongated, pointed dorsal fin. *Breeding*: Bubble nest builder. Transfer young into rearing tank, start feeding with paramecia. *Biotope*: Puddles and canals crowded with underwater and floating plants on the Southeast Asian mainland. *Similar species*: Croaking gourami (*T. schalleri*).

107

Parosphromenus deissneri

1½ inches (4 cm). *Tank*: 12 inches (30 cm). *Strata*: bottom, middle. *Water*: pH 4–5; very soft. 72–77°F (22–25°C). *Set-up*: Tank arranged in dark colors, weak circulation through an air-driven (peat) filter; thin layer of sand; small caves; floating plants only. Keep in pairs. No other fish! *Food*: Smallest live food. *Sexual differences*: Females show hardly any color. *Breeding*: Bubble nest builder (in cavities). Transfer young to a rearing tank. Start feeding with freshly hatched (!) *Artemia* nauplii. *Biotope*: Slow-moving, clear black water in marshy regions of southern Malaysia. *Similar species*: *P. filamentosus*, 1½ inches (4 cm); more robust.

Kissing Gourami (*Helostoma temminckii*)

8–12 inches (20–30 cm). *Tank*: 60 inches (150 cm). *Strata*: Middle, top. *Water*: pH 6–7.5; soft to hard; 73–81° (23–27°C). *Set-up*: Tank with large-leaved plants, floating plants. Tip on communities: Other large labyrinth fishes. *Food*: Various fine-grade dry foods (including vegetarian usually taken from the surface. *Sexual differences*: Female may be plumper. *Breeding*: Open-water spawner. Transfer eggs to a rearing tank. Start feeding young with paramecia once they swim; finest-grade dry food is also possible. *Special remarks*: There is a cultivated pink variety. The "kissing" for which this fish is famous, can be observed only rarely in an aquarium. Probably it is a form of ritual fighting, but there is no doubt that it is also part of courtship behavior. *Biotope*: Primarily still, often muddy, vegetation-choked water in Southeast Asia.
Note: The kissing gourami is an important food fish in its native areas and throughout much of the rest of Southeast Asia. It is raised in large fish ponds. In Borneo, for instance, one can buy it at any market.

Paradise Fish (*Macropodus opercularis*)

4 inches (10 cm). *Tank*: 32 inches (80 cm). *Stratum*: Middle. *Water*: pH 6–8; soft to hard; 68–79°F (20–26°C). *Set-up*: Densely planted tank, floating plants. Undemanding species. Sometimes aggressive toward others of its kind and, more rarely, toward other species. Tip on communities: Only robust fishes. *Food*: Dry and live food. *Sexual differences*: Males more colorful, with longer fins. *Breeding*: Bubble nest builder. Transfer young to a rearing tank. Start feeding with fine-grade dry food. *Biotope*: Marshy areas and canals in Vietnam and into southern China. *Similar species*: Black paradise fish (*M. concolor*).

Chocolate Gourami (*Sphaerichthys osphromenoides*)
inches (5 cm). *Tank*: 24 inches (60 cm). *Strata*: All.
Water: pH 4.5–6; very soft; 75–81°F (24–27°C). *Set-up*:
tank subdivided with roots and plants; bottom material of
boiled, flaked peat; light circulation through a peat filter.
Demanding species. Keep in small groups. Do not combine with other fishes! *Food*: Small live food, including
Drosophila. *Sexual differences*: Males have a light rim on
the anal fin. *Breeding*: Mouth brooding performed by the
female (for about 19 days). Transfer fry to a rearing tank.
Start feeding with *Artemia*. *Biotope*: Shore area of slowly
moving rivers carrying clear black water in Malaysia,
Sumatra, and western Borneo.

Orange Ctenopoma (*Ctenopoma ansorgii*)
¾ inches (7 cm). *Tank*: 24 inches (60 cm). *Strata*: All.
Water: pH 6–7.5; soft to hard; 73–81°F (23–27°C). *Set-
up*: Densely planted tank, floating plants, small roots. Tip
on communities: Only calm, small species. *Food*: Small
live food. *Sexual differences*: Males have white rim on
fins. *Breeding*: Bubble nest builder. Transfer fry to a
rearing tank. Start feeding with fine-grade dry food.
Biotope: Shore areas, with dense vegetation, of small
rivers in western Central Africa. *Similar species*: C.
fasciolatum, 3 inches (8 cm).

Tips on Care of Other Species

Betta coccina
2⅜ inches (6 cm). Tank: 16 inches (40 cm). Strata:
All. Water: pH 4.5–6; very soft; 73–79°F (23–26°C).
Dark, densely planted tank. Bubble nest builder.

Betta foerschi
2½ inches (6.5 cm). Tank: 24 inches (60 cm). Strata:
Middle, top. Water: pH 4.5–6; very soft, 72–77°F
(22–25°C). Dense planting, peat filtering, tank
arranged in dark colors. Mouthbrooder.

Betta smaragdina
2⅜ inches (6 cm). Tank: 24 inches (60 cm). Strata:
Middle, top. Water: pH 6–7.5; soft to hard; 73–81°F
(23–27°C). Tank arranged in dark colors, with small
caves, where the fish spawn. Not as aggressive as
B. splendens. Bubble nest builder.

Parosphromenus nagyi
1½ inches (4 cm). Tank: 12 inches (30 cm). Strata:
Bottom, middle. Water: pH 4.5–6; very soft; 70–75°F
(21–24°C). Peat filtering, small caves; good water
quality important (see P. deissneri). Builds bubble
nests in caves.

Pseudosphromenus cupanus
2⅜ inches (6 cm). Tank: 20 inches (50 cm). Strata:
All. Water: pH 6.5–7.5; soft to hard; 73–81°F
(23–27°C). Dense planting, caves. Undemanding
species. Builds bubble nests in caves.

Macropodus ocellatus
3 inches (8 cm). Tank: 24 inches (60 cm). Strata:
Middle, top. Water: pH 6–7.5; soft to hard; 59–68°F
(15–20°C). Undemanding species for an unheated
aquarium. Fish are wintered over at about 45°F
(8°C). Bubble nest builder.

Belontia hasselti
About 8 inches (20 cm). Tank: 48 inches (120 cm).
Strata: All. Water: pH 6–7.5; soft to hard; 73–81°F
(23–27°C). Dark hiding places; nutritious live food.
Bubble nest builder; both sexes share the brood care.

Croaking Gourami (Trichopsis vittata)
2¾ inches (7 cm). Tank: 24 inches (60 cm). Strata:
Middle, top. Water: pH 6.5–7.5; soft to hard; 73–81°F
(23–27°C). Parts of tank densely planted. Undemanding species. Bubble nest builder.

Kingsley's Ctenopoma (Ctenopoma kingsleyae)
6 inches (15 cm). Tank: 48 inches (120 cm). Stratum: Middle. Water: pH 6–7.5; soft to hard; 73–81°F
(23–27°C). Hiding places among roots; nutritious
live food. Combine only with robust fishes of similar
size. Open-water spawner.

Spotted Climbing Perch (Ctenopoma acutirostre)
6 inches (15 cm). Tank: 48 inches (120 cm). Strata:
Bottom, middle. Water: pH 6–7.5; soft to medium
hard; 73–81°F (23–27°C). Tank with hiding places
(roots); nutritious live food. Combine only with calm
fishes of similar size. Open-water spawner.

Cichlid Family

Aquarists who keep cichlids have a hard time saying what it is that fascinates them most about these fishes: their colorful appearance, the variety of species suitable for aquariums, or their behavior—especially the different kinds of brood care one can watch them perform in an aquarium. Surely all these factors contribute to making the members of this family some of the most popular aquarium fishes.

What You Should Know about the Cichlid Family

Most cichlids come from Africa and South and Central America, with a few species being found in Asia (India, Sri Lanka, Israel, and Iran). Cichlids occupy the most varied habitats, ranging from small lakes to rushing rivers. In the following pages selected species from the different areas of distribution are presented, namely:
- Lake Tanganyika cichlids, pages 112–115
- Lake Malawi cichlids, pages 116–119
- African cichlids that do not come from the "great lakes," pages 120–124
- Central American cichlids, pages 125–128
- South American cichlids, pages 129–134.

Distinguishing traits: One sign that cichlids are part of the order of Perciformes is their dorsal fin. It is made up of two parts, one with hard, spiny rays, the other with soft rays. The various species differ from each other primarily in the shape of the mouth and teeth. There are cichlids with undershot and with overshot jaws, as well as end-positioned mouths. Body shape also varies widely: It ranges from pencil-shaped to leaf-shaped. The most common shape found in cichlids is a fairly arched back, flattened sides, and end-positioned mouth.

Care: The appropriate tank arrangement is described at the beginning of each section of the different cichlid groups.

Communities: If the coinhabitants are selected with an eye to the "character traits" of the cichlids, these fish can easily be kept in a community tank. Cichlids establish territories, which they may defend very vehemently; this defense is intensified during brood care.

Dwarf cichlids generally get along fine with characins and other shoaling fishes of the upper stratum. Pairs of different dwarf cichlid species can be combined in larger tanks if they practice different methods of brood care. If that is the case, they occupy different niches in the aquarium and thus there is less competition than between two species with similar territorial and parental care behavior.

Large cichlids get along well with large Loricariidae catfishes in tanks that offer plenty of refuges. Calm species that are not very aggressive are also compatible with large shoaling fishes that do not form territories. Of course, there has to be sufficient room in the tank for the coinhabitants. Thus, the area reserved for brood care cannot take up the whole aquarium.

Water: Please consult the information given for the individual cichlid groups. Cichlids have very diverse requirements depending on their area of origin.

Aggressive behavior: Because cichlids have highly developed brood care patterns and are consequently highly territorial, aggressive behavior plays an important role in their lives. This is something the aquarist has to be prepared for: Often a pair will break up after mating, and the female, who is usually smaller, will be aggressively driven away by the male. If the tank was adequate for housing the pair beforehand, it may now be too small. In such a case, there are two options: The female can be removed, or the two partners can be separated by a pane of clear plexiglass. Small holes drilled into the glass allow the water to move back and forth between the two halves of the tank. The pair can see but not hurt each other, and often they will get used to each other again (or for the first time). If aggressive behavior (threat behavior) disappears the glass can be removed experimentally. If the pair still do not get along, they have to be separated again. For many slender species, clay or plastic tubes hung just below the water surface are a useful device. They should be slightly larger in inside diameter than the fish and a little longer. Subordinate fish can find shelter in the tubes and are not easily found by their pursuers.

Reproductive behavior: Cichlids are divided into substrate brooders and mouthbrooders.

Substrate brooders lay their eggs either openly on a surface (open-water brooders) or hidden in cavities (cavity brooders). Both these groups engage in brood care. The eggs are, for example, fanned to increase the oxygen supply. Then the hatched larvae are looked after until the contents of the yolk sac are used up and the fry swim free and eat food they find in the water. Parental care continues even beyond this point, primarily in the form of protection against predators. This is the phase that can become dangerous for other fishes in the aquarium, because the parents extend their brooding territory and can become increasingly aggressive.

Mouthbrooders pick up their eggs (either right after or even during spawning) and their larvae in their mouths. This group is called ovophile ("egg-loving") mouthbrooders. Other mouthbrooders deposit their eggs on a substrate, where they look after them until the larvae hatch. Then they pick the larvae up and keep them in the mouth until they are able to swim free. This group is called larvophile ("larva-loving") mouthbrooders. In many species parental care stops when the young are first released from the mouth, but in some cases it continues, with the young being able to swim back into the protective parental mouth when danger lurks.

Pairing of parents: There are several different bonds that can be formed:
- Monogamy: A male and a female stay together.
- Polygyny: A male stays together with a number of females.
- Polyandry (rare): A female stays together with several males.
- Agamy: The partners do not enter any lasting bond but separate again immediately after spawning.

ote: As a rule it is best to start with a small group of six
eight fish, from which—depending on the family form—
airs or harems can form.

amily forms: Here one distinguishes among:
  Parental family: Both parents share all the tasks of
 ood care; that is, they take turns doing them. Usually
 naracteristic of monogamy in open-water brooders.
  Father/mother family: The female assumes responsibil-
 ✓ for the care of the eggs and larvae, while the male
 efends the territory. Usually combined with monogamy in
 avity brooders.
  Male-with-harem family: Several females assume
 sponsibility for the eggs and larvae within the extended
 rritory of one male. The male defends the territory.
 sually combined with polygyny in cavity brooders.
  Mother or father family: Only one sex looks after the
 ood. Usually combined with agamy in ovophile
 outhbrooders.
  Extended family: The parents as well as the offspring
 om earlier spawnings perform the brood care together.
ints on breeding: Cichlids are bred in the maintenance
 nk. Artemia, dry food, and other fine-grade foods are
 upplied in addition to regular fish food. The fry are re-
 oved from the tank at the latest when the parents start
 sing interest in them and they are ⅜ to ¾ inches (1–2 cm)
 ng. They are then raised to maturity in rearing tanks.

In the photo: In cichlids, unusual
patterns of behavior are found not
only in their methods of reproduction (see text on left) but also in
their ways of procuring food.
Especially fascinating behavior
is displayed by the "sleepers" of
Lake Malawi. During the day these
brown-and-white mottled fish
lie on the bottom, apparently life-
less, often on their sides, their
coloration making them look like
decaying fish—an unusual kind
of camouflage. Other fish swim
around such a fish, suspecting
nothing, mistaking it for dead. The
predatory "sleeper" takes advantage of this lack of suspicion and
pounces on its prey.

All family forms except the pure father family occur among cichlids from Lake Tanganyika. Among these fish are also found some interesting specializations in feeding behavior, such as eating the scales and fins of other fishes.

What You Should Know about Tanganyika Cichlids

Care: There are mouthbrooders as well as substrate brooders, which are mostly cavity brooders. For the cavity brooders (except snail cichlids), rock structures which may reach to the water surface should be constructed in the back of the tank. They should contain some caves that have only one entry. For mouthbrooding species from rocky biotopes, the rock structure should include many passages for swimming through. Cichlids from sandy biotopes (sand cichlids, snail cichlids) need sandy areas with snail shells (from edible land snails). Cichlids from open-water zones (for instance, *Cyprichromis* species) need large open swimming areas.

Communities: Tanganyika cichlid species that inhabit different water strata can easily coexist in large tanks. Cichlids from sandy and from rocky habitats should be kept together only in very large tanks. If the open-water areas are not occupied by cichlids, rainbow fishes are compatible with smaller *Lamprologus*, *Neolamprologus*, and *Julidochromis* species.

Water: All Tanganyika cichlids do well in medium hard to hard, slightly alkaline (pH 7.5–9) water. They do not tolerate acid water.

Lamprologus ocellatus

2⅜ inches (6 cm). *Tank*: 20 inches (50 cm). *Stratum*: Bottom. *Water*: pH 7.5–9; medium hard to hard; 77–81°F (25–27°C). *Set-up*: Supply large shells from edible land snails, at least one per fish! The fish will bury the shells themselves. *Food*: Smallish live and fairly fine-grade dry food. *Sexual differences*: The smaller females have a white rim and the males a yellow rim on the dorsal fin. *Breeding*: Father/mother family. The young hatch about nine days after the spawning. Start feeding them with *Artemia. Biotope*: Snail shells lying in sand. *Similar species*: *Neolamprologus brevis*, 2⅜ inches (6 cm); *N. multifasciatus*, 1½ inches (4 cm).

Altolamprologus calvus

5½ inches (14 cm). *Tank*: 40 inches (100 cm). *Stratum*: Middle. *Water*: pH 7.5–9; medium hard to hard; 77–81°F (25–27°C). *Set-up*: Rock structures with narrow crevices; no spacious caves; large shells from marine snails can be substituted for rock caves. Tip on communities: Other Tanganyika cichlids, including lively ones (this species then tends to lose some of its shyness). *Food*: Insect larvae, fry, *Mysis* shrimp, larger crustaceans. No dry food. *Sexual differences*: Males bigger. *Breeding*: Cavity brooder. Father/mother family. Spawning cavity must have a long, narrow entryway. Start feeding the slowly growing young with *Artemia. Biotope*: In rocky areas with a lot of sediment, especially spots with narrow cracks. *Similar species*: *A. compressiceps*, 6 inches (15 cm).

Neolamprologus longior

4 inches (10 cm). *Tank*: 32 inches (80 cm). *Strata*: Bottom, middle. *Water*: pH 7.5–9; medium hard to hard; 77–81°F (25–27°C). *Set-up*: Rocks with caves. Keep in pairs. Tip on communities: Tanganyika cichlids with different biotope requirements, such as *Cyprichromis* species and snail cichlids. *Food*: Live and dry food. The fish keep their beautiful yellow color only if given a varied diet. *Sexual differences*: Old males develop a small hump on the forehead. *Breeding*: Cavity brooder with father/mother family. Start feeding with *Artemia*. *Biotope*: Hidden in the cracks of caves in rocky biotopes rich in sediment. *Similar species*: *N. leleupi*, 4 inches (10 cm); *N. cylindricus*, 4¾ inches (12 cm). The genus *Neolamprologus* includes many other Tanganyika cichlids often kept in aquariums. However, many of them grow larger than this species, such as *N. tretocephalus* and *N. sexfasciatus*—both about 6 inches (15 cm). These larger species require a tank of at least 40 inches (100 cm). They also need larger caves and more nutritious food than *N. longior*.

‌eolamprologus brichardi

‌nches (10 cm). *Tank*: 32 inches (80 cm). *Stratum*: ‌ddle. *Water*: pH 7.5–9; medium hard to hard; 77–81°F ‌5–27°C). *Set-up*: Rocks with caves, open swimming ‌ea in the foreground. Keep in pairs. Tip on communities: ‌chlids from different biotopes, such as sand cichlids. ‌ood: Live and dry food. *Sexual differences*: Males some- ‌nat bigger. *Breeding*: Cavity brooder living in extended ‌milies. Start feeding with *Artemia* and dry food. *Biotope*: ‌ocky areas covered with sediment. The fish feed on ‌ooplankton in the open water but brood among rock ‌vities. *Similar species*: *N. marunguensis*.

113

Blunt-headed Cichlid
(*Tropheus moorii*)
About 4¾ inches (12 cm). *Tank*: 60 inches (150 cm)! *Strata*: All. *Water*: pH 7.5–9; medium hard to hard; 77–82°F (25–28°C). *Set-up*: Rocky tank with passages through the rocks. Keep six to ten fish, among which a rank hierarchy will develop. Never keep more males than females, and never remove individuals from the tank temporarily or add new ones. T on communities: Only cichlids with similar food requirements. *Food*: Hig in roughage. Never any red mosquit larvae, *Tubifex*, or beef heart! *Sexu* *differences*: Practically indistinguishable. *Breeding*: Mouthbrooder with mother family. Start feeding with *Artemia*. *Special remarks*: There are many color varieties. *Biotope*: Rocky areas without sediment, down to a depth of 10 feet (3 m). *Similar species*: *T. duboisi*, can be kept in pairs

Golden Julie (*Julidochromis ornatus*)
3 inches (8 cm). *Tank*: 24 inches (60 cm). *Strata*: Bottom, middle. *Water*: pH 7.5–9; medium hard to hard; 77–81°F (25–27°C). *Set-up*: Rocky tank with caves. Keep in pairs. If a pair is incompatible, remove one fish, or there might be a fatality. Changes in the tank can break up a pair bond that has been formed. Tip on communities: Other Tanganyika cichlids, rainbow fishes. *Food*: Small live and fine-grade dry food. *Sexual differences*: Females slightly bigger. *Breeding*: As for *Neolamprologus brichardi*. Cavity breeder with extended family. *Biotope*: Rocky shore with low gradient. *Similar species*: Other *Julidochromis* species.

Tanganiyka Clown or Striped Goby Cichlid
(*Eretmodus cyanostictus*)
8 inches (20 cm). Tank: 40 inches (100 cm). *Stratum*: Bottom. *Water*: pH 7.5–9; medium hard to hard; 77–81°F (25–27°C). *Set-up*: Rocky zone with lots of hiding places Fish that have not paired up are very aggressive toward each other. *Food*: Vegetarian food high in roughage, sm crustaceans, mosquito larvae (not red ones). *Sexual differences*: Not distinguishable. *Breeding*: Ovophile mouth brooder with parental family. Mouthbrooding done first b female and after about 12 days by male. Start feeding with small live food. *Biotope*: Shore area with scree.

In Lake Tanganyika, yellow sand cichlids inhabit sandy areas that are often found between rocks.

ellow Sand Cichlid (*Xenotilapia flavipinnis*)
–4 inches (8–12 cm). *Tank*: 32 inches (80 cm) *Stratum*: ottom. *Water*: pH 7.5–9; medium hard to hard. 77–81°F 25–27°C). *Set-up*: Tank with sandy bottom, with a few ocks and plants in the back. In groups of a few fish, pairs ill gradually form and defend small territories. In large anks (over 48 inches or 120 cm) there is room for several airs. Tip on communities: Cichlids living in open water or a rocky zones. *Food*: Smallish live food. *Sexual differences*: The yellow is brighter in males. *Breeding*: Ovophile nouthbrooder with parental family. After spawning, the emale first does the mouthbrooding and then after about ight days passes on the eggs to the male, who continues

the parental care. Once the young swim free, both parents look after them. Start feeding young with *Artemia*. *Biotope*: Areas with sandy bottom, often among groups of rocks. *Similar species*: Other *Xenotilapia* species, as well as *Enantiopus* and *Callochromis* species. These often need larger tanks; most of them are ovophile mouthbrooders with mother families.

yprichromis leptosoma
½ inches (14 cm). *Tank*: 60 inches (150 cm). *Strata*: Middle, top. *Water*: pH 7.5–9; medium hard to hard; 7–81°F (25–27°C). *Set-up*: Sandy bottom, lots of open water for swimming. Keep in groups (more females then nales). *Food:* No red mosquito larvae; instead, small rustaceans, other mosquito larvae, vitamin-enriched dry ood. *Sexual differences*: Male more brightly colored. *Breeding*: Ovophile mouthbrooder with mother family. tart feeding with *Artemia*. *Special remarks*: Poor water uality and unbalanced diet can lead to blindness. *Biotope*: Open water above rocky bottom.

Tips on Care of Other Species

Neolamprologus buescheri
2¾ inches (7 cm). Tank: 24 inches (60 cm). Strata: Bottom, middle. Water: pH 7.5–9; medium hard to hard; 79–81°F (26–27°C). Cavity brooder with father/mother family.

Cyathopharynx furcifer
8 inches (20 cm). Tank: 72 inches (180 cm). Strata: Bottom, middle. Water: pH 7.5–9; medium hard to hard; 77–79°F (26–27°C). Keep several females with one male. Sandy bottom with just a few large stones and some plants in the back. Mouthbrooder with mother family.

Cyphotilapia frontosa
12 inches (30 cm). Tank: 60 inches (150 cm). Strata: Bottom, middle. Water: pH 7.5–9; 77–79°F (26–27°C). Large, calm cichlid. Keep one male with several females. Feed them shrimp and pieces of fish. Mouthbrooder with mother family.

Chalinochromis brichardi
4¾ inches (12 cm). Tank: 32 inches (80 cm). Strata: Bottom, middle. Water: pH 7.5–9; medium hard to hard; 77–79°F (26–27°C). Cavity brooder (see photo, page 34).

Neolamprologus calliurus
3 inches (8 cm). Tank: 24 inches (60 cm). Strata: Bottom, middle. Water: pH 7.5–9; medium hard to hard; 77–79°F (26–27°C). Polygynous snail cychlid; only the small females can get into the snail shells (see photo, page 34).

There are an estimated 500 cichlid species in Lake Malawi. This large lake of the East African Rift, which is about 375 miles (600 km) long but only 53 miles (85 km) wide, thus has probably the greatest diversity of fish species anywhere.

What You Should Know about Malawi Cichlids

Care: Most of the species commonly kept in aquariums come from the rocky sections of Lake Malawi. These rock cichlids, which are also called Mbunas, are kept in tanks with rock structures in the back reaching all the way to the water surface. Because all of them are mouthbrooders, no enclosed caves are necessary for spawning. The rocks should be piled in such a way that caves with two entries are formed. That is, a fish that swims into a cave from the front should be able to emerge at a different spot. As in Lake Tanganyika, here too are found sand cichlids and cichlids that live in the open water (Utakas). Neither of these two kinds of cichlids requires rock structures in the tank.

Reproductive behavior: All cichlids endemic to Lake Malawi are ovophile mouthbrooders with mother families (see page 111), but not all species behave the same way. All possible variations of this kind of reproductive behavior occur. Thus there are species that stop looking after their young once these are first released from the mouth, while other species readmit them. In some species the mothers form "childcare" groups. Finally, there are even some species that smuggle their offspring in among the young of large, predatory catfishes that engage in parental care. These cichlid offspring are integrated into a school of catfish fry and thus enjoy the protection of these large parent fish.

Food: Mbunas need food high in roughage in the form of vegetarian dry food and also small crustaceans. In all species, the red color is intensified if small crustaceans are fed. Other cichlids of Lake Malawi can be given all kinds of food that comes in medium to large bite sizes.

Communities: Cichlids from different biotopes can be combined only in very large tanks (at least 60 inches or 150 cm). If in addition to rock cichlids other species that are adapted to a sandy bottom or to open water are kept, make sure there is plenty of bottom area and open space for swimming in the tank. Mbunas are aggressive among each other. If they are combined with other Mbuna species or with many of their own kind, their aggression is less dangerous because it is more dissipated. With all species, one male is kept with several females.

Water: All Malawi cichlids need medium hard to hard, alkaline (pH 7.5–8.5) water. Do not use roots because they acidify the water.

The male *Sciaenochromis ahli* with their rich blue are stunningly beautiful. The females, by contrast, are an inconspicuous gray. The splendor of this fish shows up best only in a large aquarium.

Sciaenochromis ahli

About 6¼ inches (16 cm). *Tank*: 60 inches (150 cm). *Strata*: Bottom, middle. *Water*: pH 7.5–8.5; medium hard to hard; 77–82°F (25–28°C). *Set-up*: Rocky aquarium with spacious cave-like passages as well as open water for swimming. Keep one male with several females. Predatory species. Tip on communities: Utaka cichlids, sand cichlids, other calm cichlid species from Lake Malawi, catfishes. Do not combine with small fishes. *Food*: Nutritious live food, especially crustaceans. *Sexual differences*: Females are an inconspicuous gray; males, a rich deep blue. *Breeding*: Ovophile mouthbrooder with mother family. Start feeding with small *Daphnia* and dry food. *Special remarks*: This species occurs in two color variations: One has a white spot on the forehead; the other does not. *Biotope*: Transition zone between rocky and sandy areas. *Similar species*: *Tyrannochromis fuscotaeniatus*, 10 inches (25 cm), tank 80 inches (200 cm) or over. This, too, is a predatory species. *Note*: This cichlid used to be called erroneously "*Haplochromis*" *jacksoni*, a name that is still sometimes used by dealers.

Dimidiochromis compressiceps

9½ inches (24 cm). *Tank*: 72 inches (180 cm). *Stratum*: Middle. *Water*: pH 7.5–8.5; medium hard to hard; 77–82°F (25–28°C). *Set-up*: Tank with rocky areas; also, to provide refuges, tall, long-leaved, plants such as *Vallisneria*. Tip on communities: Best combined with Utaka and sand cichlids from Lake Malawi, also catfishes. No small fishes. *Food*: Nutritious live food. *Sexual differences*: Males brightly colored; females inconspicuous. *Breeding*: Ovophile mouthbrooder with mother family. Start feeding with *Artemia*; also dry food. *Biotope*: Areas with aquatic plants, especially *Vallisneria*; also reeds. The fish lurk there in diagonal position, head down, waiting for prey fish. They sometimes eat the eyes of carp. *Note*: This fish has had a bad reputation for some time as an "eye eating" cichlid, and examination of the stomach contents of wild specimens has shown that this species does in fact eat the eyes of other fishes. Fish eyes are not a major part of its diet, however; they are only a delicious special treat. Probably only the eyes of certain noncichlid species are eaten. Also, it seems likely that this particular feeding habit occurs only in the wild; so far it has not been observed in aquariums.

Copadichromis spec. "Kadango"

About 5½ inches (14 cm). *Tank*: 48 inches (120 cm). *Strata*: Bottom, middle. *Water*: pH 7.5–8.5; medium hard to hard; 77–82°F (25–28°C). *Set-up*: Sandy bottom, few rocks, plants. Leave sufficient open water for swimming! Keep one male with several females. *Food*: Live and dry food, especially small crustaceans. *Sexual differences*: females inconspicuously colored. *Breeding*: Ovophile mouthbrooder with mother family. Start feeding with *Artemia*. *Biotope*: Open water where there is zooplankton to eat (Utakas). Sexually active fish on rocks near sand, where the males build sand nests.

117

Aulonocara jacobfreibergi

4¾ inches (12 cm). *Tank*: 48 inches (120 cm). *Strata*: Bottom, middle. *Water*: pH 7.5–8.5; medium hard to hard; 77–82°F (25–28°C). *Set-up*: Tank with spacious caves with two openings. Keep one male with several females. Tip on communities: Only calm cichlids from Lake Malawi (no Mbunas); catfishes. *Food*: Live and dry food, especially crustaceans. *Sexual differences*: Females pale and inconspicuous. *Breeding*: Ovophile mouthbrooder with mother family. Start feeding with *Artemia* and dry food. *Biotope*: Grottoes in transitional zones between rocky and sandy areas. In largish caves there may be many males, but only one has full characteristic male coloring.

Cobalt Blue Cichlid or Zebra Malawi Cichlid
(*Pseudotropheus zebra*)

About 4¾ inches (12 cm). *Tank*: 48 inches (120 cm). *Strata*: All. *Water*: pH 7.5–8.5; medium hard to hard; 77–82°F (25–28°C). *Set-up*: Rocky tank with caves that have two openings. Keep one male with several females. *Food*: Live and dry food high in roughage. *Sexual differences*: Females often have different coloration; egg spots on anal fin are inconspicuous or absent. *Breeding*: Ovophile mouthbrooder with mother family. Start feeding with *Artemia* and dry food. *Special remarks*: There are many different populations that differ from each other in coloration. *Biotope*: Rocky regions free of sediment.

Labidochromis spec. "yellow"

4 inches (10 cm). *Tank*: 32 inches (80 cm). *Strata*: All. *Water*: pH 7.5–8.5; medium hard to hard; 77–82°C (25–28°C). *Set-up*: Rocky tank. Keep one male with several females. Tip on communities: In tanks of at least 40 inches (100 cm), other smallish Malawi cichlids, catfishes, or shoaling fishes (such as rainbow fishes) can be kept. *Food*: Small live and fine-grade dry food. *Sexual differences*: Males with small hump on forehead. *Breeding*: Ovophile mouthbrooder with mother family. Start feeding with *Artemia*. *Biotope*: At depths of 50 to 65 feet (15–20 m) in areas with medium-sized to large rocks.

Pseudotropheus lanisticola

2⅜–2¾ inches (6–7 cm). *Tank*: 32 inches (80 cm). *Strata*: Bottom, middle. *Water*: pH 7.5–8.5; medium hard to hard; 77–82°F (25–28°C). *Set-up*: Sandy bottom, large shells of edible land snails; also rocks. Keep one male with several females. *Food*: Small crustaceans, other small live food and fine-grade dry food. *Sexual differences*: Practically nonexistent; females often without egg spots or with spots that lack the black ring. *Breeding*: Mouthbrooder with mother family. Start feeding with *Artemia* and dry food. *Biotope*: Sandy bottom with snail shells, usually in deeper water.

Melanochromis johannii

¾ inches (12 cm). *Tank*: 40 inches (100 cm). *Strata*: All. *Water*: pH 7.5–8.5; medium hard to hard; 77–82°F (25–28°C). *Set-up*: Rocky tank. Keep one male with several females. Tip on communities: Other Mbunas. *Food*: Live and dry food high in roughage. *Sexual differences*: Females and juveniles are yellow; dominant males, deep black with light spots. *Breeding*: Ovophile mouthbrooder with mother family. Start feeding with *Artemia* and dry food. *Biotope*: Rocky shore in transitional areas between zones with and without sediment. *Similar species*: M. auratus, 4¾ inches (12 cm); M. chipokae, 6 inches (15 cm), needs a tank of at least 60 inches (150 cm).

Labeotropheus trewavasae

About 4¾ inches (12 cm). *Tank*: 48 inches (120 cm). *Strata*: All. *Water*: pH 7.5–8.5; soft to medium hard; 77–82°F (25–28°C). *Set-up*: Rocky tank. Keep one male with several females. Tip on communities: Other Mbunas. *Food*: Live and dry food high in roughage. *Sexual differences*: Females have only small egg spots or none at all on the anal fin. *Breeding*: Ovophile mouthbrooder with mother family. Start feeding with *Artemia*. *Special remarks*: There are various populations that differ from each other in coloration. *Biotope*: Rocky areas with sediment deposits and having many holes and crevices. *Similar species*: L. fuelleborni.

Tips on Care of Other Species

Placidochromis electra

6⅜ inches (16 cm). Tank: 60 inches (150 cm). Strata: Bottom, middle. Water: pH 7.5–8.5; medium hard to hard; 77–82°F (25–28°C). Sandy bottom. Ovophile mouthbrooder.

Pseudotropheus "acei"

4¾ inches (12 cm). Tank: 48 inches (120 cm). Strata: Bottom, middle. Water: pH 7.5–8.5; medium hard to hard; 77–82°F (25–28°C). Rocky tank with plenty of open water for swimming.

Pseudotropheus elongatus

4–4¾ inches (10–12 cm). Tank: 48 inches (120 cm). Strata: All. Water: pH 7.5–8.5; medium hard to hard; 77–82°F (25–28°C). Mbuna species that can—depending on which population the fish come from—be highly aggressive.

Nimbochromis livingstonii

10 inches (25 cm). Tank: 60 inches (150 cm). Strata: Bottom, middle. Water: pH 7.5–8.5; medium hard to hard; 77–82°F (25–28°C). Predatory species that lies in wait for its prey—young cichlids—lying on its side and displaying its conspicuous markings. This behavior has been interpreted as trying to look like a rotting fish. Can be combined with large species without any problems.

Protomelas fenestratus

5½ inches (14 cm). Tank: 48 inches (120 cm). Strata: Bottom, middle. Water: pH 7.5–8.5; medium hard to hard; 77–82°F (25–28°C). Peaceful species, highly recommended. Do not combine with robust Mbunas.

Gephyrochromis moorii

4¾ inches (12 cm). Tank: 48 inches (120 cm). Strata: Bottom, middle. Water: pH 7.5–8.5; medium hard to hard; 77–82°F (25–28°C). Plenty of open water for swimming, sandy bottom, rocks in the back only.

These are cichlids that do not come from the two great African lakes, Lake Malawi and Lake Tanganyika. The geographic range for each species is given under the heading "Biotope."

What You Should Know about African Cichlids
The rivers and lakes of Africa contain a diversity of cichlids that is comparable only to the diversity of river cichlids in South America. However, today this profusion of species is threatened in Africa, as it is in many other places. One sad example of this state of affairs is Lake Victoria. With a surface area of almost 26,500 square miles (69,000 km²) it is Africa's largest lake and home to several hundred cichlid species. A great portion of these species are condemned to extinction. The reason is not overfishing on the part of natives or export to aquarium fish dealers. The cause of the problem is that the lake was stocked with an alien species. Because of their size (up to 6½ feet or 2 m), Nile perch (*Lates niloticus*) were introduced into Lake Victoria. This large predator has upset the ecological balance for many small species.

Care: The smaller species not only thrive in well-planted tanks equipped with roots and small caves but also can be bred there. A tank for large species should include large flat rocks and roots arranged to create shelters and retreats for weaker fish. Place gravel around the top of the roots of robust, large-leaved plants to keep them from being dug up. No plants should be used in the case of a few species that are plant eaters (*Tilapia* species).

Communities: Most species are not too aggressive even during the brood care phase and can be combined with catfishes and shoaling fishes of the upper water strata. There are, however, some real ruffians, such as the red cichlids and some large species related to the *Tilapia* genus, that can be very aggressive and require a lot of room while engaged in parental care. Combine these bullies only with other large, robust species and with some of the larger catfishes.

Water: With the exception of a few dwarf cichlids of the genera *Nanochromis* and *Pelvicachromis*, all species accommodate to medium hard and slightly acid to slightly alkaline (pH 6–7.5) water. Cichlids from Lake Victoria prefer alkaline (pH 7.5–8.5) water.

Note: At the end of this section (on page 124) the orange chromide (*Etroplus maculatus*) from India—an outsider in this company—is described. It is one of the few cichlids found in Asia.

Purple Cichlid
(*Pelvicachromis pulcher*)
4 inches (10 cm). *Tank:* 24 inches (60 cm). *Strata:* Bottom, middle. *Water:* pH 5–7.5; soft to hard; 77–82°F (25–28°C). *Set-up:* Tank arranged in dark colors, with plants, roots, and small caves. Tip on communities: Shoaling fishes of the upper stratum; in tanks of at least 40 inches (100 cm) other smallish cichlids. *Food:* All types of fairly fine-grade foods. *Sexual differences:* Females smaller, with a shiny dorsal fin. *Breeding:* Cavity brooder with father/mother family. Start feeding with *Artemia* and dry food. *Special remarks:* There are different color variations of this species, some of which need softer, acid water. *Biotope:* Shallow areas with leaf litter, brush, and leafy plants in slow-moving or, rarely, still water in southern Nigeria.

There are several different populations of Guenther's mouthbrooder, and they grow to different sizes. This is one of the few mouthbrooders where the male assumes the brood care; that is, the eggs and yolk sac larvae are incubated by the father.

Guenther's Mouthbrooder (*Chromidotilapia guntheri*) ¾–6⅜ inches (12–16 cm); *Tank*: 32 inches (80 cm); *Strata*: Bottom, middle. *Water*: pH 6–7.5; soft to hard; 75–82°F (24–28°C). *Set-up*: Tank with fine bottom material, pebbles, and roots. Slight circulation recommended. Tip on communities: In tanks of at least 40 inches (100 cm), *Pelvicachromis* species, active shoaling fishes of the top stratum. When combined with other fishes, *C. guntheri* loses some of its shyness. *Food*: Live and dry food of all kinds. *Sexual differences*: Females smaller, with a shiny dorsal fin. *Breeding*: Ovophile mouthbrooder. Eggs and yolk sac larvae are brooded by the father. After the young swim free, both parents engage in brood care. Start

feeding with *Artemia*. Biotope: Occurs in the most varied biotopes, but usually in moving water over sandy or pebbly bottom in West Africa from Ghana to Cameroon. *Similar species*: *C. finleyi* and *C. batesii*, both 4¾ inches (12 cm). There are several different populations of both species, each with different coloration. The species also vary in their brooding behavior. *C. finleyi* is an ovophile mouthbrooder, with the parents passing the eggs back and forth, sometimes several times in the course of a day. Later they lead the young together. *C. batesii* is a larvophile mouthbrooder. Both species have more stringent requirements for water quality than *C. guntheri* and prefer soft, slightly acid water.

Pelvicachromis taeniatus
3⅜ inches (8.5 cm). *Tank*: 24 inches (60 cm). *Strata*: Bottom, middle. *Water*: pH 6–7.5; soft to medium hard; 77–82°F (25–28°C). *Set-up*: Tank arranged in dark colors, small caves, plants. Slight circulation. Tip on communities: Shoaling fishes of the top stratum. *Food*: Varied small live and fine-grade dry food. *Sexual differences*: Males bigger, with elongated fins. *Breeding*: Cavity brooder with father/mother family. Start feeding with *Artemia*. Special remarks: Some populations require soft, acid water. *Biotope*: Shore areas with leaf litter and brush mostly in clear, moving water in Cameroon and eastern Nigeria.

Nanochromis transvestitus
2⅜ inches (6 cm). *Tank*: 20 inches (50 cm). *Stratum*: Bottom. *Water*: pH 5–6.5; soft to medium hard; 81–84°F (27–29°C). *Set-up*: Tank arranged in dark colors, with roots and small caves for hiding. Tip on communities: Small characins, killifishes, and others that live in the upper water level. *Food*: Varied diet of small live and fine-grade dry food. *Sexual differences*: Females more colorful, smaller, with a striped caudal fin. *Breeding*: Cavity brooder with father/mother family. Water soft, very acid (pH 4.5–5.5). *Biotope*: In shallow, partially rocky shore areas of black water areas near Lake Maj-Ndombe, Zaire.

Anomalochromis thomasi

3 inches (8 cm). *Tank*: 24 inches (60 cm). *Strata*: Bottom, middle. *Water*: pH 6–7.5; soft to medium hard; 75–82°F (24–28°C). *Set-up*: Tank arranged in dark colors, with plants, small roots, and open areas with pebbles. In light-colored tanks the delicate beauty of this fish does not show up well. Tip on communities: Shoaling fishes of the upper stratum; in tanks of at least 40 inches (100 cm), also cavity brooding dwarf cichlids (such as *Pelvicachromis* species). *Food*: Small live and fine-grade dry food. *Sexual differences*: Often hard to tell, even in full-grown fish. Females smaller, with somewhat brighter colors. *Breeding*: Open-water brooder with parental family. Soft water; slightly acid (pH 6–6.5). Start feeding with *Artemia*. Parents often do not get along, and the pair breaks up. Try to bring them together again by using a glass panel (see page 110, under the heading "Aggressive behavior"). *Biotope*: Small, clear rivers in wooded and bushy landscapes in Sierra Leone and Liberia. *Note*: This species was earlier known as *Pelmatochromis thomasi*.

Red Cichlids (*Hemichromis spec.*)

About 4 inches (10 cm). *Tank*: 32 inches (80 cm). *Strata*: Bottom, middle. *Water*: pH 6–7.5; soft to hard; 75–82°F (24–28°C). *Set-up*: Tank arranged in dark colors, robust plants, roots. Aggressive species. Tip on communities: In tanks of at least 48 inches (120 cm), cichlids of comparable size. *Food*: Live and dry food. *Sexual differences*: Practically nonexistent. Females look plumper and slightly smaller. *Breeding*: Open-water brooder with parental family. Start feeding with *Artemia* and dry food. *Biotope*: The various species occur in small marshy bodies of water and in clear streams in West and Central Africa.

Lionhead, Lumphead, or Blockhead Cichlid

(*Steatocranus casuarius*)
About 4¾ inches (12 cm). *Tank*: 32 inches (80 cm). *Stratum*: Bottom. *Water*: pH 6.5–8; soft to hard; 75–81°F (24–27°C). *Set-up*: Tank with rock caves. Undemanding species. Keep in pairs. Tip on communities: In tanks of at least 40 inches (100 cm), shoaling fishes of the upper water level, robust cichlids. *Food*: Live and dry food (including vegetarian) of all types. *Sexual differences*: Males bigger, with bigger lumps on head. *Breeding*: Cavity brooder; both parents may take part in brood care. *Biotope*: Among stones in rapids of the lower Zaire River, Central Africa. *Similar species*: A dwarf version, *S. spec. aff. uban-guiensis*, 2¾ inches (7 cm), suited for small tanks of at least 20 inches (50 cm); see photo, page 35.

Tilapia joka

inches (20 cm). *Tank*: 48 inches (120 cm). *Strata*: Bottom, middle. *Water*: pH 6–7.5; soft to medium hard; 77–81°F 25–27°C). *Set-up*: Tank arranged in dark colors, caves, pots, robust plants. Calm species. Tip on communities: Other calm cichlids; catfishes. *Food*: Vegetarian and non-vegetarian. *Sexual differences*: Mature males dark gray with the tips of their elongated fins whitish gray. *Breeding*: Cavity brooder that uses spacious caves. Start feeding with *Artemia* and dry food. *Biotope*: Banks of small, clear rivers with lots of hiding places, Sierra Leone and Liberia.

Pseudocrenilabrus nicholsi

2¾ inches (7 cm). *Tank*: 24 inches (60 cm). *Strata*: Bottom, middle. *Water*: pH 6.5–7.5; medium hard to hard; 73–79°F (23–26°C). *Set-up*: Planted tank with open swimming area and fine-grained bottom material. Keep one male with several females. Tip on communities: Other fishes of comparable size. *Food*: Primarily small crustaceans and other live and dry food. *Sexual differences*: Males more brilliantly colored and somewhat larger. *Breeding*: Mouthbrooder with mother family. Isolate the female. Start feeding young with *Artemia*. *Biotope*: Southern part of the Zaire River watershed.

"Haplochromis" nigricans

About 4¾ inches (12 cm). *Tank*: 40 inches (100 cm). *Strata*: Bottom, middle. *Water*: pH 7.5–8.5; medium hard to hard; 73–82°F (24–28°C). *Set-up*: Tank with stones and plants. Keep one male with many females. Tip on communities: Other cichlids from Lake Victoria, catfishes. *Food*: Live and dry food. *Sexual differences*: Females smaller, paler. *Breeding*: Mouthbrooder with mother family. Isolate female. Start feeding young with *Artemia*. *Biotope*: Rocky biotopes with *aufwuchs* in Lake Victoria. *Similar species*: Other *H. spec.* species from Lake Victoria. *Note*: There are several hundred cichlid species in Lake Victoria, most of which will become extinct!

Orange Chromide (*Etroplus maculatus*)

3 inches (8 cm). *Tank*: 24 inches (60 cm). *Strata*: Bottom, middle. *Water*: pH 7.5–9; medium hard to hard; 79–84°F (26–29°C). *Set-up*: Tank with hiding places. Water with salt addition (1–2 teaspoons per 10 quarts) recommended. Keep in pairs; tanks of at least 48 inches (120 cm) can accommodate several pairs. Tip on communities: Other cichlids, catfishes. *Food*: Small live and fine-grade dry food. *Sexual differences*: Hard to detect. *Breeding*: Pair-forming substrate brooder with parental family. Start feeding with *Artemia*. *Biotope*: Shallow shore areas of still water, often in brackish lagoons, southern India, Sri Lanka.

Tips on Care of Other African Species

Nanochromis squamiceps

2⅜ inches (6 cm). Tank: 20 inches (50 cm). Stratum: Bottom. Water: pH 5.5–7.5; soft to medium hard; 77–82°F (25–28°C). Cavity brooder. Tank arranged in dark colors. Extremely low water values necessary only for breeding.

Pelvicachromis humilis

4¾ inches (12 cm). Tank: 40 inches (100 cm). Stratum: Bottom. Water: pH 6–7.5; soft to medium hard; 75–82°F (24–28°C). Demanding, calm species. Tank arranged in dark colors with lots of hiding places and sandy bottom. Cavity brooder.

Pelvicachromis subocellatus

3½ inches (9 cm). Tank: 24 inches (60 cm). Strata: Bottom, middle. Water: pH 6–7.5; soft to hard; 77–84°F (25–29°C). Care as for other *Pelvicachromis* species. Cavity brooder. Low water values are necessary for breeding.

Steatocranus tinanti

4¾ inches (12 cm). Tank: 32 inches (80 cm). Stratum: Bottom. Water: pH 6.5–8; soft to hard; 75–82°F (24–28°C). Peaceful species. Likes circulation. Cavity brooder.

Tilapia zillii

About 12 inches (30 cm). Tank: 48 inches (120 cm). Strata: Bottom, middle. Water: pH 6–9; soft to very hard; 75–86°F (24–30°C). Large cichlid, suitable only for tanks without plants. Open-water brooder with parental family.

Tilapia mariae

About 12 inches (30 cm). Tank: 48 inches (120 cm). Strata: Bottom, middle. Water: pH 6–8; soft to hard; 75–82°F (24–28°C). Calm species. Large cichlid. Combine with other large species. Cavity brooder with parental family.

Sarotherodon melanotheron

About 8 inches (20 cm). Tank: 48 inches (120 cm). Strata: Bottom, middle. Water: pH 7–8.5; medium hard to very hard; 79–84°F (26–29°C). Likes to swim a lot. Large tank. Mouthbrooder. Parental care done mostly by males, but females sometimes participate.

Lamprologus congoensis

6 inches (15 cm). Tank: 48 inches (120 cm). Stratum: Bottom. Water: pH 6.5–8; soft to hard; 75–82°F (24–28°C). Polygamous cavity brooder. Large tank. Keep one male with several females. Each fish needs a cave for hiding.

Thysochromis ansorgii

4¾ inches (12 cm). Tank: 32 inches (80 cm). Strata: Bottom, middle. Water: pH 6–7.5; soft to hard; 77–82°F (25–28°C). Care as for *Pelvicachromis pulcher*. Cavity brooder. Female with a silvery spot in the anal region.

ere are almost no dwarf cichlids among the Central
nerican cichlids. Most of them grow to a size that
quires a tank no smaller than 32 inches (80 cm).

hat You Should Know about ntral American Cichlids

re: For medium-sized to large species, many of which
e to burrow, set up the tank as follows: Large flat rocks
ng the back wall, large roots, and robust plants (such
Vallisneria gigantea). Arrange stones around the top of
e roots to prevent fish from digging them up. When you
t up the tank, be sure to create shelters and hiding
ices but still leave open space. With some cichlid spe-
s you have to replant periodically if you want the plants
look good, because these fish pull up or eat the plants.
s better to do without plants if the fish have demon-
ated an inclination to uproot them.

r smaller cichlids belonging to the "*Cichlasoma*" subge-
s *Archocentrus*, for *Thorichthys* species, and for *Theraps
eruleus*, the tank should have small caves and may be
erally planted, for these fishes leave plants alone or, if
ey dig, dig only right next to their brooding cavity.

r all species, caves and other shelters are important
cause they are the center of the spawning territory and
so offer subordinate animals a place for retreat.

ater: All Central American cichlids like medium hard to
rd, alkaline (pH 7.5–8.5) water. Most of them do not
erate acid water.

Theraps coeruleus
4¾ inches (12 cm). *Tank*: 40 inches (100 cm). *Stratum*:
Bottom. *Water*: pH 7–8.5; medium hard to very hard;
75–81°F (24–27°C). *Set-up*: Tank with big, round pebbles
that form small cavities. Strong circulation. Tip on communities: In a largish tank, a pair of *Thorichthys* (such as
T. meeki); otherwise, livebearing toothcarps (Poeciliidae).
Food: All types of fairly fine-grade food. *Sexual differences*: Males somewhat bigger, with small black dots on
the flanks. *Breeding*: Cavity brooder with father/mother
family. Start feeding with *Artemia*. *Biotope*: Preferably in
currents of clear water in various tributaries of the Río
Tulija in southern Mexico. *Similar species*: *T. lentiginosus*.

Cichlasoma" nicaraguense
inches (25 cm). *Tank*: 48 inches (120 cm). *Stratum*:
ottom. *Water*: pH 7–8.5; medium hard to very hard;
–81°F (24–27°C). *Set-up*: Caves with sandy bottom
nstructed out of fairly large rocks. Tip on communities:
her medium-sized cichlids. *Food*: Live and dry food;
so snails. *Sexual differences*: Females smaller and
ore colorful and with a flatter forehead. *Breeding*: Cavity
ooder (eggs are not sticky) with father/mother family.
art feeding with *Artemia*. *Biotope*: Transitional zone
tween sandy and rocky areas, primarily in the lakes of
caragua and Costa Rica.

Zebra or Convict Cichlid ("*Cichlasoma*" *nigrofasciatum*)
5½ inches (14 cm), some populations smaller. *Tank*:
32 inches (80 cm). *Stratum*: Bottom. *Water*: pH 7–8.5;
medium hard to very hard; 73–81°F (23–27°C). *Set-up*:
Tanks with caves formed by rocks and roots. *Food*: All
types, including vegetarian. *Sexual differences*: Males
bigger, with steeper forehead and more elongated fins.
Breeding: Cavity brooder with father/mother family. Start
feeding with *Artemia* and dry food. *Special remarks*: Many
different populations with varying appearance. *Biotope*:
Varied, from Panama to Mexico. *Similar species*: "*C.*"
septemfasciatum, "*C.*" *sajica*.

"Cichlosoma" synspilum

14 inches (35 cm). *Tank*: 80 inches (200 cm). *Strata*: Bottom, middle. *Water*: pH 7–8.5; medium hard to very hard; 75–81°F (24–27°C). *Set-up*: Tank with bulky roots and large, flat rocks in the back. No plants; this species not only burrows but also likes to chew on and eat plants. Keep in pairs. Tip on communities: A pair of large cichlid of comparable strength, but make sure that the tank is divided into two territories. *Food*: Nutritious live and dry food in big morsels and amounts, including vegetarian food. A varied diet is important, because full development of the beautiful colors depends on it. *Sexual differences*: Mature males develop an obvious lump on the forehead. *Breeding*: Open-water brooder with parental family. Start feeding with *Artemia* and dry food. With sexually mature fish, the finding of partners often gives rise to severe problems, and because of intraspecies aggression a meeting can turn into a dangerous encounter that may possibly end in the death of the weaker partner. Fish that have grown up together form pairs more easily. *Biotope*: Slow-moving, often murky water from southern Mexico to Belize. *Similar species*: "*C.*" *maculicauda*, 12 inches (30 cm); "*C.*" *bifasciatum*, 10 inches (25 cm).

Rainbow Cichlid (*Herotilapia multispinosa*)
4¾ inches (12 cm). *Tank*: 32 inches (80 cm). *Strata*: Bottom, middle. *Water*: pH 7–8.5; medium hard to very hard; 77–86°F (25–30°C). *Set-up*: Tank with robust plants; rocks for hiding places. Fine-grained bottom material. Undemanding species. Tip on communities: Only with cichlids of comparable size, including livebearers. *Food*: Vegetarian, live, and dry food. *Sexual differences*: Males have a somewhat steeper forehead. *Breeding*: Substrate brooder with a tendency to brood in cavities. Start feeding with dry food and *Artemia*. *Biotope*: Shallow, often muddy shore area with lots of vegetation; Honduras to Costa Rica.

Cichlasoma" longimanus

inches (15 cm). *Tank*: 40 inches (100 cm). *Stratum*:
ottom. *Water*: pH 7–8.5; soft to very hard; 75–84°F
4–29°C). *Set-up*: Create sizable shelters out of roots
nd stones in the back of the tank. Bottom partially sandy.
arge-leaved plants. *Food*: Small to medium-sized mor-
els of live and dry food. *Sexual differences*: Females are
naller and, during courtship period, display greater color
ontrasts. *Breeding*: Open-water brooder with parental
mily. Start feeding with *Artemia*. *Biotope*: Above sandy
 scree-covered bottom in sections, some of them fast-
oving, of the Río Choluteca, Honduras. *Similar species*:
." *rostratum*, 10 inches (25 cm), 48-inch (120 cm) tank.

"Cichlasoma" carpinte

12 inches (30 cm). *Tank*: 48 inches (120 cm). *Strata*:
Bottom, middle. *Water*: pH 7–8.5; medium hard to very
hard; 75–81°F (24–27°C). *Set-up*: Tank with large roots
and flat rocks. Large-leaved plants. Tip on communities:
Other large cichlids. *Food*: Nutritious live and dry food.
Sexual differences: Females smaller, with flatter forehead.
Breeding: Open-water brooder with parental family. Start
feeding with *Artemia*. *Biotope*: Inhabits the most varied
biotopes on the Atlantic side of northern Mexico. *Similar
species*: "*C.*" *cyanoguttatum*, 12 inches (30 cm).

**The firemouth is one of the oldest
veterans among aquarium cichlids.
Those caught in the wild, like the
pair in this photo, are more beautiful than the tank-bred ones from
Southeast Asia that are often
offered for sale.**

iremouth (*Thorichthys meeki*)

/2 inches (14 cm). *Tank*: 32 inches (80 cm). *Stratum*:
ottom. *Water*: pH 6.5–8.5; soft to very hard; 75–81°F
4–27°C). *Set-up*: Tank with roots, large-leaved plants,
ith open areas, some of them sandy. Keep in pairs. Tip
 communities: In tanks of at least 48 inches (120 cm),
veral pairs of this species can be kept. *Food*: Medium-
zed morsels of live and dry food. *Sexual differences*:
males have a black spot on the dorsal fin. *Breeding*:

Open-water brooder with parental family, though the
female is more likely to be in charge of the brood while the
male takes on the defense of the territory. Start feeding
with fine-grade dry food, later *Artemia*. *Biotope*: Shallow
shore areas (with submerged wood or rocks) of clear and
murky rivers, including areas where the water does not
move; especially in southern Mexico and in Guatemala.
Similar species: *Th. aureus* and *Th. callolepis*.

Salvin's Cichlid (*"Cichlasoma" salvini*)
6 inches (15 cm). *Tank*: 40 inches (100 cm). *Strata*: Bottom, middle. *Water*: pH 7–8.5; soft to very hard; 75–82°F (24–28°C). *Set-up*: Arrange roots, plants, and stones in such a way that there are shelters and hiding places. Aggressive species. Keep in pairs. Tip on communities: In tanks of at least 48 inches (120 cm), other medium-sized, robust cichlids; Loricariidae catfishes. *Food*: This is a predatory species that needs nutritious live food but also takes dry food. *Sexual differences*: Females smaller, with more red. *Breeding*: Open-water brooder with a tendency to brood in cavities; father/mother family. Start feeding with *Artemia*. *Special remarks*: Depending on where this fish is from, it varies in body shape, color, and size. *Biotope*: Still and moving water, both clear and murky, in Mexico and into Guatemala. Usually in places with roots and plants.

Tips on Care of Other Species

"Cichlosoma" motaguense
About 12 inches (30 cm). Tank: 60 inches (150 cm). Strata: Bottom, middle. Water: pH 7–8.5; medium hard to very hard; 77–82°F (25–28°C). Predatory species best combined with equally large, robust cichlids in a very large tank (at least 80 inches or 2 m).

"Cichlosoma" panamense
6 inches (15 cm). Tank: 32 inches (80 cm). Strata: Bottom, middle. Water: pH 7–8.5; medium hard to very hard; 75–81°F (24–27°C). Care as for *"C." nigrofasciatum*. Cavity brooder.

Neetroplus nematopus
4⅜ inches (11 cm). Tank: 32 inches (80 cm). Strata: Bottom, middle. Water: pH 7–8.5; medium hard to very hard; 75–81°F (24–27°C). Arrange hiding places among rocks. Aggressive species. Cavity brooder. During brood care phase, these fish are black with a white band on the side; in normal state the colors are reversed.

Jack Dempsey (*"Cichlasoma" octofasciatum*)
8 inches (20 cm). Tank: 48 inches (120 cm). Strata: Bottom, middle. Water: pH 7–8.5; medium hard to very hard; 77–82°F (25–28°C). Caves to hide in. Nutritious live and dry food; also vegetarian. Open-water brooder.

"Cichlosoma" sieboldii
About 8 inches (20 cm). Tank: 48 inches (120 cm). Strata: Bottom, middle. Water: pH 7–8.5; medium hard to hard; 73–81°F (23–27°C). Feed it vegetarian food! Cavity brooder.

[So]uth American cichlids have always been popular with [aq]uarists. Among them are the best known "veterans" of [ho]bbyists' tanks, namely the discus and angelfishes. Most [of] the "South Americans" come from the huge Amazon [re]gion, where the most varied water qualities occur. That [is] why different species of South American cichlids often [re]quire very different water properties.

[W]hat You Should Know about Cichlids [fr]om South America

[Ca]re: Tanks for these cichlids should be dark, with the [sp]ace well subdivided. Objects used for structuring the [sp]ace include roots and stones arranged to provide caves [for] the cavity brooders. For smaller species, coconut [sh]ells that are cut in half, with an entry hole cut out, or [pie]ces of flower pots can substitute as caves.

[La]rge-leaved plants are especially well suited for cichlid [ta]nks. Place pebbles around the top of the roots to keep [th]e fish from digging up the plants. Some cichlid species [ar]e plant eaters; they have to be kept in unplanted tanks. [Dw]arf cichlids can be kept in densely planted tanks. They [ar]e good candidates for community tanks with characins [an]d other peaceful fishes, as long as their requirements [for] water quality are kept in mind.

[W]ater: Except for a few sensitive dwarf cichlids, all [sp]ecies thrive in medium hard, acid to slightly alkaline [p]H 6–7.5) water. For breeding, however, many of them [ne]ed water that is soft and acid.

Agassiz's Dwarf Cichlid (*Apistogramma agassizii*)
4 inches (10 cm). *Tank*: 32 inches (80 cm). *Stratum*: Bottom.
Water: pH 5–6.8; very soft to medium hard; 79–84°F
(26–29°C). *Set-up*: Tank arranged in dark colors, tangle
of roots, plants, small caves. Demanding species. Tip on
communities: Shoaling fishes of the upper stratum. *Food*:
Small live and frozen food. *Sexual differences*: Males
bigger, with larger fins. *Breeding*: Cavity brooder with
father/mother family (polygynous). Soft water. Start feeding with *Artemia*. *Special remarks*: There are several color
varieties. *Biotope*: Shallow water with little current and
with leaf litter and branches on the bottom, especially in
black water along the main course of the Amazon River.

[Co]ckatoo Dwarf Cichlid

[(A]*pistogramma cacatuoides*)
[3½] inches (9 cm). *Tank*: 32 inches
[80] cm). *Stratum*: Bottom. *Water*:
[pH] 6.5–8; soft to hard; 79–84°F
[26]–29°C). *Set-up*: Tank arranged in
[da]rk colors, densely planted. Hiding
[pla]ces among roots, small caves.
[Ke]ep one male with several females.
[Tip] on communities: Shoaling fishes
[of] the upper stratum. *Food*: Live and
[dry] food in small to medium morsels.
[Se]xual differences: Females half as
[big] as males, with shorter fins. *Breed-
[in]g*: Cavity brooder with male-with-
[ha]rem family (polygynous). Start
[fee]ding with *Artemia*. *Biotope*: Shal-
[lo]w areas with leaf litter on bottom in
[sm]all moving and stagnant bodies of
[wa]ter in the Peruvian Amazon region
[(cl]ear and white water). *Similar spe-
[cie]s*: A. spec. "Bigmouth."

Among the best-known cichlids is
the colorful butterfly or ram cichli
an open-water brooder that spaw
on small stones. Both sexes take
part in parental care. The brood,
which may consist of as many as
200 eggs, is fanned and defended
by both parents together. Even
when the young have started to
swim free, both parents still prote
them and look after them for a
while.

Ram or Butterfly Cichlid (*Papiliochromis ramirezi*)
2 inches (5 cm). *Tank*: 20 inches (50 cm). *Strata*: Bottom,
middle. *Water*: pH 5–6.5; soft to medium hard; 81–86°F
(27–30°C). *Set-up*: Tank so densely planted that the
bottom area is shaded. Peaceful species. Keep in pairs.
Tip on communities: Calm fishes of the upper stratum. In
tanks of over 32 inches (80 cm) several pairs of this
species can be kept. *Food*: Small live food; also dry food.
Sexual differences: Mature males have a much-elongated
fin lobe on the anterior part of the dorsal fin. Sexually
active females have pink abdomen. *Breeding*: Open-water
brooder with parental family. Small stones serve as
spawning substrate. Soft water. Start feeding with
Artemia. *Special remarks*: Tank-bred fish from Asia grow
larger, but their brood behavior often has degenerated.
Biotope: Swampy lagoons in open savanna landscapes in
Venezuela, Colombia. *Similar species*: P. altispinosus,
3½ inches (9 cm), less demanding. *Note*: Keep up water
quality. P. ramirezi is fairly sensitive to water quality. It is
not very long-lived (about two years).

Dicrossus filamentosus
3½ inches (9 cm). *Tank*: 32 inches (80 cm). *Strata*: Bottom, middle. *Water*: pH 5–6.8; soft; 75–81°F (24–27°C).
Set-up: Planted tank with roots and cave-like hiding
places. Tip on communities: Characins of the upper
stratum. *Food*: Small live food. *Sexual differences*:
Females are smaller, with shorter fins and, during spawning phase, red ventral fins. *Breeding*: Cavity brooder with
father/mother family. Water extremely soft, acid (pH abo
5). Start feeding with *Artemia*. *Biotope*: Streams and rive
expansions of the Río Negro and the Orinoco, Brazil and
Venezuela.

Flag Cichlid (*Laetacara curviceps*)
3 inches (8 cm). *Tank*: 24 inches (60 cm). *Strata*: Bottom, middle. *Water*: pH 6–7; soft to medium hard; 79–86°F (26–30°C). *Set-up*: Densely planted tank with small roots that serve as territory borders and some stones on the fine-grained bottom material. In tanks of over 32 inches (80 cm), two pairs can be kept. Tip on communities: Small fishes of the upper stratum. *Food*: Small live food. *Sexual differences*: Mature females are smaller than males. *Breeding*: Open-water brooder with parental family. Feed first with paramecia or dry food; after a few days, with *Artemia*. *Biotope*: Along banks and in bays with little current in the entire Amazon region.

Bujurquina vittata
4¾ inches (12 cm). *Tank*: 32 inches (80 cm). *Strata*: Bottom, middle. *Water*: pH 6–7.5; soft to medium hard; 75–82°F (24–28°C). *Set-up*: Shelters formed by roots and plants in the background. Place some dry, brown beech leaves in the tank. Tip on communities: Robust characins, catfishes, smallish cichlids. *Food*: Live and dry food. *Sexual differences*: Practically nonexistent. Adult males have longer fins. *Breeding*: Larvophile mouthbrooder that deposits eggs on fallen leaves so that it can move the brood. Start feeding with *Artemia* and dry food. *Biotope*: Rivers in the watershed of the Paraná and the Paraguay Rivers in southern South America.

The Cupid cichlid charms the beholder with its delicate pastel colors. This fish comes originally from the vicinity of the Brazilian city of Santarém.

Cupid Cichlid (*Biotodoma cupido* "Santarém")
5⅛ inches (13 cm). *Tank*: 32 inches (80 cm). *Strata*: Bottom, middle. *Water*: pH 6–7.5; soft to hard; 77–82°F (25–28°C). *Set-up*: Planted tank, with roots or flat rocks to provide hiding places. Some fine bottom material with pebbles in the foreground. Keep several fish, among which pairs will form. Calm species. Tip on communities: Only calm, small to medium-sized fishes. *Food*: Small to medium live food with addition of dry food. *Sexual differences*: Males more colorful than females, with bluish iridescent bands below the eyes. Females have iridescent spots instead. *Breeding*: Open-water brooder with paren-

tal family. Small pits with pebbles in the bottom serve as spawning sites. Start feeding with *Artemia*. *Biotope*: Lakelike widenings in the Río Tapajo near Santarém; Brazilian part of the Amazon watershed—there in clear water. *Similar species*: *Biotodoma* species that are at present still assigned to *B. cupido* (except *B. wavrini*).

Brown Discus (*Symphysodon aequifasciatus*)
7 inches (18 cm). *Tank*: 48 inches (120 cm), at least
20 inches (50 cm) tall. *Stratum*: Middle. *Water*: pH 5–7.5;
very soft to medium hard; 79–86°F (26–30°C). *Set-up*:
Difficult to care for, not a fish for beginners. A tank with
large-leaved plants. Roots that reach to the water surface.
Muted lighting. Frequent changes of small quantities of
water are very important. Tip for communities: Calm
fishes; this species does not burrow or damage plants.
Food: Do not give *Tubifex*, beef heart, or red mosquito
larvae, or do so only rarely! Other live food is fine. Provide
a varied diet rich in vitamins; otherwise, this fish is likely to
get hole-in-the-head disease. *Sexual differences*: Adult
males often have a small lump on the forehead. The anal
papilla is pointed in the male, round in the female, but
during nonbreeding times the difference is hard to tell.
Breeding: Possible only in soft, acid (pH 5.5–6.5) water.
Open-water brooder using vertical substrates; parental
family. The parent fish need peace and quiet. They spawn
against carefully cleaned plant leaves or stones. A spawning produces up to 250 eggs. At 82–86°F (28–30°C) the
young hatch after three days, and six days after hatching
they swim free. The fry feed on a skin secretion of their
parents which is produced in greater quantities at this
time. From the fifth to the tenth day of swimming free the
fry are given *Artemia*, later also *Cyclops* and microworms.
But the young have to stay with their parents at least 10
days because they need the secretion provided by the
parents. Other rearing foods cannot replace it. Still, the fry
should not stay with their parents too long because they
will eventually "overgraze" their parents and damage their
slime skin. Because of their continued willingness to
provide for their brood, the parents do not drive the young
away. *Note*: Breeding this fish is not easy, but it is possible if a pair is kept in a maintenance tank with water of
the perfect properties. Another method is to place a pair in
a breeding tank (28 x 28 x 28 inches or 70 x 70 x 70 cm).
To keep the water as clean as possible, do without bottom
material and plants and provide only two flat rocks and a
spawning cone or a conical clay vase placed upside
down. Water: 1–3 DH; pH up to 6.5; 82–88°F (28–31°C).
Biotope: Sections of deep, calm water with submerged
trees in clear and white water in Amazonia. The fish live
in groups among the branches of these trees. *Similar
species*: In nature there are many forms of discus fish,
some of which are considerably more demanding than the
brown discus, among them the blue discus. There are
also many cultivated color strains (such as "royal blue"
and turquoise discus) that are the result of years of selective breeding.

ngelfish (*Pterophyllum scalare*)
inches (15 cm). *Tank*: 32 inches (80 cm), at least 20 ches (50 cm) tall. *Stratum*: Middle. *Water*: pH 5.5–7.5; oft to medium hard; 75–82°F (24–28°C). *Set-up*: Tank ith large-leaved plants, muted lighting, and roots that each to the water surface. Peaceful species that does not urrow. It tends to form shoals but is territorial during the pawning season. Keep in pairs; in tanks of at least 40 ches (100 cm), a group of about six fish can be kept. Tip n communities: Calm fishes but not too small and slener ones (such as cardinal tetras) because these may get aten. *Food*: Live and dry food. *Sexual differences*: Unnown. *Breeding*: Open-water brooder that prefers vertical urfaces. Parental family. The hatched larvae are glued ack onto the spawning substrate and later moved into ts. Both parents look after the fry. Start feeding with rtemia. *Special remarks*: There are a number of different ultivated varieties (such as the marbled, veiltail, and olden angelfish); these often have hidden traits of degenration. *Biotope*: The deeper strata of calm or moving ver sections among brush or rocks; distributed almost roughout Amazonia. *Similar species*: *P. altum* is suitable r taller, larger tanks with acid, soft water but is more fficult to care for (see photo, page 36).

Species belonging to the genus *Geophagus* do not display their full beauty until they reach maturity. Juvenile fish do not yet have the gorgeous colors and elongated fins of the adults.

Geophagus spec. aff. altifrons
0 inches (25 cm). *Tank*: 48 inches (120 cm). *Strata*: ottom, middle. *Water*: pH 6–7.5; soft to hard; 79–86°F 26–30°C). *Set-up*: Tank with fine-grained bottom material nd large shelters (roots). The fish dig through the upper ayers of sand in search of food. Tip on communities:)ther calm cichlids, catfishes, larger characins. *Food*: Mosquito larvae, small earthworms, plus dry food. *Sexual ifferences*: Males somewhat more colorful, with elonated, pointed ventral and caudal fins. *Breeding*: Ovophile nouthbrooder with parental family. When a pair has ormed, the eggs are deposited on a solid substrate and

then immediately picked up in the mouth. Start feeding with *Artemia*. *Biotope*: Probably the same as for other *Geophagus* species, namely, sandy, muddy, pebbly, or rocky areas of fairly big rivers (often near submerged wood). Exact place of origin unknown. *Similar species*: Other *Geophagus* as well as *Satanoperca* species. All *Geophagus* species used to be called *G. surinamensis*. Now we know that there are more than 10 different, similar-looking species. In spite of their external similarity, there are great differences in reproductive behavior, and the group includes both substrate brooders and mouthbrooders.

During the courtship phase the abdomen of the female *Crenicichla anthurus* is pink to red. The female alone assumes responsibility for tending the eggs and larvae, while the male defends the territory. Once the young swim free, both parents look after the offspring.

Crenicichla anthurus
10 inches (25 cm). *Tank*: 48 inches (120 cm). *Strata*: Bottom, middle. *Water*: pH 6–7.5; soft to hard; 75–82°F (24–28°C). *Set-up*: Tank with caves to hide in and plants. Keep adult fish in pairs. Juveniles are very aggressive amongst each other and should be raised in large numbers (8–10) in large tanks so that their aggression becomes dissipated. Provide pipe-shaped hiding places below the water surface for weaker fish to retreat to. Once pairs have formed, catch and remove the other fish. Tip on communities: Large, high-backed cichlids, Loricariidae catfishes. *Food*: Nutritious live food, fish. *Sexual differences*: Females have white markings on dorsal fin.

Breeding: Cavity brooder with father/mother family. Start feeding with *Artemia*. *Biotope*: Clear rivers with leaf litter on bottom and submerged wood in the Peruvian and Ecuadorian watershed of the Amazon. *Similar species*: Other *Crenicichla* species. Of these, *C. regani* and *C. notophthalmus* remain small and have been available for some time. Both measure about 4¾ inches (12 cm) but are demanding in terms of water quality (soft and acid), and the suppressed females need pipe-shaped retreats.

Paraguay Mouthbrooder (*Gymnogeophagus balzanii*) 7 inches (18 cm). *Tank*: 48 inches (120 cm). *Strata*: Bottom, middle. *Water*: pH 6.5–7.5; soft to hard; 75–82°F (24–28°C). *Set-up*: Tank with large roots and large-leaved plants in the background. Tip on communities: Only calm species such as Loricariidae catfishes, *Geophagus* cichlids and related genera. *Food*: Nutritious live and dry food. *Sexual differences*: Males develop a large lump on the head, especially if other males are present. Females are smaller. *Breeding*: Larvophile mouthbrooder; mother family. Start feeding with *Artemia*. *Biotope*: Still and often swampy water along the Paraná River and in Paraguay.

Tips on Care of Other Species

Dwarf cichlid (*Apistogramma borellii*)
2⅜ inches (6 cm). Tank: 20 inches (50 cm). Strata: Bottom, middle. Water: pH 6.5–7.5; soft to hard; 75–79°F (24–26°C). Care as for *A. agassizii*. Does not form harems.

Golden-eyed Dwarf Cichlid
(*Nannacara anomala*)
3½ inches (9 cm). Tank: 24 inches (60 cm). Strata: Bottom, middle. Water: pH 6–7.5; soft to hard; 79–84°F (26–29°C). Robust. Tends toward cavity brooding.

Oscar or Velvet Cichlid (*Astronotus ocellatus*)
14 inches (35 cm). Tank: 60 inches (150 cm). Stratum: Middle. Water: pH 6-7.5; soft to hard; 79-86 F (26-30 C). Nutritious food, such as earthworms and fish meat. Calm species.

Mesonauta insignis
8 inches (20 cm). Tank: 48 inches (120 cm). Strata: Middle, top. Water: pH 6–7.5; soft to hard; 79–86°F (26–30°C). Roots, floating plants. Vegetarian food important. Open-water brooder.

Uaru amphiacanthoides
10 inches (25 cm). Tank: 48 inches (120 cm). Strata: Bottom, middle. Water: pH 5–7; soft to medium hard; 81–86°F (27–30°C). Dark tank, roots. Calm species. Possible to keep in small groups. Vegetarian food. Open-water brooder feeding young with skin secretion like the discus fish.

eir bizarre shapes, which differ so radically from the assical fish shape, and their amusing behavior are so riguing that many catfishes have become a regular ature of community tanks. However, one should not go it to buy just any catfish. With this kind of fish it is important to know not only what kind of diet it needs but also w large it will grow. There are some small ones, like the mored catfishes, which are comfortable in tanks of 16 to ? inches (40–80 cm), but there are also big ones, such the fascinating and imposing Pterogoplichthys gibbiceps, hich grows to between 12 and 20 inches (30–50 cm) and eds a big tank 60 to 80 inches (150–200 cm) in length.

hat You Should Know about Catfishes

here are probably over 2,000 species of catfishes, and ey are thus, along with the gobies, one of the most umerous fish orders. Catfishes are found all over the obe in the most varied habitats, and a few species have ven ventured into the oceans.

atfishes belong to about 34 families. Among those of terest to aquarists are:

callichthyd and armored catfishes (Callichthyidae), hich include, among others, the genera *Corydoras*, rochis, *Dianema*, and *Hoplosternum*;

sucker-mouth armored catfishes (Loricariidae), which clude, among others, the genera *Ancistrus*, eoparacanthicus, *Peckoltia*, *Farlowella*, *Otocinclus*, turisoma, and *Rineloricaria*; and

upside-down catfishes (Mochocidae), represented by e genus *Synodontis*.

istinguishing traits: Catfishes are easy to recognize by eir barbels and their scaleless skin. Many families have eveloped bony plates instead of scales. Since catfishes, ith very few exceptions, live on the bottom, their underde is flattened and the eyes are set relatively high in the ead.

are: Nocturnal catfishes, especially, need shelters and aves into which they can retreat. Soft bottom material is articularly important for burrowing species (such as the mored catfishes) and for species that dig themselves to the bottom material (like the croaking spiny catfish, mblydoras hancocki). Set up the tank with many shelters nd plants so that there are shaded places, where the shy sh can be watched during the day. Many individuals elonging to nocturnal catfish species will come out of eir hiding places during the day at feeding time. If this is ot the case, give these "night owls" an extra feeding in e evening, after the lighting is turned off.

ote: Most of the popular Callichthyidae and Schilbeidae atfishes are diurnal and lively fish.

ater: Except for catfishes from Lake Tanganyika and ake Malawi, all species thrive in soft to medium hard and lightly acid (pH 6–7) water. Most of them also show no iscomfort in hard, slightly alkaline water.

ommunities: Catfishes are ideal candidates for commuity tanks because they inhabit niches on the bottom and helters not occupied by other aquarium dwellers. Only e combination with cichlids can sometimes become problematic if the cichlids extend their territorial claims to include the entire tank.

Behavior: There are shoaling and group catfishes that get along peacefully with each other, and there are unfriendly loners who always keep at a minimum distance from their neighbors. During the mating season many catfishes (for instance, Loricariidae) claim territories around a cave or another favored spot. This territory is defended against other members of the species, leading sometimes to violent conflict. In species that perform parental care it is usually the father who looks after the brood until the fry start foraging for food on their own.

Hints on breeding: Many catfishes will spawn in a community tank, but there are also many species that have not yet reproduced in captivity.

Species without brood care (such as the armored catfishes) attach their eggs to plants, stones, or the walls of the tank. Remove eggs carefully with a razor blade and place them in a rearing tank or a spawning box (see HOW TO page 53, "Breeding Fish"). When the young have used up the contents of their yolk sac, they are first fed with *Artemia* and microworms.

Species with brood care: The eggs are left in the maintenance tank until they hatch (in the case of *Ancistrus* species, until the fry start swimming). Then the larvae or fry are siphoned off and placed in a rearing tank (for first food, see descriptions of individual species). Very important: During the first weeks of life, part of the water has to be changed every day.

Leopard Catfish (*Corydoras trilineatus*)
2⅜ inches (6 cm). *Tank*: 24 inches (60 cm). *Stratum*: Bottom. *Water*: pH 6–7.5; soft to hard; 77–82°F (25–28°C). *Set-up*: Tank with shelters created by plants or roots; bottom material soft in places. Group fish, diurnal. Tip on communities: No larger cichlids; otherwise a good community fish. *Food*: Smallish live and dry food. *Sexual differences*: Females plumper. *Breeding*: As for *C. aeneus*, but does not enter mating mood as readily. *Special remarks*: This species is often sold as *C. julii*. *Biotope*: Above areas with soft bottom in still and moving waters of the Amazon watershed in Peru.

Some armored catfishes display some remarkable reproductive behavior patterns. The emerald catfish is an example. When mating, the male holds on to the female's barbels with his pectoral fins. During copulation, which lasts only seconds, both eggs and sperm cells are released.

Emerald or Short-bodied Catfish (*Brochis splendens*)
3 inches (8 cm). *Tank*: 32 inches (80 cm). *Stratum*: Bottom. *Water*: pH 6–7.5; soft to hard; 73–81°F (23–27°C). *Set-up*: Tank with fine-grained bottom material, shelters (roots, large-leaved plants). Diurnal species. The gorgeous, metallic emerald sheen develops only if good water quality is maintained. Tip on communities: No larger cichlids; otherwise a good community fish. *Food*: Varied diet of dry and smallish live food. *Sexual differences*: Females plumper and larger. *Breeding*: More difficult to get to spawn than *Corydoras aeneus*. These fish spawn against plant leaves and stones after a change to cooler water. Pick eggs off or remove leaves or stones and

transfer them to rearing tanks. Start feeding with *Artemia* microworms, dry food tablets. Reproductive behavior: Armored catfishes spawn in groups and will spawn in pairs only if in dire necessity. Each female needs two or three males. Spawning is preceded by intense activity. The female approaches the male from the side and presses her mouth against his pectoral area. Then the male holds fast to the female's barbels with his pectoral fins. Now a number of eggs move into the pocket-like ventral fin of the female, where they are fertilized by the male. After the partners have separated, the female attaches the eggs to a firm substrate. *Biotope*: Along banks, with dense vegetation, of slow-moving rivers in Peru, Brazil, and Ecuador.

Bronze Catfish (*Corydoras aeneus*)
2¾ inches (7 cm). *Tank*: 24 inches (60 cm). *Stratum*: Bottom. *Water*: pH 6–7.5; soft to hard; 77–82°F (25–28°C). *Set-up*: Bottom material soft in places. Diurnal species. Keep at least 5 specimens. Tip on communities: No larger cichlids; otherwise a good community fish. *Food*: Small-sized types and tablets. *Sexual differences*: Females larger and plumper. *Breeding*: Spawns against glass walls, leaves, or stones after a change to cooler water. Transfer eggs to rearing tank. Start feeding with *Artemia*, microworms, and dry food tablets. *Biotope*: Sandy areas of slow-moving rivers from Venezuela to the Río de la Plata.

Corydoras panda
2 inches (5 cm). *Tank*: 24 inches (60 cm). *Stratum*: Bottom. *Water*: pH 73–79°F (23–26°C). *Set-up*: Lightly planted tank. Good water maintenance important! Diurnal species. Keep in small groups. Tip on communities: No larger cichlids; otherwise a good community fish. *Food*: Fond of food tablets and frozen *Cyclops*; also eats small live food. *Sexual differences*: Females plumper. *Breeding*: Spawns against glass walls and in Java moss. Otherwse like *C. aeneas*. More likely to spawn during the colder half of the year. *Biotope*: Clear water with partially sandy bottom in the southern tributaries of the Peruvian Amazon.

warf Catfish or Pygmy Corydoras
(*Corydoras hastatus*)
⅜ inches (3.5 cm). *Tank*: 16 inches (40 cm). *Stratum*: iddle. *Water*: pH 6–7.5; soft to hard; 77–82°F (25–28°C). et-up: Tank with partial dense planting. Diurnal shoaling sh. Tip on communities: Small, delicate fishes. *Food*: yclops, small *Daphnia*, *Artemia*, small food flakes. exual differences: Males about ¾ inch (1 cm) smaller, immer. *Breeding*: Eggs are deposited primarily in Java oss after a water change with cooler water. Transfer ggs to a rearing tank. Start feeding with *Artemia*. iotope: In open water close to the bank in small tributar-s, Mato Grosso, Brazil. *Similar species*: C. pygmaeus.

Stripe-tailed Catfish (*Dianema urostriata*)
About 4¾ inches (12 cm). *Tank*: 40 inches (100 cm). *Strata*: Bottom, middle. *Water*: pH 6–7.5; soft to hard; 77–82°F (25–28°C). *Set-up*: Tank with roots, largish plants, floating plants. Diurnal group fish. Tip on communities: Calm fishes. *Food*: Mosquito larvae, small crustaceans, also worm foods. *Sexual differences*: Females bigger, plumper. *Breeding*: Males engage in parental care; they guard the brood in a bubble nest below the water surface. Transfer free-swimming brood to a rearing tank. Start feeding with *Artemia*. *Biotope*: Often in water left behind after flooding and in puddles along the Río Negro near Manáos. *Similar species*: D. longibarbis, 3½ inches (9 cm).

Leoparacanthicus galaxias
About 12 inches (30 cm). *Tank*: 48 inches (120 cm). *Stratum*: Bottom. *Water*: pH 6–7.5; soft to hard; 74–82°F (24–28°C). *Set-up*: Tank with many hiding places among roots. Robust plants. Tip on communities: Medium-sized and large fishes, including cichlids. *Food*: Nutritious live food, vegetables, and food tablets. *Sexual differences*: Unknown. *Breeding*: Unknown. *Biotope*: Fast-moving sections (with submerged wood) of the Río Guama and the Tocantins River, Brazil. *Caution*: Can pinch with its pointed teeth when lifted out!

Pterygoplichthys gibbiceps

12–20 inches (30-50 cm). *Tank*: 60–80 inches (150–200 cm). *Stratum*: Bottom. *Water*: pH 6.5–7.5; soft to hard; 77–86°F (25–30°C). *Set-up*: Large tank with roots in the background and some clear bottom area in the front. Very peaceful species. Is active at dusk and at night. Grazes algae everywhere but does not damage plants. Tip on communities: Gets along with smaller fishes. *Food*: Trout pellets, vegetarian food, smaller fish; also food tablets and live food. Feed in the evening: *Sexual differences*: Unknown. *Breeding*: Unknown. *Biotope*: Calm, slow-moving rivers in the watershed of the Río Negro, Brazil. These fish are found there in groups that move slowly across the bottom. *Similar species*: Spotted members of the *Hypostomus* genus. In nature, these species spawn in earth cavities. They, too, need large tanks with plenty of hiding places. *Note*: The genus name *Pterygoplichthys* will be changed in the near future.

Chaetostoma spec.

About 2¾ inches (7 cm). *Tank*: 20 inches (50 cm). *Stratum*: Substrate-dependent. *Water*: pH 6.5–7.5; soft to medium hard; 68–75°F (20–24°C); oxygen-rich. *Set-up*: Tank with circulation that moves the water across large pebbles. Tip on communities: Shoaling fishes. *Food*: Vegetarian, small crustaceans (frozen), food tablets. *Sexual differences*: Males have bigger, blockier snout. *Breeding*: Male guards eggs deposited in areas sheltered from current. Raise young in a spawning box with circulation. Feed with *Artemia*, blanched spinach, food tablets. *Biotope*: Areas with scree in rushing streams and rivers in the Andes and their foothills.

ckoltia pulcher

out 3 inches (8 cm). *Tank*: 24 inches (60 cm). *Stratum*: bstrate-dependent. *Water*: pH 6.5–7.5; soft to hard; –82°F (24–28°C). *Set-up*: Tank with refuges made up roots. Robust species. Tip on communities: Good mmunity fish; also compatible with larger cichlids. *Food*: nall live and fine-grade dry food; vegetables for rasping . *Sexual differences*: Some fish periodically develop rdened areas with bristles on the head and the caudal duncle. These are probably males. *Breeding*: Unknown; bably similar to *Ancistrus*. *Biotope*: Rivers in South nerica.

Ancistrus spec. aff. dolichopterus

5½ inches (14 cm). *Tank*: 32 inches (80 cm). *Strata*: Substrate-dependent, bottom. *Water*: pH 6–8; soft to hard; 77–84°F (25–29°C). *Set-up*: Tanks with roots and caves to hide in. Keep several males, but only in large tanks because they establish territories. Tip on communities: Even tiny fishes. *Food*: Live and dry food, vegetables. Algae eater; roots for rasping on are very important! *Sexual differences*: Females smaller, with smaller antennae on the head. *Breeding*: When the young swarm at the end of the male's brood care, raise them separately on food tablets and *Artemia*. *Biotope*: Still and moving water with submerged wood in the Amazon watershed.

Chocolate-colored Catfish

(*Rineloricaria spec. aff. lanceolata*) 5⅛ inches (13 cm). *Tank*: 24 inches (60 cm). *Stratum*: Bottom. *Water*: pH 6–7.5; soft to hard; 77–82°F (24–28°C). *Set-up*: Tank with pipe-shaped hiding places (bamboo canes, clay pipes) that are just barely wide enough for the fish to fit (spawning sites). Fine-grained bottom material; good aeration. Tip on communities: Other fishes that are not overly robust; no larger cichlids. *Food*: Food tablets, small live food, some vegetables. *Sexual differences*: Males have whiskers. *Breeding*: Males look after the spawn in the pipe-like shelters. Transfer brood to rearing tank after they swarm. Start feeding with *Artemia*. *Biotope*: Small, clear rivers in the Amazon watershed. *Similar species*: Other species of the genera *Rineloricaria* and *Dasyloricaria*.

Sturisoma aureum

12 inches (30 cm). *Tank*: 48 inches (120 cm). *Stratum*:
Bottom. *Water*: pH 6–7.5; soft to hard; 77–84°F (25–29°C)
Set-up: Some open bottom area; pieces of root placed
horizontally. Light circulation. Close monitoring of the
water is essential! *Food*: Vegetables for rasping on; also
blanched peas, small live food, food tablets. *Sexual differences*: Males have whiskers. *Breeding*: Fish usually
spawn against glass walls. Take eggs away from the
parenting father shortly before they hatch (sixth or sev-
enth day). When the contents of the yolk sac are used up
(four days after hatching), start feeding with blanched
spinach and food tablets. Good aeration in the rearing
tank important. For artificial rearing: If eggs become
detached from their substrate in hard water, siphon them
up with a hose. If the male is not tending the brood, care
fully remove the eggs that are still sticking to the substrat
with a razor blade. In either case, transfer eggs to a sma
rearing tank and add a fungicide to the water. Change
about 80 percent of the water twice a day and add fungicide to the new water. As soon as you notice that the
young are beginning to hatch or a few hours before the
time they are due to hatch according to your calculations
imitate what a brood-caring father would do and brush th
eggs very gently with a soft, fine paint brush until the egg
skins slip off. *Biotope*: On sandy or muddy bottom with
submerged wood in rivers of the Amazon watershed.

Midget Sucker Catfish (*Otocinclus spec. aff. affinis*)
1½ inches (4 cm). *Tank*: 12 inches (30 cm). *Stratum*:
Substrate-dependent. *Water*: pH 6–7.5; soft to hard;
72–79°F (22–26°C). *Set-up*: Dense plants and clear,
circulating water. Tip on communities: Fishes up to medium size and not predatory. *Food*: Vegetarian food, small
live food, food tablets. *Sexual differences*: Females are
fatter at times. *Breeding*: Has seldom succeeded. The
eggs are deposited on leaves and glass walls but not
cared for. Transfer them to a rearing tank. Start feeding
with blanched spinach, dry food. *Biotope*: Rivers with
vegetation in southeastern Brazil.

Needle catfishes have to get plenty of varied food. Because they eat at night, they have to be fed in the evening. If they are fed during the day, they may starve to death. Specimens that wander around restlessly in the tank and are thin as rails are starving!

?edle Catfishes (*Farlowella spec.*)
10 inches (15–25 cm), depending on species. *Tank*: 32
:hes (80 cm). *Stratum*: Substrate-dependent. *Water*: pH
·7.5; soft to hard; 75–82°F (24–28°C). *Set-up*: Tank with
1g roots placed horizontally. Best kept in pairs, one pair
a tank. Males establish territories and keep subordinate
ales from eating. Tip on communities: Very small fishes
at don't compete for food by foraging on the bottom.
ombination with food rivals can result in this fish's starv-
g to death! *Food*: Vegetables to rasp on and frozen live
od; food tablets. Roots for rasping on are crucial be-
_use they provide essential roughage. *Sexual differ-

ences*: Males have whiskers. *Breeding*: As for *Sturisoma
aureum*. Remove female after spawning so that the male
can proceed with brood care undisturbed. Vegetable food
essential as rearing food, but *Artemia* and food tablets
can also be tried. Artificial rearing of the eggs is possible
(as described for *Sturisoma aureum*). *Special remarks*:
There are many different *Farlowella* species, and exact
identification is difficult. *Biotope*: Shallow shore areas of
still and moving water with lots of wood or plants, throughout the Amazon region.

?ysichthys coracoideus
out 4¾ inches (12 cm). *Tank*: 24 inches (60 cm). *Stra-
m*: Bottom. *Water*: pH 6.5–7.5; soft to hard; 77–82°F
5–28°C). *Set-up*: Sandy bottom. This species likes to
urrow into wilted beech leaves. Nocturnal species. Tip on
ommunities: No small fishes. *Food*: Worms, small live
od; feed in the evening. *Sexual differences*: Females
umper. *Breeding*: Has seldom succeeded. Fish some-
mes spawn after sudden cooling through water change.
lace eggs in rearing tank; feeding with *Artemia*. *Biotope*:
mong leaves on the bottom and roots of floating plants in
ill and slowly moving water in the Amazon region.

Pimelodus pictus
About 4¾ inches (12 cm). *Tank*: 48 inches (120 cm).
Strata: Bottom, middle. *Water*: pH 6.5–7.5; soft to hard;
77–82°F (25–28°C). *Set-up*: Tank with plenty of open
water for swimming. Strong filtration that creates water
circulation. Group fish. Tip on communities: No small
fishes because they may get eaten. *Food*: Nutritious live
and dry food. *Sexual differences*: Unknown. *Breeding*:
Unknown. *Special remarks*: Suffers from lack of exercise
in tanks that are too small. *Biotope*: Above muddy, sandy,
or pebbly ground in shallow, often murky water of tributaries of larger rivers in Peruvian Amazonia.

141

Croaking Spiny Catfish (*Amblydoras hancocki*)
6 inches (15 cm). *Tank*: 32 inches (80 cm). *Stratum*:
Bottom. *Water*: pH 6–7.5; soft to hard; 77–84°F (25–29°C).
Set-up: Sand in some areas of the bottom; hiding places.
Nocturnal, peaceful species. Tip for communities: Aquarium fishes of at least medium size. *Food*: Nutritious live
and dry food; feed in the evening. *Sexual differences*: Males
have brown sprinkles on the belly. *Breeding*: Reportedly
males build nest and species engages in brood care.
Biotope: Along the bottom of still or slow-moving water in
the Amazon lowlands. *Similar species*: *Platydoras costatus*,
8 inches (20 cm); *Agamyxis flavopictus*, 6⅜ inches (16 cm);
Acanthodoras spinoissimus 6 inches (15 cm).

Black Clown Catfish or Polkadot African Catfis
(*Synodontis angelicus*)
About 9½ inches (24 cm). *Tank*: 48 inches (120 cm).
Stratum: Bottom. *Water*: pH 6–7.5; soft to hard; 75–82°
(24–28°C). *Set-up*: Tank with many roots to provide shelte
open water for swimming along the bottom. Sometimes
members of the species are incompatible. Tip on comm
nities: Fishes that are not too small (over 2½ inches or 6
cm). *Food*: Medium-sized live food, food tablets, vegeta
ian food. *Sexual differences*: Unknown. *Breeding*: Unknown. *Biotope*: Unknown. Found in the watershed of th
Zaire River in Zaire and southern Cameroon. *Similar sp
cies*: *S. nigrita*, *S. schoutedeni*.

Upside-down Catfish (*Synodontis nigriventris*)
4 inches (10 cm). *Tank*: 32 inches (80 cm). *Strata*: Middle,
top. *Water*: pH 6–7.5; soft to medium hard; 75–82°F
(24–28°C). *Set-up*: Tank with plenty of roots, well planted.
Keep in groups. Good community fish. *Food*: Primarily
black mosquito larvae but also other live food and food
tablets. *Sexual differences*: Females clearly fatter when
getting ready to spawn. *Breeding*: Has occasionally
succeeded. Simulating rainy season conditions probably
helps bring about mating readiness. Start feeding with
Artemia. *Biotope*: Along banks with vegetation of smallish
to largish rivers in the Zaire River watershed.

Cuckoo Catfish (*Synodontis petricola*)
4¾ inches (12 cm). *Tank*: 48 inches (120 cm). *Stratum*:
Bottom. *Water*: pH 7.5–9; medium hard to hard; 77–81°
(25–27°C). *Set-up*: A Tanganyika Lake tank with mouthbrooding species, such as *Tropheus*, from the rocky
zones. Keep a small group. *Food*: Live and dry food.
Sexual differences: Unknown. *Breeding*: These catfish
spawn when mouthbrooders (cichlids) spawn and sneak
their eggs in among the cichlid's eggs. The catfish brood
then feeds on the cichlid eggs and later emerges from th
mouthbrooder's mouth. *Biotope*: Rocky biotopes in Lake
Tanganyika.

Eutropiellus buffei

3 inches (8 cm). *Tank*: 32 inches (80 cm). *Stratum*: Middle. *Water*: pH 6–7.5; soft to hard; 75–81°F (24–27°C). *Set-up*: Tank with circulation. Good water maintenance important. Diurnal shoaling fish that swims a lot. Good community fish. *Food*: All types of fairly fine-grade food. *Sexual differences*: Females plumper. *Breeding*: Probably simulation of rainy season conditions plays an important role in bringing about mating readiness. Spawns against plants; does not engage in brood care. Start feeding with Artemia. *Biotope*: River banks, often in floodplains, Nigeria. *Similar species*: E. debauwi, which can be told apart from this species by the rounded tips of the caudal fin.

Ghost Catfish or Glass Catfish (*Kryptopterus minor*)
2¾ inches (7 cm). *Tank*: 32 inches (80 cm). *Stratum*: Middle. *Water*: pH 6-7.5; soft to hard; 75–82°F (24–28°C). *Set-up*: Tank with dense planting on sides and back; floating plants; light circulation. Good water maintenance important. Diurnal shoaling fish. Tip on communities: Other catfishes, shoaling fishes. *Food*: Small to medium-ized live food; is not likely to adjust to dry food. *Sexual differences*: Females plumper. *Breeding*: Thus far only accidental. Open-water spawner above plants. Simulating rainy season conditions helps during the maturing of the eggs. *Biotope*: Southeast Asia, Sumatra, Borneo.

Tips on Care of Other Species

Ancistrus spec. aff. hoplogenys
8 inches (20 cm). Tank: 40 inches (100 cm). Stratum: Substrate-dependent. Water: pH 6–7; soft to medium hard; 77–82°F (25–28°C). Tanks with roots that have big holes in which the fish spawn. Vegetables important for the fish to rasp on.

Baryancistrus spec.
About 12 inches (30 cm). Tank: 48 inches (120 cm). Stratum: Substrate-dependent (bottom). Water: pH 6–7.5; soft to hard; 79–86°F (26–30°C). Tank with roots. Vegetables important for the fish to rasp on.

Hypancistrus zebra
About 3½ inches (9 cm). Tank: 24 inches (60 cm). Stratum: Bottom. Water: pH 6–7.5; soft to hard; 77–82°F (25–28°C). Tank with round pebbles; also wood. Foods from vegetable and animal sources.

Corydoras robineae
3 inches (8 cm). Tank: 32 inches (80 cm). Strata: Bottom, middle. Water: pH 6–7.5; soft to medium hard; 75–82°F (24–28°C). Breeding is possible. Fast-growing brood.

Peppered Corydoras (*Corydoras paleatus*)
2¾ inches (7 cm). Tank: 32 inches (80 cm). Stratum: Bottom. Water: pH 6.5–8; soft to hard; 64–73°F (18–23°C). Tank with sand and broad-leaved plants. Food tablets and small live food. Robust species.

Hoplo Catfish or Spotted "Callichthys" (*Hoplosternum thoracatum*)
7 inches (18 cm). Tank: 40 inches (100 cm). Strata: All. Water: pH 6–7.5; soft to hard; 77–86°F (25–30°C). Calm fish for a community tank with medium-sized fishes. Bubble nest builder.

Microglanis iheringi
2¾ inches (7 cm). Tank: 20 inches (50 cm). Stratum: Bottom. Water: pH 6–7.5; soft to medium hard; 75–82°F (24–28°C). Dark, densely planted tank. Mosquito larvae and *Tubifex*. Small fishes.

Mystus micracanthus
About 4 inches (10 cm). Tank: 40 inches (100 cm). Strata: Bottom, middle. Water: pH 6–7; soft to hard; 79–84°F (26–29°C). Community tank with medium-sized fishes. Dark tank; caves for hiding; plants.

Synodontis brichardi
8 inches (20 cm). Tank: 48 inches (120 cm). Stratum: Bottom. Water: pH 6–7.5; soft to hard; 73–81°F (23–27°C). Tank with circulation. Sometimes aggressive among each other.

Pangasius spec.
Over 40 inches (1 m). Tank: circular aquarium holding at least 1,500 gallons (6,000 L). Stratum: Middle. Water: pH 6–7.5; soft to hard; 77–84°F (25–29°C). This species is sold despite its size! Keeping it in a living room aquarium is sheer cruelty to animals.

Most gobies are marine fishes, but many are found in the brackish water of estuaries and in fresh water as well.

What You Should Know about Gobies

There are about 2,000 species of gobies, which makes them one of the largest fish groups. The two biggest and best-known families are the Eleotrididae (the "sleepers") and the Gobiidae ("true" gobies).

Characteristic traits: The body of most species is elongated and somewhat compressed laterally. Usually there are two dorsal fins. The ventral fins of the "true" gobies are usually grown together and form a suction disk that enables the fish to attach themselves to stones and other stationary substrates. Eleotrididae have separate ventral fins.

Care: Most gobies like hiding places. Depending on the species, small hiding places and shelters formed by rocks, wood, or plant thickets are appropriate. Many species happily accept pipes with an inside diameter that is just slightly bigger than their girth. Pieces of flowerpots pressed into the bottom material are also accepted as spawning sites. For shy species, a cover of floating plants is advisable. Most species have to be fed live food.

Water: Although many goby species are found in very soft water, medium hard to hard water that is neutral to alkaline is recommended for them in an aquarium. For species that occur in brackish water, the aquarist should add some sea salt (about 1 ounce [30 g] per 10 quarts of water).

Communities: Bottom-dwelling gobies can be combined without any problems with fishes of the middle and upper water strata. Fishes that are very active may become food rivals against whom the gobies are unable to assert themselves. On the other hand, gobies (especially the "sleepers") are quite predatory and capable of swallowing fishes almost as long as themselves. Gobies should not be combined with fishes that establish territories on the bottom (cichlids, many catfishes).

Behavior: Being territorial and having developed distinct brood care habits on the part of the male, gobies display a rich repertoire of behavior. If several males of the same species are kept in a fairly large tank, one can often observe intimidation displays and fighting. To prevent serious injuries, provide a large number of hiding places.

Hints on breeding: Most gobies spawn in hidden caves. Parental care normally ceases when the larvae hatch. Only species that produce a small number of large eggs can be reared easily, because the young immediately start eating *Artemia* and other easily obtainable foods. The fry have to be raised separated from their parents. The easiest method is to move the eggs, along with the substrate to which they are attached, to a rearing tank shortly before the larvae hatch. Attempts to breed species with free-swimming larvae have succeeded only rarely to date.

Euctenogobius badius

4 inches (10 cm). *Tank*: 32 inches (80 cm). *Stratum*: Bottom. *Water*: pH 6.5–8; medium hard to hard; 77–81°F (25–27°C). *Set-up*: Tank with river sand as bottom material. Fish dig and search for food in the sand. Each fish needs a hiding place. Tip on communities: No robust fishes. *Food*: Fine-grade dry and live food that sinks to the bottom. *Sexual differences*: Males have a bigger mouth. *Breeding*: The females spawn in the caves of the males. Nobody has yet succeeded in raising the tiny brood. *Special remarks*: Males fight with mouths gaping wide open. *Biotope*: Rivers on the Atlantic side of northern South America, probably over sandy bottom.

Rhinogobius wui

2 inches (5 cm). *Tank*: 16 inches (40 cm). *Stratum*: Bottom. *Water*: pH 6–7.5; medium hard to hard; 59–77°F (15–25°C). *Set-up*: Tank with some circulation. Many small hiding places around which the males claim small territories. Tip on communities: Small fishes that like circulation. *Food*: Small live food; no dry food. *Sexual differences*: Males have red lines on the gill lamellae; body and fins more brightly colored. *Breeding*: Raise young in separate tank on *Artemia*. *Biotope*: Small rivers in hilly country in southern China and Hongkong.

ьhlamydogobius eremius

⅜ inches (6 cm). *Tank*: 16 inches (40 cm). *Stratum*: ьottom. *Water*: pH 7–8.5; medium hard to hard; 70–79°F ⁈1–26°C). *Set-up*: Tank with many small caves along the ьottom. Keep one male with several females; in a tank of ⁈ least 24 inches (60 cm), two males can be kept. Tip on ьmmunities: Small fishes of the middle and upper strata. ⁈ood: Live and dry food, filamentous algae. *Sexual differ-* ⁈nces: Males bigger, more colorful. *Breeding*: Raise ьoung in a separate tank on *Artemia* and dry food. ⁈iotope: Various biotopes in the vicinity of Lake Eyre and ⁈ inlets in central Australia.

Tateurndina ocellicauda

2 inches (5 cm). *Tank*: 16 inches (40 cm). *Strata*: Bottom, middle. *Water*: pH 6–7.5; soft to medium hard; 79–84°F (26–29°C). *Set-up*: Well planted tank with several small caves. Keep one or two males with several females. This species also likes to be in the open water. *Food*: Live food as well as dry food. *Sexual differences*: Males have longer posterior rays on the second dorsal and the anal fins. *Breeding*: Males assume parental care of the eggs (which are deposited in a cave or on a substrate) and of the larvae. Raise the young in a separate tank on *Artemia*. *Biotope*: Clear, slowly moving water with plentiful vegetation, in New Guinea.

ьrachygobius doriae

¾ inches (4.5 cm). *Tank*: 16 inches (40 cm). *Strata*: All. ⁈ater: pH 7.5–8.5; medium hard to hard; 81–86°F (27– ⁈0°C). *Set-up*: Tank without circulation; small brooding ьavities (snail shells, short pieces of pipe). Keep 10 or ьore fish. Tip on communities: Only small, peaceful fishes ⁈uch as other small gobies or glass perch). *Food*: Daph-ьia, *Cyclops*, *Artemia*, and small mosquito larvae. *Sexual* ⁈ifferences: Females plumper. *Breeding*: Move eggs to ьearing tank. Start feeding the larvae with rotifers. *Biotope*: ьrackish water, with plants among which the fish, which ⁈therwise swim in open water, hide; western Indonesia.

Tips on Care of Other Species

Butis butis
6 inches (15 cm). Tank: 32 inches 80 cm). Strata: Bottom, middle. Water: pH 7–8; medium hard to hard; 77–82°F (25–28°C). Predatory species; needs nutritious live food. Add sea salt to the water.

Mogurnda mogurnda
4–6¾ inches (10–17 cm). Tank: 32 inches (80 cm). Strata: Bottom, middle. Water: pH 6.5–8; medium hard to hard; 74–81°F (24–27°C). Nutritious live food. Do not combine with small fishes.

Hemieleotris latifasciatus
3–4¾ inches (8–12 cm). Tank: 32 inches (80 cm). Strata: Bottom, middle. Water: pH 6.5–7.5; soft to hard; 77–82°F (25–28°C). Peaceful species that likes to retreat into dense vegetation.

Stiphodon elegans
2 inches (5 cm). Tank: 24 inches (60 cm). Stratum: Bottom. Water: 6.5–7.5; soft to hard; 73–82°F (23–28°C). This species has a blue neon stripe. Requires circulation and algae *aufwuchs*.

Stigmatogobius sadanundio
3 inches (8 cm). Tank: 24 inches (60 cm). Strata: Bottom, middle. Water: pH 7–8.5; medium hard to hard; 77–82°F (25–28°C). Add sea salt to the water.

All the fishes that do not fit in any of the big groups dis-cussed in the preceding pages are brought together here under the heading "Oddities." They belong to the most varied and often very small families and orders.

What You Should Know about Odd Fishes

It is worthwhile paying some attention to odd fishes even if they do not catch one's eye with brilliant colors. Many of these fishes display interesting 'oddities' of behavior or appearance. Here are a few examples:

Fishes with electric organs: Some New World members of the orders Gymnoformes and Mormyriformes have weak electric organs and sensory cells that respond to electrical stimuli (electroreceptors). The electric organs constantly emit weak electric impulses that create an electric field around the fish. Objects and creatures that enter this field bring about changes in the field, which a fish senses through its electroreceptors. This way a fish knows what is going on in its vicinity even if it cannot see. Electric eels and elephant fishes are thus able to find their way about and forage for food at night or in murky water. These fishes, however, use their electric organs not just for taking in their surroundings and locating prey but also for communicating with each other by means of electric impulses.

Usually only species that emit weak impulses are kept in an aquarium. This weak electric current does not disturb other fishes and is also harmless for humans. There are fishes, though—not suitable for home aquariums—that emit powerful electric shocks when catching prey. Among these is the electric eel (*Electrophorus electricus*), which sends out shocks of over 500 volts and over 1 ampere.

Primordial fishes: Bichirs (Polypteridae) and reed fishes (both of the order Polypteriformes) are among the geologically oldest fishes kept in aquariums. They have existed virtually unchanged for many millions of years. Their larvae, like those of newts, have external gills that disappear in time.

Predators with perfect camouflage: Among these is the South American leaf fish (*Monocirrhus polyacanthus*). With its brownish color, it looks just like a dry leaf as it lies in wait or slowly approaches its prey in a diagonal, head-down position. It hunts for small fishes, which it practically sucks up into its mouth, which is huge in comparison to its overall size.

Blue perch are a solitary, quiet fish that should not be combined with other species. They are unable to compete successfully for food in a community tank.

Blue Perch (*Badis badis*)
2¾ inches (7 cm). *Tank*: 20 inches (50 cm). *Strata*: Middle, bottom. *Water*: pH 6–7.5; soft to hard; 77–82°F (25–28°C). *Set-up*: Densely planted tank with roots and small caves. Solitary, calm fish that cannot hold its own against food rivals in a community tank. Do not combine with other fishes! *Food*: Small live food; has to be gradually accustomed to frozen food. *Sexual differences*: The belly of the female is rounded in profile. *Breeding*: After the eggs are laid, the male alone looks first after the eggs and then after the larvae in small caves. Once the young swim free, feed them *Artemia* nauplii. *Special remarks*: There is also a red subspecies from Burma (*Badis badis burmanicus*) in which aquarists are showing increasing interest. *Biotope*: Still and slow-moving water with lots of vegetation, India. *Note*: The Badidae family is closely related to the labyrinth fishes.

Channa orientalis

 inches (15 cm). *Tank*: 32 inches (80 cm). *Strata*: bottom, middle. *Water*: pH 6–7.5; soft to hard; 73–79°F (23–26°C). *Set-up*: Planted tank with plenty of hiding places, light circulation, and diffused lighting. Keep in pairs. Tip on communities: Other calm, large fishes, but only as long as this species does not engage in brood care, because then the parents are extremely aggressive. *Food*: Nutritious live food. *Sexual differences*: Females are plumper. *Breeding*: Mouthbrooder that forms lasting pair bond. Male does mouth brooding; once the young swim free, the mother feeds them unfertilized eggs until they are a couple of inches long. Start feeding the young with small live food. *Biotope*: In fast-moving sections of small rainforest streams on Sri Lanka. *Similar species*: C. gachua. This species, which differs from *C. orientalis* by having ventral fins, does not feed its numerous young. is found in slower-moving parts of the same rivers (more likely downstream). *Note*: The unusual method of feeding larvae on eggs practiced by *C. orientalis* is an example of adaptation to the environment. Probably it evolved because there is not enough food for the young available in the biotope. The parents do better because they eat large insect larvae as well as small fish. They are thus able to build up food reserves for their offspring in the form of food eggs."

South American Leaf Fish

(*Monocirrhus polyacanthus*)
4 inches (10 cm). *Tank*: 24 inches (60 cm). *Stratum*: Middle. *Water*: pH 5–6.5; soft; 79–84°F (26–29°F). *Set-up*: Large-leaved plants, roots, dark bottom material, hiding places for weaker females if kept in pairs in small tanks. Do not combine with other fishes. *Food*: Mosquito larvae, small fish. No dry food. *Sexual differences*: Females developing spawn are somewhat rounder. *Breeding*: The males look after the eggs, which are deposited on a leaf. Start feeding with *Artemia*. *Biotope*: Shore vegetation of slow-moving or still water, Amazonia.

Indian Glass Perch (*Chanda ranga*)
2 inches (5 cm). *Tank*: 20 inches (50 cm). *Stratum*:
Middle. *Water*: pH 7–8.5; medium hard to hard; 75–82°F
(24–28°C). *Set-up*: Tank arranged in dark colors, with
dense, feathery-leaved plants. No wood from bogs.
Shoaling fish. Tip on communities: Only small, delicate
fishes. *Food*: *Daphnia*, *Cyclops*, *Artemia*. *Sexual differences*: Males are dark with iridescent blue rims on anal
and dorsal fins during spawning season. *Breeding*: Males
form small territories at spawning time. Fish spawn on
plants. Start feeding the hatching young with very small
live food (*Cyclops* nauplii) in high concentration. *Biotope*:
Fresh water and brackish water, Southeast Asia.

Reed Fish or Snake Fish
(*Calamoichthys calabaricus*)
12 (36?) inches (30 [90?] cm). *Tank*: 40 inches (100 cm).
Stratum: Bottom. *Water*: pH 6–7.5; soft to hard; 79–86°F
(26–30°C). *Set-up*: Tightly covered tank because these
snake-like fish escape easily. Dense planting. Hiding
places among roots. Keep two to five specimens. Tip on
communities: Only medium-sized to large fishes, but no
large cichlids. *Food*: Nutritious live food, fish meat cut in
strips. *Sexual differences*: Males have bigger, olive-
colored anal fin; this fin is ochre-colored in females.
Breeding: Unknown. *Biotope*: Marshy, vegetation-choked
water in the Niger delta.

Polypterus senegalus
12 inches (30 cm). *Tank*: 48 inches (120 cm). *Stratum*:
Bottom. *Water*: pH 6–7.5; soft to hard; 79–84°F (26–29°C).
Set-up: Hiding places in the back of the tank. Several fish
can be kept, best in pairs. These fish can become very
friendly. Tip on communities: Only medium-sized fishes.
Food: Nutritious live food, but also fish flesh cut in strips.
Sexual differences: The male's anal fin is wider. *Breeding*:
A water change with water a few degrees cooler will
stimulate spawning. Collect the scattered eggs and place
in a rearing tank. Start feeding with *Artemia* and soon with
larger food. The young have external gills. *Biotope*:

Marshy, vegetation-choked water in West and Central
Africa. *Similar species*: *P. ornatipinnis*, 18 inches (45 cm).
Note: This genus belongs to the order Polypteriformes,
which occurs only in Africa and is one of the oldest fish
groups, having existed unchanged for many million years.
Polypterus have a well developed sense of smell. With
slightly raised head they "sniff" if they sense that there is
food in the tank they have not yet located.

In its homeland, *Mastacembelus erythrotaenia*, which grows to about 40 inches (1 m), is a table fish. Because these large fish are aggressive toward each other in a tank, it is better to keep only one. It can be combined with large, deep-bodied fishes, such as vegetarian Serrasalmidae.

Mastacembelus erythrotaenia

Up to about 3 feet (1 m). *Tank*: 48 inches (120 cm). *Stratum*: Bottom. *Water*: pH 6–7.5; soft to hard; 75–82°F (24–28°C). *Set-up*: Dark tank with soft bottom material, dense planting, and hiding places (preferably clay pipes). Susceptible to ectoparasites. Tip on communities: Vegetarian Serrasalmidae; no small, slender fishes. *Food*: Nutritious live food, fish flesh, small dead fish. *Sexual differences*: Unknown. *Breeding*: Unknown. *Biotope*: Moving water, often with thick plant cushions and/or soft bottom, Southeast Asia. *Similar species*: *Macrognathus* spec. and a small *Mastacembelus* species have been bred in tanks. They are plant spawners that deposit

spawn in cushions of floating plants, such as *Ceratopteris pteridoides* or *Riccia fluitans*. Several males court one female. The eggs measure over 1/24 inch (1 mm). Start feeding with *Artemia* and small *Cyclops*. The young grow fast. Do not overfeed because the fry die if they overeat.

In the course of courtship and during spawning, glass knife fish emit "electrical" songs. With the aid of an amplifier, a loudspeaker, and two electrodes, we can hear these "songs."

Glass Knife Fish (*Eigenmannia lineata*)

About 10 inches (25 cm). *Tank*: 48 inches (120 cm). *Strata*: Middle, top. *Water*: pH 6–7.5; soft to hard; 77–84°F (25–29°C). *Set-up*: Cover of floating plants, preferably *Pistia stratiotes*. Keep a small group of four or five fish, preferably one male and three or four females. Unlike other knife fishes, this species is diurnal. Tip on communities: Only fishes of the bottom stratum or peaceful shoaling fishes that do not pull on fins. *Food*: Mosquito larvae. *Sexual differences*: Males larger, with a thicker caudal peduncle. *Breeding*: Stimulate spawning by imitating rainy season conditions with soft water (Kirschbaum method).

Gravid females spawn in the matted roots of "their" floating plant. Pick off the eggs and transfer them to a rearing tank. Start feeding them with *Artemia*. *Biotope*: Underneath meadows of floating plants in tropical South America. *Similar species*: Other *Eigenmannia* species that grow larger. Members of this genus are hard to tell apart; several species are imported. *Note*: The fish in this photo is a juvenile.

Butterfly Fish (*Pantodon buchholzi*)
4 inches (10 cm). *Tank*: 32 inches (80 cm). *Stratum*: Top.
Water: pH 6–7.5; soft to hard; 81–86°F (27–30°C). *Set-up*: Tank arranged in dark colors with partial cover of
floating plants. Cover well because this fish jumps; leave
four to eight inches (10–20 cm) between the water surface
and the cover. Tip on communities: Fishes of the lower
level; no fishes that pull on fins. *Food*: Large insects; also
small fish. No dry food. *Sexual differences*: Males have a
peculiarly shaped, concave anal fin. *Breeding*: Spawns
below water surface. Remove the floating eggs and transfer them to a rearing tank. Start feeding with *Artemia*.
Slight water circulation through an air stone is important
so that there are always enough *Artemia* carried close to
the surface where the brood is. Keep the water level low
in the rearing tank for the same reason. *Special remarks*:
This fish was given its name because of its fins, which
look like butterfly wings. The broad pectoral fins, which
resemble moth's wings, help the fish stay in the air on its
short flights above the water. *Biotope*: Still and slow-
moving water with dense shore vegetation, where these
fish catch insects below the water surface; West and
Central Africa.

African Knife Fish (*Xenomystus nigri*)
8–12 inches (20–30 cm). *Tank*: 40 inches (100 cm). *Strata*:
Bottom, middle. *Water*: pH 6–7.5; soft to hard; 79–84°F
(26–29°C). *Set-up*: Each fish needs its own hiding place
(such as clay pipes). Keep singly in tanks of 40 inches
(100 cm), in pairs in tanks over 48 inches (120 cm). *Food*:
Nutritious live food; also food tablets. *Sexual differences*:
Females have a more rounded belly. *Breeding*: Spawns in
holes and cracks. Transfer eggs to a rearing tank. Start
feeding with *Artemia*. *Special remarks*: These fish emit
barking sounds during courtship. *Biotope*: Still and slow-
moving water in West and Central Africa.

The very obvious proboscis, or trunk, which serves as a tactile organ, gave the long-nosed elephant fish its name. These fish are extremely intelligent and make great demands on the aquarist. Unfortunately this sensitive species is often improperly kept. Only experienced aquarists should include this fish in their aquariums.

Long-nosed Elephant Fish (*Gnathonemus petersi*) 9 inches (23 cm). *Tank*: 40 inches (40 cm). *Strata*: Bottom, middle. *Water*: pH 6–7.5; soft to hard; 75–81°F (24–27°C). *Set-up*: Tank with clay pipes as hiding places and shelters among wood or stones for every fish. Keep only one specimen in a 40-inch (100 cm) tank; a tank of at least 60 inches (150 cm) is needed for three fish because they defend their territories very aggressively against their fellows. Nocturnal species. Tip on communities: Small to medium-sized species; no cichlids! *Food*: Mosquito larvae, soaked *Tubifex*. Feed after the lights are turned off, otherwise these nocturnal fish starve if they have to compete for food. *Sexual differences*: Unknown. *Breeding*:

Unknown. *Special remarks*: Elephant fish, like electric eels, use electricity to communicate and orient themselves. *Biotope*: Moving water with submerged wood, from Nigeria to Cameroon. *Similar species*: Campylomormyrus tamandua, about 16 inches (40 cm). *Note*: The long-nosed elephant fish is used by water departments to test the quality of drinking water. Its electric charges change when water quality declines. This fish reacts more sensitively than many chemical measuring methods.

Green Pufferfish (*Tetraodon nigroviridis*) 8 inches (20 cm). *Tank*: 40 inches (100 cm). *Strata*: Bottom, middle. *Water*: pH 7.5–8.5; medium hard to hard; 75–82°F (24–28°C). *Set-up*: Hiding places among roots and stones; robust plants. Often bites. Best kept singly. Addition of salt (2 teaspoons of table salt per quart) recommended. Tip on communities: Only largish, robust fishes. *Food*: Nutritious live food; cleans up snails. *Sexual differences*: Unknown. *Breeding*: Unknown. *Special remarks*: Usually wrongly called *T. fluviatilis*. *Biotope*: Coastal areas in Indonesia. *Similar species*: *T. biocellatus*, ⅜ inches (6 cm); easier to combine with other species.

Tips on Care of Other Species

Apteronotus albifrons
About 10 inches (25 cm). Tank: 40 inches (100 cm); Strata: Bottom, middle. Water: pH 6–7.5; soft to hard; 77–82°F (25–28°C). Each fish needs a hiding place, preferably clay pipes.

Elephant Fish (*Pollimyrus isidori*)
About 3 inches (8 cm). Tank: 32 inches (80 cm). Strata: Bottom, middle. Water: pH 6–7.5; soft to hard; 77–82°F (25–28°C). Only live and frozen food. Can be encouraged to build nests and spawn through the "Kirschbaum method" of simulating rainy season conditions. Aggressive amongst each other.

Doryichthys martensi
5 inches (13 cm). Tank: 16 inches (40 cm). Strata: Bottom, middle. Water: pH 6–7.5; soft to hard; 79–84°F (26–29°C). Keep this species, like all freshwater pipefishes, by itself in a densely planted tank. Feed only with small live food, such as *Artemia*.

Carinotretraodon lorteti
2¾ inches (6 cm). Tank: 20 inches (50 cm). Strata: Bottom, middle. Water pH 6–6.5; soft to medium hard; 74–82°F (24–28°C). Sandy bottom with a rock, feathery-leaved plants. No other fishes. Aggressive toward its fellows as well as toward other species.

Thousand Dollar Knife Fish (*Notopterus chitala*)
40 inches (100 cm). Tank: 100 inches (250 cm). Strata: Bottom, middle. Water: pH 6–7.5; soft to hard; 75–82°F (24–28°C). Predatory.

Index

Page numbers in **boldface** type indicate color photos. **C1** = front cover; **C2** = front cover flap; **C3** = inside front cover flap; **C4** = inside front cover; **C5** = inside back cover; **C6** = inside back cover flap; **C7** = back cover flap; **C8** = back cover.

A

Acanthodoras spinoissimus, 142
Acanthophthalmus anguillaris. See Pangio anguillaris
Acanthophthalmus kuhlii. See Pangio kuhlii
Acanthophthalmus myersi. See Pangio myersi
Acanthophthalmus semicinctus. See Pangio semicinctus
Acanthopsis spec., **1,** 92, **92**
Acanthopsoides, 92
Accessories (aquarium), 22
Acidic, 62
Acidifier, 62
Acidity (pH)
  measuring, 12–13
  of water, 12
Aequidens curviceps. See Laetacara curviceps
Aequidens dorsiger. See Laetacara dorsiger
Aequidens vittata. See Bujurquina vittata
African knife fish, 150, **150**
Agamy, 59
Agamyxis flavopictus, 142
Agassiz's dwarf cichlid, 129, **129**
Alestes longipinnis. See Brycinus longipinnis
Alfaro cultratus, 97, **97**
Algae, 62
Algae-eater, 91, **91**
Alkaline, 62
Alnoldichthys spilopterus, 75, **75**
Alternanthera reineckii, **C5,** 27
Altolamprologus calvus, 112, **112**
  compressiceps, 112
Amblydoras hancocki, 142, **142**
Ambulia, **C5,** 27
Ameca splendens, 98, **98**
Ammania gracilis, **C5,** 28, 160
Ammonia (NH_3), 14–15, 62
Ammonia poisoning, 43–44
Ammonium (NH_4), 16
Ampullaria spec., 73
Anabantoidea, 105
Anal fin, 61

Ancistrus spec. aff. dolichopterus, 139, **139**
  hoplogenys, 143
Andropodium, 62
Angelfish, **2/3, 36,** 133, **133**
Angola barb, 84, **84**
Anomalochromis thomasi, 122, **122**
Anostomus anostomus, 80, **80**
Anubias barteri var. *nana,* **C5,** 29, **31**
Aphyosemion australe, **C3,** 101, **101**
  bualuanum kekemense, 104
  fallax, 101
  gardneri, 100, **100**
  sjoestedti, 101, **101**
  striatum, 100, **100**
Apistogramma agassizii, 129, **129**
  borellii, 134
  cacatuoides, 129, **129**
  spec. "Bigmouth," 129
Aplocheilichthys macropthalmus, 102, **102**
Aplocheilus panchax, 103, **103**
Aponogeton crispus, 28
Apteronotus albifrons, 151
Aquarium
  accessories for, 22
  chore schedule for, 24
  decorating materials for, 22
  filtration for, 21–22, 64
  fish for, 23–24
  heaters for, 20–21
  lighting for, 20
  plants for, 26–29, **30–31**
  safety around, 18, 20
  setting up, 22–23
  tank for, 18
  See also Biotope aquarium
Arnoldichthys spilopterus, 75, **75**
Arnold's red-eyed characin, 75, **75**
Arrowhead, 28
Artemia, **20,** 55, 62
Ascites, 62
Astronotus ocellatus, 134
Atherinidae, 89
Atyopsis moluccensis, 73
Aufwuchs, 62
Aufwuchs-eating cichlids, **33**
Aulonocara jacobfreibergi, 118, **118**

Awaous strigatus. See Euctenogobius badius

B

Bacopa caroliniana, **C6,** 27
Bacteria, 62
Badis badis, 146, **146**
  burmanicus, 146
Balantiocheilus melanopterus, 85
Bala shark, 85
Banana plant, **25**
Barbs, **C2, C3,** 81–85, **81–85**
Barbus barilioides, 84, **84**
  jae, 84
  conchonius. See Puntius conchonius
  nigrofasciatus. See Puntius nigrofasciatus
  oligolepis. See Puntius oligolepis
  pentazona. See Puntius pentazona
  semifasciolatus "schuberti." See Puntius semi-fasciolatus "schuberti"
  tetrazona. See Puntius tetrazona
  titteya. See Puntius titteya
Barclaya longifolia, 29, **31**
Baryancistrus spec., **43,** 143
Basic. *See* Alkaline
Beckford's pencil fish, 79, **79**
Bedotia geayi, 89, **89**
Belonesox belizanus, 99
Belontia hasselti, 109
Betta coccina, 109
  foerschi, 109
  imbellis, **C3, C8,** 107, **107**
  picta, 107
  pugnax, 107, **107**
  smaragdina, 109
  splendens, **19,** 107, **107**
Biotodoma cupido "Santarem," **C4,** 131, **131**
  wavrini, 131
Biotope, 62
Biotope aquarium, 32, 62
  for black-water Southeast Asian fishes, **36,** 37
  for rainforest stream, 37
  for rock cichlids from Lake Malawi, 33, **33**
  for rocky rapids fish, 35, **35**

for rocky Tanganyika tank with sandy area, 34, **34**
for sand/open-water of Great African Lakes, 32, **32**
for South American root biotope, 36, **36, 37**
for Southeast Asian still water, 36–37
Black Amazon, 28
Black clown catfish, 142, **142**
Black-finned pearl fish, 104
"Black molly," 96, **96**
Black neon tetra, 80
Black phantom tetra, 75, **75**
Black tetra, 77, **77**
Black-water, **36,** 37, 62
Bleeding heart tetras, **2/3**
Blockhead cichlid, 123, **123**
Blue discus, 37
Blue gourami, 105, **105**
Blue panchax, 103, **103**
Blue perch, 146, **146**
Blunt-headed cichlid, 114, **114**
Body covering, 60
Body shape, 60–61
Boehlkea fredcochui, 80, **80**
Boeseman's rainbow fish, 87, **87**
Bog roots, 62
Bolbitis heudelotii, 29
Botia eos, 90
  lecontei, 90
  lohachata, 93
  macracantha, 91, **91**
  modesta, 90, **90**
  morleti, 93
  sidthimunki, 90, **90**
  striata, 93
Bottom-dwellers, 60
Bottom material, 22
Bottom spawners, 57, 62
Brachydanio albolineatus, 85
  nigrofasciatus, 84
  rerio, **C3,** 84, **84**
Brachygobius doriae, 145, **145**
Breeding
  breeding (spawning) tank, 52, 54, 62
  feeding the brood, 53, 55
  ongoing, 53
  parent fish selection, 50
  spawning, 50–52

spawning boxes, 54
transferring eggs, larvae, or fry, 52–53
See also Reproduction
Brine shrimp, **20**, 62, 73
Broad-leaved rotala, 27
Brochis splendens, 136, **136**
Bronze catfish, 136, **136**
Brood-care species, 52–53, 58–59, 62
Brown discus, 132, **132**
Brycinus longipinnis, 74, **74**
Bujurquina vittata, 131, **131**
Bunocephalus coracoideus. See Dysichthys coracoideus
Butis butis, 145
Butterfly cichlid, 130, **130**
Butterfly fish, 150, **150**

C
Cabomba
caroliniana, 27
piauhyensis, **31**
Calamoichthys calabaricus, 148, **148**
Callichthyidae, 135
Callistus tetra, 76, **76**
Callochromis, 115
Camallanus, 46, 62, 63
Campylomormyrus tamandua, 151
Cape Lopez lyretail, 101, **101**
Carbonate hardness, 10, 63
Carbon dioxide (CO$_2$), 13–14, 63
fertilization with, 63
poisoning with, 42
Cardinal flower, 27
Cardinal tetra, **23**, 79, **79**
Care mistakes, list of, 45
Caridina spec., 73
Carinotetraodon lorteti, 151
Carnegiella strigata, 80, **80**
Catfishes, **1**, 135–142, **135–142**
Cation exchanger, 63
Caudal fin, 61
Celebes rainbow fish, 88, **88**
Ceratophyllum demersum, **C6, C8**, 29
Ceratopteris
pteridoides, 29, **30**
thalictroides, 28
Ceylonese fire barb, 82, **82**
Chaetostoma spec., **59**, 138, **138**
Chalinochromis brichardi, **34**, 115
Chanda ranga, 148, **148**
Channa
gachua, 147
orientalis, **73**, 147, **147**

Characidium spec., 76, **76**
Characiformes, 81, 90
Characins, **C3**, 74–80, **74–80**
Characodon lateralis, 99
Checkered barb, 83, **83**
Chemistry (water), 16–17
Cherry barb, 83, **83**
Chilatherina
bleheri, 88, **88**
fasciata, 89
Chlamydogobius eremius, **1**, 145, **145**
Chocolate-colored catfish, 139, **139**
Chocolate gourami, 109, **109**
Chore schedule, 24
Chromidotilapia
batesii, 121
finleyi, 121
guntheri, 121, **121**
"Cichlasoma"
aureum. See Thorichthys aureus
bifasciatum, 126
biocellatum. See Chiclasoma biocellatum
callolepis. See Thorichthys callolepis
carpinte, 127, **127**
cyanoguttatum, 127
longimanus, 127, **127**
maculicauda, 126
meeki. See Thorichthys meeki
motaguense, 129
nicaraguense, 125, **125**
nigrofasciatum, **C4**, 125, **125**
octofasciatum, 128
panamense, 129
rostratum, 127
sajica, 125
salvini, **15**, 128, **128**
septemfasciatum, 125
sieboldii, 128
synspilum, 126, **126**
Cichlids, **C3, C4**, 110–111, **111**
from Africa, 120–124, **120–124**
from Central America, 125–128, **125–128**
from Lake Malawi, 116–119, **116–119**
from South America, 129–134, **129–134**
from Tanganyika, 112–115, **112–115**
Clear water, 63
Clown loach, 91, **91**
Cobalt blue cichlid, 118, **118**
Cockatoo dwarf cichlid, 129, **129**

Colisa
chuna, 106, **106**
fasciata, 106
lalia, **12, 13**, 106, **106**
sota. See Colisa chuna
Commercial foods, 55
Communities, 63
Community tank, 63
Complete desalting, 63
Congo tetra, 74, **74**
Convict cichlid, **C4**, 125, **125**
Coolie loach, 91, **91**
Coontail, 29
Copadichromis
borleyi, 117
spec. "Kadango," 117, **117**
Copeina arnoldi. See Copella arnoldi
Copella arnoldi, 77, **77**
Copperleaf, **C5**, 27
Corydoras
aeneus, 136, **136**
hastatus, 137, **137**
julii. See Corydoras trilineatus
paleatus, 143
panda, 136, **136**
pygmaeus, 137
robineae, 143
trilineatus, 135, **135**
Costia, 63
Courtship display, 63
Crenicara filamentosa. See Dicrossus filamentosus
Crenicichla
anthurus, 134, **134**
notophthalmus, 134
regani, 134
Croaking gourami, 109
Croaking spiny catfish, **40**, 142, **142**
Crossocheilus siamensis, 93
Crushed coral, 63
Crustaceans, 39, 73
Cryptocoryne, 160
affinis, **C6**
balansae, 28
wendtii, 28
X willisii, 28, **30**
Crystalwort, 29, **30**
Ctenopoma
acutirostre, 109
ansorgii, 109, **109**
fasciolatum, 109
kingsleyae, 109
Cuckoo catfish, 142, **142**
Cupid cichlid, **C4**, 131, **131**
Cyathopharynx furcifer, 115
Cyclops, 63
Cynolebias nigripinnis, 104
Cyphotilapia frontosa, 115
Cyprichromis leptosoma, 115, **115**

Cyprinidontiformes, 100
Cypriniformes, 81, 90
Cyprinodon macularius, 104, **104**
Cyrtocara
ahli. See Sciaenochromis ahli
borleyi. See Copadichromis borleyi
compressiceps. See Dimidiochromis compressiceps
electra. See Placidochromis electra
fenestratus. See Protomelas fenestratus
fuscotaeniatus. See Tyrannochromis fuscotaeniatus
livingstonii. See Nimbochromis livingstonii
moorii, **33**
spec. "Kadango." See Copadichromis spec. "Kadango"

D
Danio
aequipinnatus, 84, **84**
devario, 84
regina, 84
Danios, **C3**, 81–85, **81–85**
Daphnia, 63
Darter characin, 76, **76**
Dasyloricaria, 139
Dermogenys pusillus, 99, **99**
Desert pupfish, 104, **104**
Diamond tetra, **41**, 80
Dianema
longibarbis, 137
urostriata, 137, **137**
Diapteron fulgens, 104
Dicrossus filamentosus, 130, **130**
Didiplis diandra, 28
Diet
dry food, 38
feeding rules, 40
live food, 38–40
vegetable food, 40
vitamin supplements, 40
Diffuser, 63
Dimidiochromis
compressiceps, 117, **117**
Discus, **C1, 37, 44**
Diseases
camallanus infestation, 46
diagnosis and treatment aids, 47
disinfecting tank, 47
formalin bath for, 46
heat therapy for, 46
hole-in-the-head disease, 46

153

intestinal flagellates, 46
killing a fish, 47
medications for, 46
recognizing and treating, 42
salt bath for, 46
veterinarian trip, 46
See also Poisoning
Disinfecting, 47
Dorsal fin, 61
Doryichthys martensi, 151
Drosophila, 40, 55, 64
Dry food, 38, 64
Dry season, 64
Dust food, 64
Dwarf catfish, 137, **137**
Dwarf cichlid, 134
Dwarf gourami, **12/13,** 106, **106**
Dwarf loach, 90, **90**
Dwarf rasbora, 82, **82**
Dysichthys coracoideus, 141, **141**

E
Echinodorus
amazonicus, 28, 160
bleheri, 28
cordifolius, 29
horemanni, **31**
osiris, 29, **30**
parviflorus, 28
tenellus, 28
Ectoparasites, 64
Egg-layers, 56
with brood care, 58–59
without brood care, 57
Eggs, 52, 56
Eigenmannia
lineata, 149, **149**
spec., 51
Electrical accidents, 18, 20
Electrical conductivity, 12, 64
Eleotridae, 144
Elephant ear, 29
Elephant fish, 151
Elephant-trunk fishes, **1,** 90–93, **90–93**
Emerald catfish, 136, **136**
Emperor tetra, 79, **79**
Enantiopus, 115
Enchytraeus, 55
Endoparasites, 64
Epalzeorhynchus
bicolor, 93, **93**
erythrozorus, 93
frenatus, 93, **93**
kallopterus, 93, **93**
siamensis. See
Crossocheilus siamensis
Epiplatys dageti monroviae, 101, **101**
Eretmodus cyanostictus, **51,** 114, **114**

Erpetoichthys calabaricus.
See Calamoichthys
calabaricus
Etroplus maculatus, 124, **124**
Euctenogobius badius, 144, **144**
Eutropiellus
buffei, 143, **143**
debauwi, 143
vanderweyeri. See
Eutropeillus buffei

F
False loosestrife, 27
Family, 64
Family relationships, 59
Fanwort, 27, **31**
Farlowella spec., 141, **141**
Feeding rules, 40
Filtration, 64
air-driven inside filters, 21
biological, 21
materials for, 21–22
mechanical, 21
motorized filters, 21
Fin-eating cichlid, **58**
Fin rot, 64
Fin-sucker catfish, **58**
Firemouth, **C8,** 127, **127**
Fish
buying and introducing, 23–24
rules for combining species, 24
Fish filets, 40
Fish tuberculosis, 64
Flag cichlid, 131, **131**
Flame tetra, 76, **76**
Floating fern, 29
Flying fox, 93, **93**
Flying foxes, 90–93, **90–93**
Foam, 21
Food
for brood, 53, 55
dry, 38, 64
dust for rearing, 64
live, 38–40, 66
vegetable, 40, 69
Food animals, 38–40, 55
Formalin bath, 46
Frozen food, 38, 64
Fruit flies, 40, 55
Fry, 52, 56, 64

G
Gambusia affinis, 99
Garnet tetra, 80
Gas exchange, 64
Gasteropelecus sternicla, **2/3**
General (total) hardness, 10, 65
Genus, 65

Geophagus spec. aff.
altifrons, **4, 5,** 133, **133**
Gephyrochromis moorii, 119
Giant danio, 84, **84**
Gill flukes, 65
Gills, 60
Girardinus metallicus, 98, **98**
Glass knife fish, 149, **149**
Glossolepis
incisus, **C4,** 89, **89**
wanamensis, 89
Glowlight tetra, 78, **78**
Gnathonemus petersi, 151, **151**
Gobies, **1,** 144–145, **144–145**
Gobiidae, 144
Golden-eyed dwarf cichlid, 134
Golden julie, 114, **114**
Golden pheasant gularis, 101, **101**
Gonopodium, 65
Goodeidae, 94
Green pufferfish, 151, **151**
Group fish, 65
Guenther's mouthbrooder, 121, **121**
Guppy, 96, **96**
Gymnocorymbus ternetzi, 77, **77**
Gymnogeophagus balzanii, 134, **134**
Gymnotiformes, 146
Gyrinocheilus aymonieri, 91, **91**

H
Haplochromis, 116
ahli. See Sciaenochromis
ahli
borleyi. See
Copadichromis borleyi
compressiceps. See
Dimidiochromis
compressiceps
electra. See Placido-
chromis electra
fenestratus. See Proto-
melas fenestratus
fuscotaeniatus. See
Tyrannochromis
fuscotaeniatus
livingstonii. See Nimbo-
chromis livingstonii
moorii. See Cyrtocara
moorii
multicolor. See Pseudo-
crenilabrus multicolor
spec. "Kadango." See
Copadichromis spec.
"Kadango"
Hardness (water)
carbonate, 10, 63

changing, 11–12
conductivity and, 12
for fish, 11
general (total), 10, 65
levels of, 10
measuring, 11
noncarbonate, 10, 66
for plants, 11
Harlequin fish, 81, **81**
Hasemania nana, 78, **78**
Hatchetfish, **2/3**
Head, 60
Head-and-tail-light tetra, 80
Heaters, 20–21
Heat therapy, 46
Heliosoma spec., 73
Helostoma temminckii, 108, **108**
Hemichromis
lifalili, 122
spec., 122, **122**
Hemieleotris latifasciatus, 14?
Hemigrammus
bleheri, 78, **78**
erythrozonus, 78, **78**
ocellifer, 80
pulcher, 80
rhodostomus, 78
Hemirhamphidae, 94
Hemirhamphodon
pogonognathus, 99
Hengel's rasbora, 81, **81**
Herichthys
carpintis. See "Cichlasoma
carpinte
cyanoguttum. See
"Cichlasoma"
cyanoguttum
Herotilapia multispinosa, 126, **126**
Heterandria formosa, 97, **97**
Heteranthera zosterifolia, **C5,** 27
Hole-in-the-head disease, **44,** 46, 65
Honey gourami, 106, **106**
Honey rainbow fish, 89
Hoplosternum thoracatum, 143
Hornwort, **C6, C8,** 29
Humic acids, 65
Humpbacked limia, 99
Hydrocotyle leucophala, **C5,** 28
Hygrophila
corymbosa, **C6,** 29
difformis, 27
polysperma, 27
Hypancistrus zebra, 143
Hyphessobrycon
bentosi, 75, **75**
bifasciatus, 76
callistus, 76, **76**

erythrostigma, **2/3**, 75
flammeus, 76, **76**
herbertaxelrodi, 80
Hypostomus, 138

I

Ichthyophtirius multifiliis
 ("ich"), 65
Ilyodon furcidens, 99
Indian glass perch, 148, **148**
Inpaichthys kerri, **C3**, 79, **79**
Insurance, 18
Intestinal flagellates, 46, 65
Ion exchangers, 65
Ions, 65
Iriatherina werneri, 88, **88**

J

Jack Dempsey cichlid, 128
Java fern, 29, **33**
Java moss, 29
Jewel rainbow fish, 87, **87**
Jewel tetra, 76, **76**
Julidochromis ornatus, 114,
 114

K

Killifishes, **C3**, 100–104,
 100–104
Killing a fish, 47
Kingsley's ctenopoma, 109
Kirschbaum method, 51–52,
 65
Kissing gourami, **52/53**, 108,
 108
Kryptopterus
 bicirrhis, 143
 minor, 143, **143**

L

Labeo bicolor. See
 Epalzeorhynchus bicolor
Labeotropheus
 fuelleborni, 119
 trewavasae, 119, **119**
Labidochromis spec. "yellow,"
 C3, 118, **118**
Labyrinth fishes, **C3**,
 105–109, **105–109**
Laetacara curviceps, 131,
 131
Lamprichthys tanganicus,
 103, **103**
Lamprologus, 112, **112**
 congoensis, 124
Larvae, 52, 56, 65
Lateral line organ, 61
Lebistes reticulatus. See
 Poecilia retulata
Leiocassis siamensis, 143
Leopard catfish, 135, **135**
Leporacanthicus galaxias, 1,
 137, **137**

Leptotilapia tinanti. See
 Steatocranus tinanti
Lighting
 fluorescent, 20
 mercury vapor, 20
Limia nigrofasciata, 99
Limnophila sessiliflora, **C5**,
 27
Lionhead cichlid, 123, **123**
Little Amazon, 28
Livebearers, 1, 56, 94–99,
 94–99
Live food, 38–40, 66
Loaches, **1**, 90–93, **90–93**
Lobelia cardinalis, 27
Long-finned characin, 74, **74**
Long-nosed elephant fish,
 151, **151**
Loosestrife, 27
Loricariidae catfishes, **43**,
 135
Ludwigia repens, 27
Lumphead cichlid, 123, **123**
Lyre-tailed panchax, **C3**, 101,
 101

M

Macrognathus spec., 149
Macropodus
 chinensis. See Macro-
 podus ocellatus
 concolor, 108
 ocellatus, 109
 opercularis, 108, **108**
Malayan half-beak, 99, **99**
Malayan snail, **20**, 73
Malpulutta kretseri, 109
Marbled hatchetfish, 80, **80**
Marsh-purslane, 27
Mastacembelus
 erythrotaenia, 149, **149**
Mbunas, 33, **33**, 66, 116–119,
 116–119
Medication
 furazolidon in, 46
 malachite green solution in,
 46
 poisoning from, 44
Megalomphodus
 megalopterus, 75, **75**
 sweglesi, 75
Melanochromis
 auratus, 119
 chipokae, 119
 johannii, 33, 119, **119**
Melanoides spec., 73
Melanotaenia
 boesemani, 87, **87**
 lacustris, 89
 splendida, 89
 trifasciata, 87, **87**
Melanotaeniidae, 89
Mesonauta insignis, 134

Metabolism, 66
Metallic livebearer, 98, **98**
Methynnis argenteus, 80
Microgeophagus ramirezi.
 See Papiliochromis
 ramirezi
Microglanis iheringi, 143
Microsagittaria, 28
Microsorium pteropus, 29
Midget livebearer, 97, **97**
Midget sucker catfish, 140,
 140
Mochocidae catfish, **C8**, 135
Moenkhausia
 pittieri, **41**, 80
 sanctaefilomenae, 77, **77**
Mogurnda mogurnda, 145
Monocirrhus polyacanthus, **1**,
 146, 147, **147**
Monogamy, 59
Mormyiformes, 146
Mosquito fish, 97, **97**, 99
Mosquito larvae, 38, 66
Mouthbrooders, 58–59, 66
Mud plantain, **C5**, 27
Mussels, 40
Myriophyllum brasiliense, 27
Mystus micracanthus, 143

N

Najas guadelupensis, 29
Nannacara anomala, 134
Nannocrycon eques. See
 Nannostomus eques
Nannostomus
 beckfordi, 79, **79**
 eques, 80
 trifasciatus, 79
Nanochromis
 squamiceps, 124
 transvestitus, 121, **121**
Needle catfish, 141, **141**
Needle sagittaria, 28
Neetroplus nematopus, 129
Nemacheilus notostigma, 93
Nematobrycon palmeri, 79,
 79
Neolamprologus
 brevis, 112
 brichardi, 113, **113**
 buescheri, 115
 calliurus, **34**, 115
 cylindricus, 113
 elongatus. See
 Neolamprologus brichardi
 leleupi, 113
 longior, **C3**, 113, **113**
 marunguensis, **11**, 113
 multifasciatus, 112
 savoryi elongatus. See
 Neolamprologus brichardi
 sexfasciatus, 113
 tretocephalus, 113

Neolebias ansorgii, 75, **75**
Neon disease, 66
Neon tetra, **23**, 48–49
Nimbochromis livingstonii,
 111, 119
Nitrate (NO_3), 15, 66
Nitrite/nitrate poisoning, 44
Nitrite (NO_2), 66
Nitrogen, 66
Nomorhamphus liemi, 99, **99**
Noncarbonate hardness, 10,
 66
Nothobranchius
 guentheri, 102
 rachovii, 102, **102**
Nymphaea zenkeri, 29, **31**
Nymphoides aquatica, 25

O

Oddities, 146–151, **146–151**
Oodinium, 66
Open-water spawners, 57, 66
Orange chromide, 124, **124**
Orange ctenopoma, 109, **109**
Order, 66
Organic waste products, 66
Oryzias latipes, 89, **89**
Oryziidae, 89
Oscar cichlid, 134
Otocinclus spec. aff. affinis,
 140, **140**
Ovoviviparous, 56, 66
Oxidator, 67
Oxygen (O_2), 13, 67

P

Pachypanchax playfairii, 104
Pakistani loach, 93
Pangasius spec., 143
Pangio
 anguillaris, 93
 kuhlii, 91
 semicinctus, 91
 spec., 91, **91**
Pantodon buchholzi, 150, **150**
Papiliochromis
 altispinosus, 130
 ramirezi, 130, **130**
Paracheirodon
 axelrodi, **23**, 79, **79**
 innesi, **23**, 79
Paradise fish, 108, **108**
Paraguay mouthbrooder,
 134, **134**
Paramecia, 55, 67
Parosphromenus
 deissneri, 108, **108**
 filamentosus, 108
 nagyi, 109
Parotocinclus maculicauda,
 140
Parrotfeather, 27
Pearl gourami, 106, **106**

155

Peat, 67
Peat filtering, 21, 67
Peckoltia pulcher, 139, **139**
Pellets, 38, 67
Pelmatochromis thomasi.
    See *Anomalochromis*
        thomasi
Pelvicachromis
    humilis, 124
    pulcher, 120, **120**
    subocellatus, 124
    taeniatus, **C4,** 121, **121**
Penguin fish, 77, **77**
Peruvian longfin, 104, **104**
Petitella georgiae, 78
pH, 12–13, 67
    buffering, 67
Phallichthys amates, 99
Phalloceros caudimaculatus,
    99
Phenacogrammus interrup-
    tus, 74, **74**
Photosynthesis, 67
Pike livebearer, 99
Pike-top minnow, 99
Pimelodus pictus, 141, **141**
Pistia stratiotes, 29
Placidochromis electra, 119
Plants, **30–31**
    for background, 27–28
    epiphytic, 29
    floating, 29
    for sides and middle, 28
    solitary, 28–29
Platy, **1,** 95, **95**
Platydoras costatus, 142
Playfair's panchax, 104
Plecostomus. See
        Hypostomus Poecilia
    latipinna, 97
    reticulata, 96, **96**
    sphenops, 96, **96**
    velifera, 97, **97**
Poeciliidae, 94
    ollimyrus isidori, 151
Pointed-mouth molly, 96, **96**
Poisoning
    ammonia, 43–44
    carbon dioxide, 42
    from medication, 44
    nitrite/nitrate, 44
    from tap water, 44
Polkadot African catfish, 142,
    142
Polyandry, 59
Polygyny, 59
Polypterus
    ornatipinnis, 148
    senegalus, 148, **148**
Popondetta furcata. See
        Pseudomugil furcatus
Priapella intermedia, 98, **98**
Pristella riddlei, **2/3**

Procatopus
    nototaenia, 102
    similis, 102, **102**
Proteins, 67
Protomelas fenestratus, 119
Pseudocrenilabrus
    multicolor, 123
    nicholsi, 123, **123**
Pseudogastromyzon cheni,
    92, **92**
Pseudomugil
    furcatus, 89, **89**
    gertrudae, 89
    mellis, 89
Pseudomugilidae, 89
Pseudopiplatys annulatus, 104
Pseudosphromenus cupanus,
    109
Pseudotropheus
    "*acei,*" 119
    aurora, 118
    "Bright Blue," **39**
    elongatus, 119
    lanisticola, **57,** 118, **118**
    zebra, 118, **118**
Pterogoplichthys gibbiceps,
    138, **138**
Pterolebias peruensis, 104,
    104
Pterophyllum
    altum, **36,** 133
    scalare, **2, 3,** 133, **133**
Puntius
    conchonius, 85
    johorensis, 83
    nigrofasciatus, 85
    oligolepis, 83, **83**
    pentazona, 83, **83**
    semifasciolatus, 83, **83**
    tetrazona, 84, **84**
    titteya, 83, **83**
Purple cichlid, 120, **120**
Purple-headed barb, 85
Pygmy chain, 28

R
Rachbow's nothobranch, 102,
    102
Rainbow cichlid, 126, **126**
Rainbow fishes, **C4,** 86–89,
    86–89
Rainy season, 50–52, 67
Ram cichlid, 130, **130**
Ramshorn snail, **20,** 73
Rasbora
    espei, 81
    hengeli, 81, **81**
    heteromorpha, 81, **81**
    maculata, 82, **82**
    pauciperforata, 82, **82**
    trilineata, 82, **82**
    urophthalma, 82
    vaterifloris, 82, **82**

Rearing tank, 67
Red cichlid, **9,** 122, **122**
Red-finned loach, 90, **90**
Red fresh-water crab, **20,** 73
Red lamp-eye, 102, **102**
Red-line rasbora, 82, **82**
Red-tailed silverside, 89, **89**
Reed fish, 148, **148**
Reproduction
    in egg-laying species, 56
    in livebearers, 56
Reverse osmosis, 69
Rhinogobius wui, 144, **144**
Riccia fluitans, 29, **30**
Rice fishes, 86, 89, **89**
Rineloricaria, 139
    spec. aff. lanceolata, 139,
        139
Rivulus
    agilae, 103, **103**
    xiphidius, 103, **103**
Rocks, 22
Roots, 22
Rosy barb, 85
Rotala macrandra, 27
Rotifers, 68
Roughage, 68

S
Sagittaria subulata, 27
Sailfin molly, 97, **97**
Salmon-red rainbow fish, **C4,**
    86, **86**
Salt bath, 46
Salts, 68
Salvinia auriculata, 29
Salvin's cichlid, **15,** 128, **128**
Sand cichlid, **32**
Sarotherodon melanotheron,
    124
Satanoperca, 133
Sawbwa resplendens, 85
Schubert's barb, 83, **83**
Sciaenochromis ahli, 116,
    116
Scientific name, 68
Scissortail, 82, **82**
Seasonal fish, 68
Shinnersia rivularis, 28
Shoaling fishes, 68
Short-bodied catfish, 136,
    136
Siamese fighting fish, **19**
Silversides, **C4,** 86–89,
    86–89
Skin flukes, 68
Slender-leaved Amazon, 28,
    160
Snail cichlid, **34, 57**
Snails, 68, 73
Snake fish, 148, **148**
South American leaf fish, **1,**
    147, **147**

Spawning, 50–52
    boxes for, 54
    rhythm of, 50, 68
    substrates, 68
    tank for, 54, 62
Species tank, 68
Sphaerichthys osphro-
    menoides, 109, **109**
Splash tetra, 77, **77**
Spotted climbing perch, 109
Spotted danio, 85
Spotted-eyed velvet cichlid,
    70/71
Spotted rasbora, 82, **82**
Steatocranus
    casuarius, 123, **123**
    spec. aff. ubanguiensis, **35,**
        123
    tinanti, 124
Steel-blue aphyosemion,
    100, **100**
Stigmatogobius sadanundio,
    145
Stiphodon elegans, 145
Striped danio, **C3,** 84, **84**
Striped dwarf shrimp, **20,** 73
Striped goby cichlid, 51, 114,
    114
Striped headstander, 80, **80**
Stripe-tailed catfish, 137, **137**
Sturisoma aureum, 140, **140**
Substrate-dependent, 68
Substrate spawners, 57, 69
Sucker-mouth armored
    catfish, **59**
Sucking loach, 91, **91**
Sulfates, 69
Sumatra barb, 84, **84**
Sunset platy, **C8,** 95, **95**
Surface dwellers, 61
Swim bladder, 69
Swimming free, 69
Swordfern, 29
Swordplant, 29
Swordtail, 94, **94**
Symphysodon aequifasciata,
    C8, 132, **132**
Synodontis, **C8**
    angelicus, 142, **142**
    brichardi, 143
    nigrita, 142
    nigriventris, 142, **142**
    petricola, 142, **142**
    schoutedeni, 142

T
Tanganicodus irascae, 114
Tanganyika clown, 51, 114,
    114
Tanganyika lamp-eye, 103,
    103
Tanichthys albonubes, 85,
    85

Tank
  breeding (spawning), 52, 62
  cover for, 18
  decorating, 22
  disinfecting, 47
  rearing, 67
  setting up, 22–23
  size of, 18
  species, 68
Tap water poisoning, 44
Tateurndina ocellicauda, 145, **145**
Telmatherina ladigesi, 88, **88**
Tetraodon
  biocellatus, 151
  fluviatilis, 151
  lorteti. See Carinotetraodon lorteti
  nigroviridis, 151, **151**
  palembangensis. See Tetraodon biocellatus
  somphongsi. See Carinotetraodon lorteti
  steindachneri. See Tetraodon biocellatus
Thayeria
  boehlkei, 77, **77**
  obliqua, 77
Theraps
  coeruleus, 125, **125**
  lentiginosus, 125
Thermometer, 21
Thorichthys
  aureus, 127

callolepis, 127
meeki, **C8,** 127, **127**
Thousand dollar knife fish, 151
Three-lined rasbora, 82, **82**
Thysia ansorgii. See Thysochromis ansorgii
Thysochromis ansorgii, 124
Tiger barb, 84, **84**
Tilapia
  joka, 123, **123**
  mariae, 124
  zillii, 124
Tilapia melanotheron. See Sarotherodon melanotheron
Toxins, 14–15
Trace elements, 69
Trichodina, 69
Trichogaster
  leeri, 106, **106**
  trichopterus, 105, **105**
Trichopsis
  pumila, 107, **107**
  schalleri, 107
  vittata, 109
Tropheus
  duboisi, 114
  moorii, 114, **114**
Tubifex, 39, 69
Tufa, 69
Tyrannochromis fuscotaeniatus, 116

U
Uaru amphiacanthoides, 134
Upside-down catfish, 142, **142**
Utakas, 69

V
Vallisneria
  gigantea, 28
  tortifolia, 28
Variegated platy, **C8,** 95, **95**
Vegetable food, 40, 69
Velvet cichlid, 134
Ventral fin, 60
Vesicularia dubyana, 29
Veterinarian visit, 46
Vitamins, 40
Viviparous, 56, 69

W
Water
  acidity (pH) of, 12–13
  ammonia in, 14–15
  carbon dioxide in, 13–14
  chemistry of, 16–17
  conductivity in, 12
  damage from, 18
  hardness of, 10–12
  nitrate in, 15
  oxygen in, 13
  properties of, 69
  quality of, 10
Water fern, 28
Water hyssop, **C6,** 27
Water lettuce, 29

Water pennywort, **C5,** 28
Water purslane, 28
Water snail, 73
Water sprite, 28
Water wisteria, 27
White cloud minnow, 85, **85**
White water, 69
Whiteworms, 55
Wrestling half-beak, 99, **99**

X
Xenomystus nigri, 150, **150**
Xenotilapia, 115
  flavipinnis, 115, **115**
  ochrogenys, **32**
Xenotoca eiseni, 98, **98**
Xiphophorus
  helleri, 94, **94**
  maculatus, **1,** 95, **95**
  variatus, **C8,** 95, **95**
X-ray fish, **2/3**

Y
Yellow lamp-eye, 102, **102**
Yellow sand cichlid, 115, **115**
Yolk sac larva, 56, 69

Z
Zebra cichlid, **C4,** 125, **125**
Zebra danio, 84, **84**
Zebra loach, 93
Zebra Malawi cichlid, 118, **118**
Zooplankton, 69

Literature and Addresses

Books

Braemer, Helga, and Ines Scheurmann. *Tropical Fish.* Barron's Educational Series, Inc., Hauppauge, New York, 1983.

Hansen, J. *Making Your Own Aquarium.* Bell and Hyman, 1979.

Hawkins, A.D., ed. *Aquarium Systems.* Academic Press, 1981.

Hellner, Steffen. *Killifish.* Barron's Educational Series, Inc., Hauppauge, New York, 1990.

Pinter, Helmut. *Labyrinth Fish.* Barron's Educational Series, Inc., Hauppauge, New York, 1986.

Rampshorst, J. D. van, ed. *The Complete Aquarium Encyclopedia.* Phaidon, 1978.

Scheurmann, Ines. *The New Aquarium Handbook.* Barron's Educational Series, Inc., Hauppauge, New York, 1986.

———. *Water Plants in the Aquarium.* Barron's Educational Series, Inc., Hauppauge, New York 1987.

Stadelmann, Peter. *Tropical Fish.* Barron's Educational Series, Inc., Hauppauge, New York, 1991.

Sterba, G. *The Aquarists' Encyclopedia.* Blandford, 1983.

Ward, Brian. *Aquarium Fish Survival Manual.* Barron's Educational Series, Inc., Hauppauge, New York, 1985.

Zurlo, Georg. *Cichlids.* Barron's Educational Series, Inc., Hauppauge, New York, 1991.

Magazines

Aquarium Fish Magazine
P.O. Box 6050
Mission Viejo, CA 92690

Freshwater and Marine Aquarium
144 West Sierra Madre Boulevard
Sierra Madre, CA 91024

Practical Fishkeeping Magazine
RR1, Box 200 D
Jonesburg, MO 63351

Tropical Fish Hobbyist
One TFH Plaza
Third and Union Avenues
Neptune City, NJ 07753

Specialty Societies

American Cichlid Association
P.O. Box 32130
Raleigh, NC 27622

American Killifish Association
903 Merrifield Place
Mishawaka, IN 46544

American Livebearer Association
50 N. Second Street
St. Clair, PA 17970

British Cichlid Association
33 Kirkmeadow
Bretton
Peterborough. PE3 8JG
England

British Discus Association
P.O. Box 9168
Canton, OH 44711-9168
or
41 Pengwern,
Llangollen.
Clwyd. LL20 8AT
England

Catfish Association of North America
Box 45
Rt. 104A
Sterling, NY 13156

International Fancy Guppy Association
2312 Pestalozzi
St. Louis, MO 63118

North American Discus Society
P.O. Box 5145
Lakeland, FL 33807

North American Fish Breeders Guild
4731 Lake Avenue
Rochester, NY 14612

Photo Credits

Büscher: pp. 11, 32, 34 (above; below), 51 (above), 115 (below), 130 (below); Elias: pp. 12, 13, 52, 53; Ettrich: pp. 73, 147 (above); Hartl: pp. 99 (above), 148 (below); Hellner: pp. 93 (right, above), 101 (above), 103 (left, below); Hieronimus: pp. 1 (right, middle), 147 (below); Horsthemke: pp. 144 (above), 145 (below); Kahl: inside front cover flap (right, above), pp. 2/3, 6/7, 23, 25, 30, 31, 48/49, 76 (above), 77 (left, below), 78 (left, above), 84 (left, below), 85, 90 (below), 91 (above), 93 (left, above), 108 (right, above; below), 129 (below), 136 (above), 141 (right, below), 158/59, 160, inside back cover, inside back cover flap, back cover (right, above); Linke: inside front cover (left middle,), pp. 1 (right, above), 9, 19, 75 (right, above), 83 (right, above; left, below), 88 (below), 94, 95 (left, above; right, above), 96 (left, above), 97 (above), 98 (left, below), 106 (above; left, below), 107 (left, above; right, above), 109 (below), 112 (above), 121, 122 (below), 123 (left, below), 130 (above), 136 (right, below); back cover (right, below); Meyer: pp. 96 (right, above), 98 (right, below); Nieuwenhuizen: front cover, front cover flap, inside front flap (left, above), pp. 1 (left, above; left, middle), 20 (right, above), 36 (left, above), 41, 70/71, 74 (above), 75 (left, above; right, below), 76 (left, below), 77 (left, above), 79 (left, above; left, below), 80, 81, 82, 83 (left, above), 84 (left, above; right above and below), 87, 89 (right, above), 92, 95 (below), 96 (below), 97 (left, below), 99 (below), 101 (right, below), 102 (below), 103 (left, above; right, below), 106 (right, below), 107 (right, below), 108 (left, above), 109 (above), 117 (above), 118 (left, above), 120, 131 (left, above), 132, 135, 136 (left, below) 137 (above), 138 (above), 139 (right, above; below), 140 (below), 141 (left, below), 142 (left, below), 143 (above), 145 (left, above; right, above), 146, 149 (below), back cover (left, above and middle), back cover flap; Reinhard: pp. 83 (right, below), 90 (above) 93 (below), 127 (right, above), 142 (right, above), 149 (above), 150, 151, back cover (left, below); Rösler: inside front flap (left, below), pp. 100 (above) 107 (left, below), 122 (above); Scheinert: p. 44; Schliewen: pp. 35 (below), 43 (below); Schmelzer: pp. 113 (above), 115 (above); Schraml: pp. 75 (left, below), 88 (left, above), 97 (right, below), 114 (above), 123 (right, below), 124 (above); Seegers: pp. 76 (right, below), 79 (right, below) 89 (left, above and below), 100 (below), 101 (left, below), 102 (left, above; right, above), 103 (right, above), 104 (below); Sommer: inside front cover flap (left, middle) pp. 1 (below), 51 (below), 104 (above), 105 140 (above), 141 (above), 148 (left, above); Spreinat: inside front cover (right, above), inside front flap (right, middle), pp. 33, 37, 39, 57, 58 (right) 74 (below), 86, 88 (right, above), 111 112 (below), 113 (below), 117 (below

18 (right, above); 119 (right), 133
(above), 142 (right, below); Staek:
p. 36 (right), 114 (left, below; right,
below), 116, 118 (right, below), 124
(below), 129 (above); Stawikowski:
inside front cover (left, below; right,
middle), inside front cover flap (right,
below), pp. 15, 35 (above), 40, 43
(above), 118 (left, below), 119 (left),
123 (above), 125 (left, below; right,
below), 126 (below), 128, 131 (right,
above; below); Werner: pp. 4/5, 20
left, above; middle, above and below;
right, below), 58 (left), 59, 77 (right,
below), 78 (right, above; below), 79
(right, above), 91 (left, below; right,
below), 98 (left, above; right, above);
125 (above), 126 (above), 127 (left,
above; below), 133 (below), 134, 138
(below), 139 (left, above), 142 (left,
above), 143 (below), 144 (below), 148
(right, above).

Photos on covers

Front cover: Discus fish
(*Symphysodon aequifasciata*).
Back cover: *Betta imbellis* (above,
left); hornwort (*Ceratophyllum
demersum*) (above, right); variegated
sunset platy (*Xiphophorus
variatus*), cultivated variety (middle,
left); mochocidae catfish (*Synodontis
spec.*) (below, left); firemouth
(*Thorichthys meeki*) (below, right).

The Author

Ulrich Schliewen has been a passion-
ate aquarium hobbyist since early
childhood. He studied biology with
special concentration on zoology at
the University of Munich and has had
close contact with the Max Planck
Institute for Ethology and the Zoologi-
cal State Collection in Munich. He has
also traveled to South America, Central Africa, and Southeast Asia to
study fish in their natural environment.
Mr. Schliewen is on the editorial board
of *DCG-Info*, the publication of the
German Cichlid Society, and has
published articles in aquarists'
magazines.

Note of Warning

In this book, electrical equipment commonly used with
aquariums is described. Please
be sure to observe the safety
rules on page 20; otherwise,
there is a danger of serious
accidents.
Before buying a large tank,
check how much weight the
floor of your apartment can
support in the location where
you plan to set up your
aquarium (see page 18).
Sometimes water damage
occurs as a result of broken
glass, overflowing, or a leak in
the tank. An insurance policy
that covers such eventualities is
therefore highly recommended
(see page 18).
Make sure that children (and
adults) do not eat any aquarium
plants. These plants can make
people quite sick. Also make
sure that fish medications are
out of reach of children.
Avoid contact of the eyes, skin,
and mucous membranes with
caustic chemicals. In case of a
contagious disease (such as fish
tuberculosis), do not touch infected fish or reach into the tank
with your bare hands. The spines
below the eyes of loaches and
the fin spines of some catfish
species can inflict wounds.
Because these punctures can
trigger an allergic reaction, you
should immediately see a physi-
cian if you get hurt.

English translation © Copyright 1992
by Barron's Educational Series, Inc.

© Copyright 1991 by Gräfe and Unzer
Verlag GmbH, Munich, Germany
The title of the German book is
Wasserwelt Aquarium

Translated from the German by Rita
and Robert Kimber

All rights reserved.
No part of this book may be reproduced in any form, by photostat,
microfilm, xerography, or any other
means, or incorporated into any
information retrieval system, elec-
tronic or mechanical, without the
written permission of the copyright
owner.

All inquiries should be addressed to:
Barron's Educational Series, Inc.
250 Wireless Boulevard
Hauppauge, NY 11788

Library of Congress Catalog Card
No. 92-19277

International Standard Book
No. 0-8120-1350-6

Library of Congress
Cataloging-in-Publication Data

Schliewen, Ulrich.
  [Wasserwelt Aquarium. English]
  Aquarium fish / Ulrich Schliewen ;
[translated from the German by Rita
and Robert Kimber].
      p.   cm.
  Includes index.
  ISBN 0-8120-1350-6
  1. Aquarium fishes.   2. Aquariums.
I. Title.
SF457.S3413   1992
639.3'44—dc20   92-19277
                               CIP

PRINTED IN HONG KONG
6 7 8 9 0   4900   12 11 10

Plants for the Aquarium

Ammania gracilis

Cryptocoryne balansae

Flower of a *Cryptocoryne*

Slender-leafed Amazon (*Echinodorus amazonicus*)

Beautiful Aquarium Plants

Plants add beauty to an aquarium, but they also fulfil
some important practical functions, one of them
being to reduce products of animal metabolism. If
plants are to thrive, they have to be properly taken
care of. What matters in the care of aquarium plants
explained on pages 26–29.